𝔄 𝔥𝔢𝔞𝔱𝔥𝔢𝔫 𝔑𝔞𝔱𝔦𝔬𝔫 𝔈𝔟𝔞𝔫𝔤𝔢𝔩𝔦𝔷𝔢𝔡.

HISTORY

OF THE

SANDWICH ISLANDS MISSION.

BY

RUFUS ANDERSON, D. D., LL. D.

LATE FOREIGN SECRETARY OF THE BOARD.

LONDON:
HODDER AND STOUGHTON.
27 PATERNOSTER ROW.
1872.

PREFACE.

WHEN the author retired from official life in 1866, after a connection of somewhat more than forty years with the foreign correspondence of the American Board, it was with the hope of making such use of his experience in the work of missions as would subserve the interests of the missionary cause. Accordingly, in the year 1869, he published a volume, which grew out of a series of Lectures to students in Theological Seminaries, entitled, " Foreign Missions, their Relations and Claims."

Another work, requiring more time and labor, was urged upon him by the following vote of the Prudential Committee, namely: " That, inasmuch as Dr. Anderson is better acquainted than any other person, with the origin, progress, and results of the missionary work, as conducted by the Board, and also with its methods, aims, and principles, the Committee hereby express their earnest desire, that he prepare for publication a History of the Board to the present time." Every reasonable facility has been afforded for the preparation of such a work. But the lectures required an unexpected amount of time in their preparation, their delivery in various Seminaries, and their ultimate publication; and there were other duties, growing out of the relations of a long public life, which it did not seem right wholly to disregard.

It was not until after some progress had been made in writing the history of other missions, that the author, in view of the uncertainties of life, yielded to what seemed to him the prior claims upon him of the Sandwich Islands Mission, and came to the resolution to make it his first duty to prepare the history of that mission. As compared with other missions under the care of the Board, this one had passed through an experience in some respects very peculiar. Regarded as an experiment in missions, it is believed to be especially instructive in its history. The results are certainly remarkable. While we see more of the foreign element in the government of the Islands, than we could desire, we are permitted to recognize it as an independent and constitutional government, with a native sovereign at its head, and a government as confessedly cognizant of God's law and the gospel, as any one of the governments of Christian Europe; and, what is more, with a Christian community of self-governed, self-supporting churches, embracing as large a proportion of the people, and as really entitled to the Christian name, as the churches of the most favored Christian countries.

It is a question of the highest interest, by what means this great amount of moral, social, and civil life was there developed.

This History is designed to answer that question; and it will be done by a simple statement of facts, as they have become known to the author, from his correspondence and intercourse with the mission during almost the entire period of its existence.

There is no published history of the Sandwich Islands Mission subsequent to the year 1845, twenty-five years ago. The work published by the author, in 1864, entitled, "The Hawaiian Islands, their Progress and Condition under Missionary Labors," is to a large extent a personal narrative of the events and results

of an official visit to the Islands, in the previous year. While necessarily embodying
brief references to many historical facts, it
made no pretensions to being a history of the
mission.

It was objected to Neander, the ecclesiastical historian, that he wrote with too much
reference to influencing the opinions and conduct of his own and succeeding ages. The
author confesses to the same desire and aim.
Missions are a science, in a process of development. Their history is, from the beginning, a
lesson for those now engaged in the missionary
work; and it is allowable to the historian,
while correctly stating his facts, to indicate
their bearing on his own times.

Were the narrative in this volume subjected
to the rigid demands of chronology, it would
have been unnecessarily prolonged, and deprived of the freedom allowable to history, as
distinguished from mere annals. The reader
will see, moreover, how inexpedient it would
have been to go into biographical sketches of
so large a number of missionaries. A single
chapter will suffice for that department; especially as the reader will find, at the close of

the volume, the leading events in the lives of all the missionaries, so far as the facts were attainable.

There was more reason for carefully illustrating the triumphs of divine grace in the lives and characters of the more prominent native converts; and the strength and consistency of Christian character in many of the early converts, may well awaken our surprise. Nor, if we follow the native Christians into their foreign missions, shall we withhold our admiration from those who are, for the most part, converts of the second generation.

The author gratefully acknowledges his obligations to the Rev. AUGUSTUS C. THOMPSON, D. D., long a member of the Prudential Committee, and to the Rev. ISAAC R. WORCESTER, the able editor of the "Missionary Herald," for judicious and highly valued criticisms, extended through nearly the entire volume. He is also under obligation to the Rev. LUTHER H. GULICK, M. D., late Corresponding Secretary of the Board of the Hawaiian Evangelical Association, and now in this country, who favored him with many valuable facts and suggestions.

Among the available sources of information, the author would mention Dr. Joseph Tracy's "History of the American Board," brought down to the year 1842. Besides the great accuracy of that compend, it performed the invaluable service of reducing the multitudinous facts to their proper chronological order, and thus saved a vast amount of labor to all future historians. The Rev. Hiram Bingham's "Residence of Twenty-one Years in the Sandwich Islands," brings the history of the mission down to the year 1845, and is sufficiently full, and generally accurate. It forms a closely printed octavo volume of more than six hundred pages. The Rev. Sheldon Dibble's "History of the Sandwich Islands," published at the Islands in 1843, a duodecimo volume of four hundred and fifty pages, is an excellent authority. Mr. James Jackson Jarves's "History of the Sandwich Islands," 1843 (Honolulu, 1847), is the best of all the histories of those Islands, and was written in a fair and friendly spirit towards the mission; but stops many years short of the present time. I have made marginal references to these works, where it seemed needful to state my authori-

ties; but having free access to original documents in the archives of the Board, I have not
often deemed it needful to refer to the "Missionary Herald," which, after all, is the grand
store-house of materials for the history of the
missions of the American Board.

Freed from the cares of official life, the
writer finds a healthful excitement, as well as
a congenial and he trusts useful employment,
in reviving the recollection of facts, once
very familiar, and recording them for the use
of the generation now coming upon the great
field of Christian action. The present volume
contains, perhaps, all it is needful now to say
concerning the wonderful work of God's grace
at the Sandwich Islands. The "Memorial Volume," prepared ten years ago, but not in the
historical form, gives a condensed and comprehensive view of the "First Fifty Years of
the American Board," as a missionary institution.

A history of all the missions of the Board,
written after the manner of the Mission to the
Sandwich Islands, will require three volumes.
The author hopes, by classing kindred missions
in a connected historical view, to avoid the

unpleasant repetition, which must otherwise
be inevitable. He can hardly expect, at so
late a period of life, to go over the whole
ground, including the missions among the ab-
origines of this country; but, in any event,
the results of his labors will be available for
the completion of the work by some other
competent person; and he feels assured the
Prudential Committee will see that there be
no unnecessary delay. The materials for the
history are abundant, rich, and easy of access.

September, 1870.

CONTENTS.

THE MISSIONARIES.

CATALOGUE OF PUBLICATIONS.

THE SANDWICH ISLANDS MISSION.

CHAPTER I.

PRELIMINARY.

The Pacific Ocean was not known to the Christian world until after the discovery of America by Columbus; and was first seen by Balboa, *Discovery of the Pacific* in 1513, from the summit of the range of *Ocean.* mountains along the Isthmus of Darien. Magellan was the first to enter it, which he did in 1520, through the strait known by his name. This intrepid commander lost his life in a quarrel with natives on the Philippine Islands, discovered by him; but one of his ships accomplished the voyage around the world, the first of those voyages that demonstrated the spherical form of the earth. These discoveries were all made in the service of Spain. Magellan was followed, though long afterwards, by Quiros, Tasman, Byron, Wallis, Bougainville, La Perouse, Cook, and others. Captain Cook was the discoverer of the *Discovery of the Sandwich* Sandwich Islands in 1778, two hundred and *Islands.* eighty-six years after the discovery of America, and two years after the declaration of independence by the United States.

Thus was the way prepared for sending the gospel to those immense insular regions, extending more than five thousand miles north and south, and nearly four thousand miles east and west.

This island world is divided by the equator. On The island world. the north, going westward, are the Sandwich Islands, the Marshall and Gilbert, the Caroline, Ladrone, Pelew, and Philippine Islands. On the south are the Marquesas, the Paumatu and Austral, the Society and Georgian, the Harvey, Tonga, Samoa and Feejee Islands, New Caledonia, the New Hebrides, the Solomon Islands, and New Zealand.

Very little is known concerning this insular world prior to the time of its discovery by Europeans. That the inhabitants of Polynesia had a common Origin of the Polynesians. descent is inferred from their community of form, features, language, manners, and customs. There can be little doubt of the Malayan descent of the people north of the equator, and in Southern Polynesia, including the Tonga and Samoa groups and New Zealand. The complexion of the Feejeeans indicates a descent from the black and copper-colored races.[1] The people of New Caledonia, New Hebrides, and the Solomon Islands, are kindred to the negro race.

The language of the various islands properly called Polynesia is radically the same, and would seem to have been derived from the Malayan stock; yet Mr. Ellis is of opinion that, if Polynesia were peopled from thence, the natives must have possessed better vessels and more accurate knowledge of navigation than they now exhibit, to have made their way against the trade-winds within the tropics, blowing constantly from east to west with but tran-

---

[1] *Wilkes' Exploring Expedition*, vol. iii. p. 74.

sienᵗ and uncertain interruptions. On the other hand, there are facts to show that this could easily have been done from the east.

Imparting the Christian religion does not seem to have entered the thoughts of any of those Europeans who directed or performed the early voyages to the Pacific Ocean. Their aim was the advancement of secular knowledge. Yet it _{Aim of the discoverers.} was the published accounts of their voyages which at length awakened an interest in some of the best Christian people of England to send the gospel to those remote regions.

In 1797, the London Missionary Society purchased a ship and freighted it with missionaries for the Society Islands, in the _{The first mission.} South Pacific Ocean. Thus was commenced the first Protestant mission to the Pacific. The commencement was auspicious, but so many years of darkness followed that the mission came near being abandoned. At the close of 1812, morning suddenly broke, and was followed by a glorious day. Other islands and groups of islands were successively occupied, and other missionary societies followed, — the Wesleyan in 1826, the Presbyterian Church of Nova Scotia in 1848, and the Reformed Church of Scotland in 1852.

The Report of the London Society for 1866 gives a wonderful account of the progress of _{Marvelous success.} the gospel in the South Pacific. It states that sixty years before there was not a solitary native Christian in Polynesia; and that then it would be difficult to find a professed idolater in the islands of Eastern or Central Polynesia, where Christian missionaries have been established. "The hideous

rites of their forefathers have ceased to be practiced.
Their heathen legends and war songs are forgotten.
Their cruel and desolating tribal wars, which were
rapidly destroying the population, appear to be at
an end.   They are gathered in peaceful village communities, and live under recognized codes of law.
They are constructing roads, cultivating their fertile lands, and engaging in commerce.   On the
return of the Sabbath, a very large proportion of
the people attend the worship of God, and in some
instances more than half the adults are recognized
members of Christian churches.   They educate their
children, endeavoring to train them for usefulness
in after life.   They sustain their native ministers,
and send their noblest sons as missionaries to the
heathen lands which lie farther west.   While the
people have not the culture, the wealth, the refine-
ment of the older nations of Christendom, those
islands are no longer to be regarded as a part of
heathendom.   They have been won from its do-
mains, and added to those of Christendom."

When Vancouver visited the Sandwich Islands,
in the years 1792–1794, Kamehameha was
the most powerful among a number of independent chiefs on the island of Hawaii.
He afterwards conquered the whole of his native
island, and the entire group, and founded the dynasty which now rules the Hawaiian Islands.   He
was a strong-minded, sagacious warrior and despot,
and availed himself of the civilization within his
reach, so far as he could make it subservient to his
ambition.   He built forts and mounted guns upon
them; had soldiers armed with muskets, and drilled

after the European fashion ; had a score of vessels,
none of them large, the first keel being laid by
Vancouver in 1794; and encouraged mechanic arts.
But the people were slaves to the chiefs, Rules as a
and the chiefs and people were slaves to despot.
the king. Every man held his land, and the fruits
of his labor, and indeed all his possessions, at the
will of his superiors.

Human sacrifices formed a part of the religion of
the Islands, and all had a superstitious ap- The religion.
prehension of being prayed to death by
some one, or injured by enchantments. But the
most intolerable part of the religious sys- The tabu.
tem was the *tabu*. It made specified days,
places, persons, and things sacred, and death was
the penalty for its violation. Under this unnatural
and cruel institution, men and women, husbands and
wives could not eat together; and women, even the
highest female chiefs, were prohibited, on pain of
death, from eating the flesh of swine, several species
of fish, and some kinds of fruits. If, by reason of
rank or otherwise, they might expect to escape the
death penalty from men, for infringing the tabu, the
priests taught them to believe they would not escape
destruction from the offended gods.

They had doubtless heard from foreign residents,
navigators, and traders, that it was not so in other
countries; indeed foreigners were all arrayed against
the tabu, and strengthened their testimony by the
force and immunity of their own example. But idolatry remained unbroken until after the Kamehameha dies
death of Kamehameha, which occurred on a heathen.
the 8th of May, 1819, at the age of sixty-six. And
there is the strongest reason for believing that he

died without having had so much as a ray of the
gospel shine into his dark mind.[1]

The religion of the Islands, in their pagan state,
was so interwoven with the tabu system,
that the one could not be given up without
the other. The destruction of the tabu was like
destroying the key-stone of an arch; the whole structure of tabu-rites and idol-worship fell at once into
ruins. This was not the result of intelligent deliber-
ation, but came gradually and imperceptibly, as the
result of a train of circumstances and of many and
various influences, some of them existing long before the death of Kamehameha. Immediately on his
death, the leading chiefs requested Kaahumanu, the
most influential of the late king's wives, to dispense
with the usual ceremonies, and allow them to disregard the tabu, but she did not consent. On that
and succeeding days, however, many of the common
people of both sexes ate together, and not a few of
the women ate forbidden fruits. Some of the female
chiefs partook even of swine's flesh, an article most
strictly tabued; and, to be consistent, they treated
with contempt their idol gods. The calamities threatened by the priests not coming upon them, they
were no longer restrained by fear. But while the
king, Keopuolani, and Kaahumanu continued to ad-
here to the tabu, the charm was not broken. When
the ceremony of the king's coronation was over,
Kaahumanu said to him, "Let us henceforth disregard the restraints of tabu;" but he was silent.
Keopuolani, the king's mother, then sent for her

Overthrow of the tabu.

---

[1] See Rev. Wm. Ellis's *Vindication of the American Mission on the
Sandwich Islands, and an Appeal in relation to the Proceedings of Bishop
Staley and the Reformed Catholic Mission at Honolulu.* London, 1866.

youngest son, yet a mere child, to come and eat with her, and thus break the tabu. The king led the little fellow to his mother, to see if no evil followed the transgression. Not seeing any, he said, "It is well to renounce tabu, and for husbands and wives to eat and dwell together;" yet he himself cautiously refrained. Soon after the king undertook, while in a state of intoxication, to consecrate two heathen temples, but there was the greatest confusion in the customary rites, and the grossest violations of the rules of tabu. In the midst of these unsuccessful ceremonies, he received a message from Kaahumanu, advising him to break the tabu and renounce the idols. Scarcely knowing what he did, he practically assented by eating dog's flesh with the females, drinking rum with the female chiefs, and smoking with them from the same pipes. As soon as this became known, the people broke loose from all restraint. Messengers were sent to all parts of the kingdom, and the king of the remotest isle, and the common people in all the islands, obeyed the message with eagerness.[1]

Yet there were many who followed the king's example with fear, and some actually rebelled. One of the highest chiefs raised the stand- A consequent rebellion. ard of revolt, and was joined by many of the priests and a considerable number of chiefs and people; but he was soon slain in battle, as was also his heroic wife, fighting by his side. The idolatrous party being thus overthrown, there was boundless rage against

[1] This account of the overthrow of idolatry differs from the commonly received statements, and is based, mainly, upon the very competent authority of the Rev. Sheldon Dibble, in his excellent History, published at the Sandwich Islands in the year 1843.

the idols, which had failed to render aid to their
Destruction worshippers in the day of battle. Some
of the idols
and temples. were cast into the sea, some were burned;
though it afterwards appeared that not a few were
concealed on Hawaii, in the pits and caves that
abound on that island. The temples were everywhere demolished, and the priest who had been
most active in the rebellion was slain.

It should be specially noted, that this strange
The result of event resulted from no religious motive
no religious
motive. whatever, much less from the influence of
Christianity, but from a desire to be more free in the
indulgence of the baser appetites and passions. Yet
there was in it a manifestly overruling Providence.
Missionaries of the cross were on their way, even
Singular co- then, to erect on these islands the banner
incidence. of the Prince of Peace. The remarkable
coincidence of the two events calls for grateful recognition. Had the mission embarked earlier by a
few months, or had the revolution occurred a few
months later, the mission would have arrived amid
the alarms and danger of war, and perhaps would
have been rejected by the jealous islanders. The
missionaries had no anticipation of such an occurrence when they left their country, and the islanders
knew nothing of their coming until they arrived.
Thus was accomplished at once at the Sandwich
Islands, what at the Society Islands had cost the
labors and sufferings of fifteen years.

The population had already suffered a large reduc-
Population tion. When the Islands were discovered,
of the isl-
ands. it was estimated at 400,000. This estimate was doubtless excessive; yet when I traversed
the group, eighty-five years after, I saw numerous

traces of deserted villages, and of grounds once under cultivation, then lying waste. The first missionaries estimated the population of the group at
130,000, and that of Hawaii at 85,000. The wars of
Kamehameha did much to depopulate; but a disease which the historian of Captain Cook acknowledges to have been introduced by the seamen of his
ships, must have done much more. Cer- Depopulation,
and how it
tainly, when the gospel came with its reno- was stayed.
vating powers, the social and moral condition of the
islanders was at the lowest point of degradation.
But for the introduction of Christianity, staying the
destructive tide, the fifty years since that time would
have sufficed to reduce the nation to a few fragments
in the mountain recesses.

CHAPTER II.

THE FOREIGN MISSION SCHOOL.

1816 — 1826.

THE Foreign Mission School for educating heathen
An experiment. youths in this country, established in the
year 1816, was intimately connected with
the rise of the Hawaiian Mission. It was also the
first decisive experiment made of educating such
youths in the midst of an advanced Christian civilization, to be helpers in missions to their barbarous
pagan countrymen.

The school had its origin in a singularly interesting youth named Obookiah, a native of the Sandwich
Henry Oboo- Islands, born about the year 1795. His
kiah birth-place was on Hawaii. For some reason he was induced to take passage in an American
ship, whose commander brought him to New Haven
in Connecticut. This occurred in the year 1809.
The college buildings attracted his attention, and,
learning their object, he was found one day, by the
Rev. Edwin W. Dwight, weeping on the threshold
of one of the buildings, because there was no one to
instruct him. The excellent man had compassion
on him, and became his instructor. Samuel J. Mills
coming to New Haven soon after, with his mind full
of the idea of missions to heathen lands, wrote
Gordon Hall the same year (1809), proposing that
Obookiah be sent back to reclaim his own country-

men, and that a Christian mission accompany him.
On the return of Mills to his father's house in Tor-
ringford, he took Obookiah with him; and afterwards took him to Andover, where no small interest
was awakened among the people of God on his behalf,
and where he was believed to have become the subject of renewing grace. Meanwhile other youths
were found, not only from the Sandwich Islands, but
from other parts of the world, and in such numbers
as seemed to call for a school specially de- Origin of the
signed for their instruction. The subject school.
was brought before the American Board in 1816, by
a committee from a meeting of gentlemen at New
Haven, and the Board appointed the Hon. John
Treadwell, Rev. President Dwight, James Morris,
Esq., Rev. Dr. Chapin, and Rev. Messrs. Lyman
Beecher, Charles Prentiss, and Joseph Harvey,
agents to devise a plan for a school, and to carry
it into execution. Cornwall, in Connecti- Its location.
cut, was selected as the most suitable place,
and the people of the town gave an academy building
and other property, valued at twelve hundred dollars.
A house for the principal was purchased by the
agents, another for a boarding-house, and about
eighty-five acres of land for a training farm. Obookiah was among the first pupils, and Mr. Dwight,
his earliest Christian friend, was employed as its
first principal, until the Rev. Herman Daggett
should be able to take charge. The school opened
with twelve pupils, of whom seven were from the
Sandwich Islands.

The object of the Seminary, as set forth in its
Constitution, was, — "The education, in Object and
our own country, of heathen youths, in such pupils.

manner as, with subsequent professional instruction, will qualify them to become useful missionaries, physicians, surgeons, schoolmasters, or interpreters; and to communicate to the heathen nations such knowledge in agriculture and the arts as may prove the means of promoting Christianity and civilization."

Nine of the pupils, in 1823, were from the Sandwich Islands, fifteen from half as many Indian tribes, three were Chinese, two were Greeks, one was a New Zealander, one a Malay, one a Portuguese, one a Jew, and three were Anglo-Americans.

Obookiah died on the 17th of February, 1818,
Death of
Obookiah.
and no one doubted his preparation for that event. Nor had he lived in vain. Chiefly through him a general interest had been awakened in the salvation of his kindred according to the flesh, and a mission to the Islands was made certain.

Seventeen of the thirty-one heathen youths ad-
The school
highly
prized.
mitted to its privileges, from 1817 to 1820, gave evidence of piety which was at the time satisfactory, and from the first the school excited a lively interest in the religious community. This interest extended to foreign lands. The Baron de Campagne of Basle, in Switzerland, remitted $876 toward its support. The very high estimate that was put upon it by the Christian community is shown by the annual Report of the Board at that time, which declares that the school was regarded with peculiar favor in all parts of the country, and that it would ever be fostered by the Board with parental care. Designed, as it was, to fit young persons who should come to the United States from the darkness, corruptions, and miseries

of paganism, to be sent back to their respective nations with the blessings of civilized and Christianized
society; with the useful sciences and arts; with the
purifying light of salvation, and with the hopes of
immortality; the Board believed that the relative
importance and eventual utility of the infant seminary could hardly be estimated too highly. Mr.
Daggett discharged the duties of principal for six
years, until 1824, when declining health Principals of
the institu-
constrained him to resign, and his place tion.
was supplied by the Rev. Amos Bassett, D. D. The
school stood, necessarily at that early period, on a
basis that was purely theoretical; and upon that
basis the question was raised, whether it Its theoretical basis.
might not be expedient to remove it to
the vicinity of some large city, where the students
would be less secluded from society. In such a
position, however, they would have been unfitted,
by acquiring the tastes and habits of city life, for a
happy and useful residence among their uncivilized
countrymen. The Board discussed the question,
and resolved to consider the school as permanently
established at Cornwall. There appears to have
been no thought at that time of its ultimate discontinuance. Yet the difficulties in working the
system were gradually developing, and at length
proved to be insurmountable. These were Result of experience.
distinctly brought out in 1825, at the meeting of the Board in Northampton. Some of the
difficulties were these. It was not found easy to
decide what to do with the youths, after their education was completed. It was now known, also,
that those who had returned to their native lands
failed to meet the expectations of their friends. The

abundant provision for them while in this country, added to the paternal attentions they everywhere received, had been a poor preparation for encountering neglect and privations among their uncivilized brethren; and the expense of maintaining them, when returned, in any tolerable state of comfort, was much greater than it would have been had they never been habituated to the modes of life in an improved state of society. In short, the indications of Providence seemed clearly to teach, that the best education for heathen youths, and indeed the only suitable education, having reference to their success as teachers of their uncivilized brethren, must be given through the instrumentality of missionary institutions in their respective countries. The expediency of continuing the school was referred by the Board to a committee, which was to report to the Prudential Committee after visiting Cornwall; and the Prudential Committee was empowered then Its discontinuance. to act definitely on the subject. The result was a discontinuance of the school in the autumn of 1826.

A simultaneous effort to train Greek and Armenian youths in this country, for the most part in the ordinary academies and schools, and some of them even in colleges, proved equally unsatisfactory; and the experiment has never been repeated.

This experiment was worth much more than it Value of the experiment. cost. The school at Cornwall was the immediate occasion, as has been said, of the mission to the Sandwich Islands; and it served, at one period, as a convincing proof to the more intelligent Cherokees and Choctaws, of the really benevolent feelings of the whites toward the Indians.

In our own community, it promoted feelings of kindness toward the heathen generally, and gave opportunity for the display of native talent, which was in
a high degree interesting to the friends of human
improvement. It attracted the attention of many to
missionary exertions, who would otherwise have remained ignorant of them.   Nor was it the least of
its good influences, that it so early determined the
expediency of restricting the efforts for training a
native agency to the countries which were to be
evangelized.

CHAPTER III.

THE mission to the Sandwich Islands was commenced in the year 1820, twenty-three years after that to the South Pacific, and more than forty years
Origin of the mission. after the discovery of the Islands by Captain Cook. The first trace of it, in the prospective plans of the Prudential Committee, occurs as early as 1816. Obookiah died in 1818. When the time came for establishing the mission, three Hawaiian youths in the Foreign Mission School at Cornwall, named Thomas Hopu, William Tenui, and John Honuri, were described, in a Report of the Board, as instructed in the doctrines and duties of Christianity, and made partakers, as was charitably hoped, of spiritual and everlasting blessings. These youths
The missionaries. became connected with the mission as native helpers. Messrs. Hiram Bingham and Asa Thurston, from the Andover Theological Seminary, were ordained as missionaries at Goshen, Conn., on the 29th of September, 1819. The sermon was preached by the Rev. Heman Humphrey, afterwards President of Amherst College, from Joshua xiii. 1: "There remaineth yet very much land to be possessed." Besides these, the mission contained a physician, Dr. Holman; two schoolmasters, Messrs.

Whitney and Ruggles; a printer, Mr. Loomis; and a farmer, Mr. Chamberlain. All these were married men, and the farmer took with him his five children.

The members of the mission, at the time of receiving their public instructions from the Board in Park-Street Church, were organized into a mission church, including the three islanders. There existed then no doubt as to the expediency of such a step. But experience afterwards showed, that embodying the missionaries and native helpers in the same ecclesiastical organization served to complicate and retard the development of a purely native Christian community, and to embarrass and delay the independent existence and action of the native churches. More than forty years elapsed before the independence of the Hawaiian churches was practically acknowledged by the missionaries.

Another error, naturally committed in the necessary absence of experience so near the outset of this enterprise, was the comparative estimate put upon mere civilizing agencies. Hence the sending of a farmer as part of the mission to the Islands. It was supposed that the natives would at once profit by improvements in tillage such as an American farmer would be able to introduce. But the facts did not correspond with those anticipations, and the farmer returned after three years. The causes of failure in this enterprise, however, were not wholly in the native population. A tropical sun operated unfavorably upon the white laborer. There were, besides, unexpected difficulties in training a family of children, that had been transplanted from our Christian community into the corrupting scenes

2

which were daily presented among that heathen
people. It should here be stated, that three years
later the first reinforcement of the mission was providentially detained several months longer than was
thought desirable; and during this detention, a
farmer and some mechanics, who had been in contemplation for it, were all withdrawn by various
causes. This was regarded at the time as a misfortune, but the knowledge afterwards obtained changed
the aspect of the case.

The mission sailed from Boston on the 23d of
October, 1819, in the brig *Thaddeus*, Captain Blanchard. On the 30th of March, after a
voyage of somewhat more than five months,
the snowy summit of Mauna Kea, on Hawaii, was
seen above the clouds, at a distance of eighty miles.

The voyage.

Up to this time, the missionaries had expected to
find the old King Kamehameha ruling the Islands
with despotic power, and zealously upholding idolatry. They expected to see the temples
standing; to witness the baleful effects of
idolatrous rites; to be shocked by day with the sight
of human sacrifices, and alarmed at night by the out-
cries of devoted victims. They expected to encounter
a long and dangerous opposition from the powerful
priesthood of paganism. They expected to hear the
yells of savage warfare, and to witness bloody battles,
before idolatry would be overthrown and the peaceful religion of Jesus Christ established. No anticipations were more reasonable, yet not one of them
was realized. Their first information from
the shore was, that Kamehameha had died,
and that his successor had renounced the national
superstitions, destroyed the idols, burned the tem-

Anticipa-
tions of the
missionaries.

Agreeable
surprise.

ples, abolished the priesthood, put an end to human sacrifices, and suppressed a rebellion which arose in consequence of these measures; and that peace once more prevailed, and the nation, without a religion, was waiting for the law of Jehovah.

The royal residence was then at Kailua, on the western or leeward side of Hawaii, and the ship *Thaddeus* reached that place with the mis- Reception. sionaries on the 4th of April, 1820. They found the son of Kamehameha, who had succeeded him, a young man of dissolute habits, but of good personal appearance, intelligent, frank, and humane. Happily he had judicious and influential counselors. These were Ke-o-pu-o-la'-ni and Ka-a-hu-ma'-nu, both queen-mothers; Ka-la-ni-mo'-ku, the prime minister, popularly known at that time among foreigners by the name of "Billy Pitt;" and Ku-a-ki'-ni, brother of Kaahumanu, to whom foreigners had given the name of "John Adams," and who afterwards became the governor of Hawaii. Keopu-olani was the king's mother, and ranked higher, in native estimation, than any other person on the whole group, in consequence of her preëminently royal parentage. Kaahumanu had been the favorite wife of the old Kamehameha, and had no superior in mental power; and Kamehameha, probably for prudential reasons, had associated her in the government with Liholi'ho, which was the name of the king; and this position she held till her death.

Liholiho had friendly feelings towards the missionaries; but having abolished one religion without any religious motives, he seemed in no haste to come under the restraints of another. He was himself a polygamist; and seeing the missionaries each with

only one wife, he was apprehensive of the demands
that might be made upon him.

To hasten a decision, the missionaries deemed it
expedient to request only for permission to remain
on trial one year. This, after some delay, was
Stations oc- granted. As the result of further nego-
cupied. tiations, the company was allowed to
occupy stations at Kailua on Hawaii, at Honolulu
on Oahu, and at Waimea on Kauai.

Near the close of 1820, the king and what may be
called his court removed from Kailua to Honolulu,
Honolulu on Oahu, which thenceforward became the
the capital. capital of his kingdom. It was then a
mere straggling village of grass hovels. Kuakini
remained at Kailua as governor of Hawaii, but his
value as a ruler and as a friend of the mission had
not yet been developed. Mr. and Mrs. Thurston,
deeming themselves not sufficiently protected at
Kailua, followed the king to Honolulu. They were
naturally rendered somewhat apprehensive by an
Singular ex- event that occurred previous to the king's
perience of departure. A vile heathen priest laid his
Mrs. Thurs-
ton. rough hands on Mrs. Thurston, while her
husband was in school. Breaking instantly away,
she fled to her natural protector. Scarcely were
they both returned and seated in their dwelling,
when the priest reëntered; but he was glad to flee
from the powerful arm of a man, who at Yale College
had been voted the most athletic in his class. It is
an interesting fact, that this was the only insult of
the kind ever offered by natives of the Islands to
missionary ladies.

The Hawaiian language had been so far reduced

to a written form in 1822, that the printing-press came into use. At the opening of the year, the first sheet was printed, containing the rudiments First print- of the language. This was an interesting ing. event to the king, the chiefs, and the mission. The alphabet contained only twelve letters, five of them vowels and seven consonants; but these twelve let- ters expressed all the vernacular sounds. Every syllable ended with a vowel, and each letter had one sound only. Spelling was thus made easy, and so was learning to read and write. This was within two years from the arrival of the mission. A month later, Mr. Bingham received a letter from Kuakini, who had succeeded in mastering the contents of the first printed sheet. Epistolary correspondence was thus commenced in the Hawaiian lan- Native cor- guage, and opened a new source of pleas- respondence. ure and advantage to the chiefs and people, of which hundreds soon availed themselves.[1]

Unfriendly foreigners were endeavoring, about this time, to undermine the confidence of Providential interposi- the rulers and people in the mission, and tion. they were able to exert some influence on the more ignorant and credulous. Two things were asserted, (1) That the missionaries at the Society Islands had taken away the lands from the natives, and reduced them to slavery, and that the American mission- aries, if suffered to remain at the Sandwich Islands, would pursue the same course. (2) That the resi- dence of American missionaries was offensive to the King of England; and that if they were not sent

[1] A syllabic alphabet, like that of the Cherokee Indians, of ninety-five characters, is said to have been among the possibilities; but it would not have been so simple and convenient as the one adopted. — See *Bingham's History*, p. 154.

away, the English monarch would soon give the islanders proof of his anger. This latter assertion was of course made by natives of England.

It was easy to see that the influence of these falsehoods would be destroyed, should respectable gentlemen from England and the Society Islands come to Honolulu, and state facts as they were. How this was to be brought about, no one could see. Yet the evil was obviated in its very crisis, and in the ordinary course of divine providence.

Vancouver had promised Kamehameha, that a vessel should be sent him by the English government. This promise had been overlooked or disregarded for the space of thirty years. Instructions were then given to the colonial government of New South Wales, to send a schooner as a present to the Hawaiian king. The captain in charge of this vessel touched at the Society Islands on his way, and there found the Rev. Daniel Tyerman and George Bennett, Esq., two respectable English gentlemen, who had been sent by the London Missionary Society as a deputation to the missions in the South Pacific Ocean. As the captain proposed to touch at the Marquesas Islands in the vessel which accompanied the one destined for Liholiho, after executing his mission at the Sandwich Islands, it was resolved to send two native chiefs as missionaries to the Marquesas, and that the Rev. William Ellis, an intelligent English missionary at the Society Islands, should accompany them to superintend their incipient operations; and the gentlemen of the deputation resolved to go with them. This whole company were thus to visit the Sandwich Islands on their way to the Marquesas.

Arriving at Honolulu, about the middle of April, 1822, Liholiho and his chiefs had repeated interviews with the Society Islanders, their language being substantially like the Hawaiian, and they described the true character and influence of the English missionaries in their own country. The English gentlemen, also, informed the government of the friendly disposition of the English monarch and people. Thus the misrepresentations of the foreigners were effectively exposed. The good influence was perpetuated by the settlement, at the request of the chiefs and the American mission, of the Society Islanders and of Mr. Ellis at the Sandwich Islands; though the latter still retained his connection with his Society in England. The deputation left the Islands in August, after an agreeable and useful visit of four months.

Mr. Ellis soon became master of the Hawaiian dialect, and was the first to enjoy the privilege of preaching freely to the people. A valuable accession. Auna, the most capable of his Tahitian assistants, was even more fluent in the use of the language.

Kaahumanu, the second in the government, had for a considerable time refused to avail herself of the advantages for intellectual Kaahumanu an iconoclast. culture afforded by the mission; yet, in a tour she made through Hawaii, she searched out and destroyed a large number of idols. More than a hundred were collected from caves in different parts of the island, and committed to the flames.

The English deputation strongly advised to the licensing of Thomas Hopu as a preacher of Native ministry. the gospel. The mission declined doing it, however, and it was long before they were ready to

CHAPTER IV.

CONDITION OF THE PEOPLE.

THE chief men of the nation had come under a civilizing influence to a certain degree. The odor-Civilization iferous sandal-wood used in the religious among chiefs. worship of China, was a monopoly of the government, and the trade was in its full vigor. Merchants gladly brought to the islands whatever insured an extravagant price from the king and his chiefs. This continued until the outlays of the government no longer left it the means of paying.

A public and formal reception was given to the first reinforcement of the mission, in what might Formal re- be called the palace, a large thatched build-ception to the first re- ing, said to resemble in its appearance a inforcement. Dutch barn; with a door at each end, windows in the sides, and Venetian shutters, but no glass. The interior formed one apartment. The side-posts, the pillars supporting the ridge-pole, and the rafters, were fastened together by cords made from the husk of the cocoanut. The floor was of mats, and chandeliers hung suspended between the pillars. Mahogany tables, sofas, chairs from China, mirrors, and two full-length portraits of the king, completed the conveniences and decorations of the room.[1]

At Kailua, on Hawaii, the king's hall of audience,

[1] Stewart's *Residence at the Sandwich Islands*, p. 79.

if such it might be called, where he first received
the missionaries, was a contrast to this. ^{The contrast at Kailua.}
It was described as a dingy, unfurnished
building made of thatch. And when his Majesty
came on board the brig at that place, to dine with
the only company of white women he had ever seen,
his clothing, in accordance with the taste and
fashion of the timè, was a narrow girdle around
his waist, a green silk scarf over his shoulders, a
string of large beads on his otherwise bare neck,
and a wreath of feathers on his head; without coat,
vest, pants, or shirt, without hat, gloves, shoes, or
stockings. The best shelter he was then able to
offer the twenty-two persons composing the mission,
was " a large barn-like, thatched structure, without
floor, ceiling, partition, windows, or furniture."

At the reception of the first reinforcement at
Honolulu, three years later, the dress of the king
and of his chiefs of both sexes was after the civilized
fashion.

It is not a pleasant duty to describe the moral
condition of these islanders, as it was when Christian labor among them commenced; but the subsequent triumphs of divine grace cannot be appreciated without such a description.

The intemperate habits of the king were a sore
trial, not only to the missionaries, but also ^{Habits of the king.}
to many of his chiefs and people. When
he visited the *Thames*, to return the call made
upon him by the gentlemen of the reinforcement,
he was sober, in fine health and spirits, handsomely
dressed, and easy in his manners, his whole deportment being that of a gentleman. Some weeks
after this, a royal dinner was given, and numerously

attended, with a great show of court dresses and
Hawaiian ceremonies.   Mr. Stewart describes a procession he saw, as one which, from the richness
and variety of dress and colors, would have formed
an interesting spectacle to visitors from civilized
countries.   Yet the king and his suite made a sorry
exhibition.   They were nearly naked, on horses without saddles, and so intoxicated as scarcely to be able
to retain their seats as they scampered from place
to place, in all the disorder of a troop of bacchana-
lians.   A body guard of fifty or sixty men, in shabby
uniform, attempted by a running march to keep
near their sovereign; while hundreds of ragged
natives, filling the air with their hootings and
shoutings, followed the chase.[1]   The dull and mo-
notonous sounds of the native drum and calabash in
the progress of this festival, the wild songs and the
pulsations of the ground under the tread of thousands in the dance, fell on the heart of the missionaries with saddening power, since they knew
them to be associated with exhibitions that might
not be described.

When the mission was commenced, the common
The common people were everywhere at the lowest point
people. of social degradation.   They deemed themselves well off with a mat braided from rushes or
leaves, a few folds of native cloth for a cover at
night, a few calabashes for water and po-i, a rude
implement or two for cultivating the ground, and
the instruments used in their simple manufactures.
A species of arum called *kalo*, and the sweet potatoe,
with occasionally a fish eaten raw, constituted their
usual food.   The banana was cultivated to some

[1] Stewart's *Residence*, p. 94.

extent, and a few cocoanuts; and bread fruit trees grew here and there on Maui and Hawaii, and perhaps on the other islands. Their animal food was the flesh of swine and dogs; the tabu, when it was in force, allowing only the dogs to women. Arrowroot grew on the islands, but the people did not know how to manufacture it; also the sugar-cane, but it was not much cultivated, and they had not learned how to convert it into sugar and molasses. A narcotic root, called *awa*, was much used for purposes of intoxication. The dwellings of the common natives were made of a few upright poles, brought from the forest on their shoulders, and covered with leaves or grass. A low opening served for a door, another for a window, and the floor was of dry grass. A mat answered for table, chairs, and bed, and the head was pillowed on a smooth stone from the beach, or a block of wood. The inmates of the little hut, four or five in number, male and female, with a mere apology for clothing, crowded around the one calabash, and with their fingers drew from it their favorite po-i.

We shall not be surprised at the poverty and degradation of the people, when we con- Their moral template their extreme moral debasement. debasement. Their licentiousness would be incredible, but for the weight of testimony. The intercourse of the sexes was all but promiscuous.

Husbands had as many wives as they pleased, and a similar liberty was allowed to the wives. The ties of consanguinity in marriage were disregarded. Indeed it may be said that marriage and the family constitution were unknown. It was common for parents to give their children away to others as soon as they were born. Very few took care of their own children. As a general thing, there was no desire for children; and if a child was born, the parents were ready to give it away to almost any one who would take the trouble of it. If no one could be found willing to take it, a very common practice was to strangle it, or bury it alive. It was estimated by foreigners, who came first among the people and had the best opportunity of judging, that at least two thirds of the infants perished by the hands of their own parents.[1]

The evils consequent on this kind of life were increased by intercourse with early visitors from foreign lands, who introduced a disease, that so poisoned the physical constitution of the nation, that not even the gospel has been able to do more hitherto, than greatly to retard its destructive influence.

Nor were the Sandwich Islands an exception to the Their cruel-ties. inspired declaration, that the "dark places . of the earth are full of the habitations of cruelty." Like other heathen, the Hawaiians were strangers in great measure to the feelings of sympathy, tenderness, and pity. The distressed, instead of calling forth compassion, were objects of ridicule and abuse. If one had lost an eye, an arm, or was otherwise maimed, or was bereft of reason, he became to others an object of sport, especially to the children, who were not slow to make his misfortune the subject of boisterous mirth. If a man was dispossessed of his land and property by his chief, it was a fit opportunity for others to seize whatever little articles remained. If his house was

---

[1] Dibble's *History*, p. 127.

consumed by fire, his neighbors were ready to carry off any property they could rescue from the flames. When fathers or mothers became aged or infirm, it was not uncommon for the children, in order to rid themselves of the burden, to cast them down a precipice, or to bury them alive. The miseries of the sick were enhanced, not only by the desertion of friends, and the want of every comfort, but also by the cruel and superstitious treatment they received from pretended physicians or officious quacks. Instead of looking with pity upon maniacs, it was a common practice to put them to death by stoning.[1]

[1] Dibble's *History*, pp. 129-131.

CHAPTER V.

1821–1824.

How to improve the social life of a nation so demoralized and degraded, was a problem not
easy of solution. Uncouth manners were to
be corrected, and modes of dress and living
to be improved. Only married missionaries could do
this. Living models of domestic Christian life were
indispensable. How great the trial of patience was
to the earliest of the female missionaries, is well
described by Mr. Bingham. "Just look," he says,
"into the straw palace of a Hawaiian queen in the
first or second year of our sojourn among them, and
see a missionary's wife waiting an hour to
get her to turn from her cards to try on a
new dress for which she has asked. Then, on trial,
hear her laconic and supercilious remarks, — '*pilikia
— hemo — hana — hou*' (too tight — off with it — do
it over); then, see her resume her cards, leaving the
lady, tired and grieved, but patient to try again; and
when successful, to be called on again and again for
more. Look again, as another year passes on, and
you may see the same woman at her writing-desk,
her maidens around her, under the superintendence
of the same teacher, learning to ply the scissors and
needle, making silk dresses for her majesty, and a

How to improve the social life of the people.

A call for patience.

pet hog, like a puppy, shaking the folds of the silk for sport, and demonstrating how civilization and barbarism can walk hand in hand, or lie down together in queens' palaces. Within another year, Kamamalu, Kapiolani, Kaahumanu, Ke- Encouraging kauluohi, Kinau, Keopuolani, Kalakua, progress. Kekauonohi, Liliha, Keoua, Kapule, Namahana, and others, threw around them an air of rising consequence, by the increase, not only of foreign articles of clothing, but of furniture, — a chair, a table, a workstand, a writing-desk, a bedstead, a glass window, partitions, curtains, etc., noticing, and attempting to imitate what, in the mission families, attracted their attention, or appeared sufficiently pleasing, useful, and available to induce them to copy."[1] Yet very few chiefs had the means to purchase the variety of useful articles created by the arts of civilized life; and if farms had been freely given the common people, they had neither the ability to purchase the implements needful for their cultivation, nor the skill and enterprise to make a good use of such implements.

The mission was divinely guided in the right way. The ladies had been well educated, not only Value of missionary in the schools of their native land, but in wives. domestic habits. Their households were an illustration of Christian life. They were a pattern of what Christian wives and mothers ought to be. They showed the native women how to make garments for themselves and for their children, and had the patience to persevere in showing them until those women had learned the art. The presence of wellordered Christian families at central points, was thus

[1] Bingham's *History*, p. 170.

3

greatly helpful to the gospel, which was the main agency for elevating the social condition.

It is due to the mission families earliest on the ground, that some of their inconveniences should be mentioned. Their first houses were mere thatched huts, like those of natives. A single low room served for parlor, study, receiving room, bedroom, and pantry. The cooking was done in an adjoining shed, or in the open air. The missionaries soon improved upon these houses, enlarging them, dividing them into rooms, laying floors, and making windows and doors; yet it was not until their health had suffered, that they were able to exchange the leaking thatch for sun-burnt brick, stone, or wood. After fourteen years, a majority of the families still lived in thatched houses; and it was only by a very gradual process that the several apartments obtained their appropriate furniture. Yet the progress was doubtless more stimulating to the natives from having been so gradual. For a time, the travelling of the missionaries, if by land, was on foot; if by water, it was generally in crowded, uncomfortable, poorly navigated native vessels. Horses, since become so common on all the islands, had not then been pressed into service. Milk could not be had for several years, even for young children. Salt beef and pork, with hard bread, and flour obtained from ships, were their main dependence. Of course these inconveniences gradually disappeared.

Trials of the mission families.

It was perhaps well that the natives educated at the Cornwall School failed as interpreters. Having been taught through the medium of the English language only, and knowing far less the force and meaning of English words than was

Failure of interpreters.

supposed, they had gained but a very few ideas, and many of these were confused and incorrect. The missionaries were thus obliged to apply all their energies to the speedy acquisition of the Hawaiian language, and to communicating thoughts directly through that medium. Efforts were made to instruct a few natives in the English language, but it was soon found best to employ the whole strength of the mission in efforts to save the multitude through the native tongue.

The missionaries were able to preach in 1823. Mr. Ellis, returning with his family from Tahiti, had the free use of the language; and the two as- *Improvement in public* sistants he brought with him were soon *worship.* able to exhort, pray, and teach. Changing a few hymns from the Tahitian dialect, Mr. Ellis introduced them into public worship, much to the gratification of the natives. From this time, hymns were in great demand, and were multiplied as fast as possible. The hymn-book went through several editions.

The arrival of the second reinforcement gave rise to the inquiry, whether the great island of *Hawaii ex-* Hawaii should not be occupied. Hence the *plored.* well-known exploring tour of Messrs. Ellis, Bishop, and Goodrich around that island.

The king and his young brother, with twelve chief men and as many chief women, were now *Hopeful indi-* learning to read and write. A little half- *cations.* sister of the king died, and received Christian burial at his request. In February, Liholiho enjoined upon his prime minister to secure the observance of the Sabbath, and imposed a fine on those who were found working that day. A crier went round on Saturday evening, proclaiming the new law.

In the year 1821, Liholiho performed a characteristic act of daring, in crossing the channel
between Oahu and Kauai, a hundred miles
broad and swept by the trade-winds, in an open sail-
boat, and landing defenseless on what might have
proved a hostile territory. He was received, however,
with the utmost respect by Kaumualii (Tamoree),
the King of Kauai, who went so far as to make a formal surrender to him of the supreme control of
the island. After they had visited the several parts
of it in company, Liholiho invited Kaumualii on
board a vessel which had come to him from Oahu,
and they sailed at once for Honolulu. The ruler of
Kauai never again saw his native isle, though allowed to retain his title, and to be held in
honor. Having discarded Kapule, his wife,
on the charge of unfaithfulness, he became the husband of Kaahumanu. Vancouver had been favorably
impressed by the promising appearance of Kaumualii
while a youth, and he had more than answered the
expectations of that intelligent navigator. Sedate,
dignified, courteous, and honorable in his dealings,
he was respected by foreigners, beloved by his people,
and esteemed by all who knew him. He was also a
patron, friend, and coadjutor of the mission. At
length finding himself seriously ill, he settled his
worldly business with composure; and, though not
exhibiting a high degree of religious joy, he showed
that four years of instruction had not been in vain.
Messrs. Ellis and Stewart, his spiritual advisers,
regarded him as manifesting a becoming humility,
and a degree of calm reliance on the Saviour. He
died on the 26th of May, 1824; and his remains, in accordance with his request, were

taken by Kaahumanu to Lahaina, and deposited by
the side of Keopuolani. The funeral services, previously performed at Honolulu, were in keeping with
the native demands for one of his rank, at that stage
of the national civilization. He was laid in state.
His splendid war-cloak, covered with small, smooth,
bright feathers, red, yellow, and black, in fanciful
patterns, and a tippet of similar fabric, decorated
his couch; and a coronet of feathers encircled his
brow. The body, partly covered with velvet and satin,
was thus exposed to the observation of his friends,
then inclosed in a coffin covered with black velvet.
Chiefs, foreigners, members of the mission family,
and others, assembled at the residence of Kaahumanu, where prayer was offered, hymns were sung,
and a sermon was preached by Mr. Ellis, from the
Saviour's injunction, " Be ye also ready."

CHAPTER VI.

KEOPUOLANI.

1823.

In March, 1823, Hoapili, the husband of Keopuolani, being appointed governor of Maui, desired to be
supplied with books, that he and his wife might
pursue their studies. For a domestic chaplain, they
took with them Pu-aa-i-ki, better known as Blind
Bartimeus, who appeared, even then, to possess
more spiritual light than any other native on the
Islands, and of whom a more particular account will
be given hereafter. At this time, Keopuolani made
Her new   the following declaration : " I have followed
views of the the custom of Hawaii in taking two hus-
marriage re-
lation.   bands, in the time of our dark hearts. I
wish now to obey Christ, and to walk in the right
way. It is wrong to have two husbands, and I
desire but one. Hoapili is my husband, and hereafter my only husband." Before leaving Honolulu,
she requested of the mission, that she might have
the presence of a missionary at Lahaina. Accordingly Messrs. Stewart and Richards, of the reinforcement, were assigned to that post. She also
took with her Taua as her teacher, the most intelligent of the Society islanders.

The people of Lahaina, acting under these new
influences, soon built two houses for the missiona-

ries, of ample proportions, and commenced building a house for public worship. While thus Builds a church at Lahaina. employed, the chattering natives were heard to say, contrasting their present service with their old one of building temples for their bloody idols, "The house of God — the house of prayer — good, very good."

The closing scenes in the life of this woman form an epoch in the mission, and in the history of the nation, and it is proper that some special account be given of her.

Keopuolani was born in the year 1778, in the district of Wailuku, on the northeast side Her royal descent. of the island of Maui. The family, on the father's side, had ruled on the island of Hawaii for many generations; and on the mother's side, had long governed Maui, and for a time also Lanai, Molokai, and Oahu. Intermarriages for successive generations had intimately connected the two families. Her paternal grandfather was the Hawaiian king, whom Captain Cook was leading by the hand when he was killed by the jealous natives. Her grandmother, the guardian of her early years, was a daughter of the king of Maui, and the wife who threw her arms around her husband's neck while he was walking with Captain Cook, and thus gave opportunity to the natives for their fatal attack.

She became the wife of Kamehameha at the early age of thirteen, and was the mother of eleven Her marriage. children, only two of whom lived to attain the kingly office. So sacred was her person, that her presence in the wars of Kamehameha did much to awe the enemy. In early life, she never walked abroad, except at evening, and then all who saw her prostrated themselves to the earth.

Kamehameha had other wives, and it does not appear that she was particularly a favorite, except as she was much the highest chief on the Islands. She was amiable and affectionate, while her husband was not remarkable for these qualities. Keopuolani was strict in the observance of the tabu, but mild in her treatment of those who had broken it, and they often fled to her for protection. She was said, by many of the chiefs, never to have been the means of putting any person to death.

In the year 1822, while at Honolulu, she was very Her conver- ill, and her attention seems to have been sion. then first drawn to the instructions of the missionaries. Though much opposed in this by some of the chiefs, she was resolute. What she did to secure this instruction, when removing to Lahaina in 1823, has already been stated. Her Christian character developed steadily from that time. Notwithstanding her necessary cares, and her interruptions from company, she daily found time for learning to read; nor was she less diligent in searching for divine truth. So decided was her stand in favor of Christianity, that many of the people and some of the chiefs were offended, but their opposition only gave her the more opportunity to show the firmness of her principles, and the strength of her attachment to the Christian cause. Even the king, her son, who had arrived from Honolulu, and to whom she was much attached, sought at times to draw her away from her Christian teachers. On one occasion she replied to him as follows: "Why do you call my foreign teachers bad? They are good men, and I love them. Their religion is good; our old religion is good for nothing. Their ways

are all good, and ours are bad. Are not their instructions the same as formerly? You then said
they were good, and told me I must regard them,
and cast away all my old gods. I have done as you
said; and I am sure I have done well. But you
now disregard the true religion, and desire me to do
the same. But I will not. I will never leave my
teachers. I will follow their instructions, and you
had better go with me, for I will never again take
my dark heart."

The illness of Keopuolani assumed a threatening
form in the last week of August, 1823. In Dangerous
consequence of this, the chiefs began to illness.
assemble, agreeably to their custom. Vessels were
despatched for them to different parts of the Islands,
and one was sent by the king to Honolulu for Dr.
Blatchley. In the evening of September 8th, under
the apprehension that she was dying, a messenger
was sent to the mission family, and several of them
repaired immediately to her house. As soon as she
heard the voice of the females, she extended her
hand to them with a smile, and said "*Maikai!*" —
"Good," — and added, "Great is my love to God."
In the morning she was a little better, and conversed
with her husband, Hoapili, on the goodness of God
in sparing her life to see his servants, and hear his
words, and know his Son. To the prime Her charge
minister, Kalanimoku, on his arrival, she to the prime minister.
said: "I love Jesus Christ. I have given myself
to him to be his. When I die, let none of the evil
customs of this country be practiced. Let not my
body be disturbed. Let it be put in a coffin.[1] Let

---

[1] At the death of chiefs, their bodies were always cut in pieces, the flesh
burnt, and the bones preserved. These were committed to the care of

the teachers attend, and speak to the people at my interment. Let me be buried, and let my burial be after the manner of Christ's people. I think very much of my grandfather, Taraniopu, and my father Kauikeouli, and my husband Kamehameha, and all my deceased relatives. They lived not to see these good times, and to hear of Jesus Christ. They died depending on false gods. I exceedingly mourn and lament on account of them, for they saw not these good times."

There is much more related of her that would interest the reader, but for which there is not room. *Her baptism.* She was anxious to receive Christian baptism, but there was no missionary then at Lahaina sufficiently conversant with the native language, to venture on administering the rite, for the first time, in the presence of so large a proportion of the national intelligence. Messrs. Stewart and Richards had not even a competent interpreter.

some chief, and during his life were venerated or worshipped. When the chief died who had charge of the bones, they were secretly conveyed to some unknown place, and nothing more was heard of them. In rare cases, however, they were preserved for two generations. The prevalence of this practice accounts for Keopuolani's charge respecting her remains. The evil customs of which she spoke, were of the most criminal kind. It had from time immemorial been the practice, at the death of high chiefs, for all the people to indulge with impunity and without restraint, in every kind of wickedness. They threw off the little clothing which they usually wore, and none had even custom to shield them from the most open assault. A man might steal from any place with impunity. Neighbors who were at enmity, might take any revenge they could get. It was no crime for a man to burn his neighbor's house, put out his eyes, take his life, or that of any of his family. Promiscuous lewdness prevailed extensively. Knocking out each others' teeth was a common and almost universal practice, during the days of mourning. But if by any means a man was so fortunate as not to lose any of his teeth, by the violence of another, he would, with a sharp pointed stone, dig them out himself ; for it was a disgrace to any man not to lose some teeth at the death of a high chief. In consequence of these customs, there were few men in that age who had not lost some of their fore teeth.

They regarded her as a fit subject for baptism, but were unwilling to administer the ordinance without some means of communicating with her and with the people, so that there might be no danger of misunderstanding on so interesting an occasion. They feared lest there should be erroneous impressions as to the place the ordinance held in the Christian system. Happily, Mr. Ellis arrived just in season, and the dying woman was thus publicly acknowledged as a member of the visible church. The king and all the heads of the nation listened with profound attention to Mr. Ellis's statement of the grounds on which baptism was administered to the queen; and when they saw that water was sprinkled on her in the name of God, they said, "Surely she is no longer ours. She has given herself to Jesus Christ. We believe she is his, and *Her death.* will go to dwell with him." An hour afterwards, near the close of September 16, 1823, she died.

The gross irregularities customary on such an occasion had been forbidden by the queen herself and by the prime minister. But it was deemed expedient to allow the customary wailing, and it did not entirely cease until after the burial.

The funeral solemnities, at the request of the chiefs, were conducted according to Christian usages. The church not being large *Her funeral.* enough to hold the people, the service was near it, in a beautiful grove of kou trees. A low platform had been erected for the preacher, on which was a table, and chairs were provided for the missionaries. The corpse was placed on a bier near the table, and around it were gathered the bearers, mourners, chiefs, missionaries, and respectable foreigners, nearly all of whom wore badges of mourning. The number of people present was believed to exceed three thousand.   Mr. Ellis preached from Rev. xiv. 13: "Blessed are the dead which die in the Lord." After the service, a procession of about four hundred followed the corpse to a tomb prepared for it, built of stone, and all the while minute guns were fired from ships in the roads. Thousands, on both sides of the way, gazed at the solemn pageant as it passed, to most of whom it was new. The spectacle was transient, but the influence of that death and burial has never ceased to be felt by the Hawaiian nation.

The king was affected, for a time, by the death of Effect on the his mother, and by her exhortations, and king. sought to avoid the snares that were evidently laid for him by a foreigner of some standing. He was overcome at last by the artful offer of cherry brandy, with the assurance that it would not harm him. He tasted, and came once more under the power of the destructive poison. The vessel which took Mr. and Mrs. Thurston back to Kailua, conveyed also the king, on what proved to be his last visit there.

CHAPTER VII.

1823 – 1825.

LIHOLIHO, shortly after the death of his mother, came to the determination to visit England and the United States. As he could not be dissuaded from this, his more sagacious chiefs desired *The departure.* him to have the benefit of a trustworthy interpreter and counselor, and interested themselves, in concurrence with the king and his favorite wife Kamamálu, who was to accompany him, to secure the services of Mr. Ellis. But Captain Starbuck, master of the English whale-ship *L'Aigle*, who had offered the king and his suite a free passage, refused to take Mr. Ellis, and for reasons that appeared wholly insufficient. Five natives composed the suite of the king, among whom were his favorite wife already mentioned, Boki governor of Oahu, and Kekuanaoa, afterwards governor of the same island, and father of the late king, and of the one now occupying the throne.

The party embarked at Honolulu, on the 27th of November, 1823, amidst the loud and passionate lamentations of the natives crowding the *Parting addresses.* shores. In parting, the king renewed his recommendation to his people to attend on the instructions of the missionaries. Kamamálu was eloquent. The daughter of Kamehameha,—still in

comparative youth, tall, portly, and of queen-like
presence, — turned to the people and exclaimed: " O
heavens, earth, mountains, ocean, guardians, subjects, love to you all.   O land, for which my father
bled, receive the assurance of my earnest love."

This movement of the king seemed unpropitious
Beneficent   at the time, but it soon proved to be an
results.   important step favoring the progress of the
gospel. His wayward and dissipated habits had been
a serious hindrance. His departure placed the reins
of government at once in the hands of Kaahumanu
as regent, and of Kalanimoku as her minister; and
they, with the concurrence and aid of such chiefs as
Kuakini, Hoapili, Kapiolani, Naihe, and others, were
earnest in promoting schools, the observance of the
Sabbath, and general attention to missionary instruction.

The departure of the chiefs for their homes, on
A pleasing   the breaking up of their consultation, was
spectacle.   a fine spectacle, as beheld from the mission
houses. Embarking in eight brigs and schooners,
mostly owned by themselves, and under native com-
manders, and leaving the harbor in regular and
quick succession, with their white sails all spread to
the brisk trades, they afforded a striking illustration
of their advance in navigation.

There were then no overland mails, no telegraphs,
The king's   so that nothing was heard from the king
arrival in   for many months. He arrived in England
England.
in May, 1824, and was wholly unexpected. Yet his
reception by the government was kind, and quarters
were provided for him and his suite at public expense. He received some attention from statesmen
and others, and was taken to the theatre and pleas-

ure gardens, and amused with various exhibitions,
but saw little or nothing of religious men. In June,
before the time appointed for an audience with
George IV., the whole party was prostrated by the
measles. The highest medical skill was
called in, but the king and queen both died. His death.
The others recovered.

Thus closed the career of Kamehameha II., at the
age of twenty-seven, after a reign of little more than
five years. It was rendered memorable by
the overthrow of idolatry throughout his Character.
dominions, and by the introduction of Christianity.
Liholiho inherited from his mother a frank and generous disposition, and under more favoring circumstances, might have escaped the ruin which came
upon him. Being regarded from childhood as presumptive heir to the throne, he was always attended
by a numerous retinue, whose business it was to grat-
ify his wishes and minister to his pleasures. Worse
than this were the temptations to convivial and intemperate habits from nominally Christian men of
depraved morals. Desperately arrayed as those men
were against the gospel, and tardy as Kaahumanu
was in coming forward for its support, we may well
admire the grace of God that withheld Liholiho
from anything like a declared opposition. While
practically sanctioning drunkenness, polygamy, adultery, and incest, he yet authorized the introduction
of a system of religion which inculcated equity,
temperance, chastity, benevolence, and the love and
service of God. The amiable wife, whose death
probably hastened his own, may be numbered among
the friends of the reformation, then in progress.

The survivors were favored with an audience by

the British sovereign at Windsor Castle, and were
_{Audience at Windsor Castle.} received with courtesy. He counseled them
to respect the missionaries, to regulate
their own affairs, but not to look for his protection,
except from the encroachments of foreign powers.

The bodies of the king and queen, inclosed in
_{The bodies sent to the Islands.} triple coffins, were sent to the Islands, with
the survivors, in the frigate *Blonde*, under
the command of Lord Byron. The frigate arrived
at Honolulu on the 6th of May, 1825, having previously touched at Lahaina. The sad news had
reached the Islands early in March, by an American
whale-ship. This gave the chiefs time for preparing
the minds of the people. Kaahumanu and the prime
minister wrote letters to the several islands, with
kind salutations to the chiefs, missionaries, and
people, apprising them of the national bereavement;
proposing a season of humiliation and prayer on that
account; exhorting them to seek consolation in the
good word of God; and enjoining on the chiefs to
keep the people quiet, and to remain at their posts
until they should be sent for.

The arrival of the *Blonde*, in May, 1825, of course
_{Their recep- tion.} occasioned a degree of excitement, but
Christian influences predominated. The
first resort of rulers and people was to the church,
where appropriate religious exercises were held.
The building was filled to overflowing. The landing of the officers and scientific gentlemen of the
frigate, was on the following morning. The reception was in a large audience room, lately erected,
and appropriately furnished. The dignified courtesy
of Lord Byron, and the Christian civility of Kaahumanu and Kalanimoku, reflected honor on the coun-

tries they represented. At the instance of the prime minister, Mr. Bingham was unexpectedly called on to lead in prayer, which he did, first in the English language and then in the Hawaiian. The levee was followed by a suitable collation.

Funeral ceremonies were deferred until the chiefs could be collected from the different islands. Funeral The pageant was one befitting royalty, and ceremonies. the services were strictly Christian. The royal remains were placed in a temporary repository, from whence they were afterward transferred to a simple mausoleum of stone, erected for the purpose.

The chiefs, now generally assembled, held a national convention, at which Lord Byron and A national the missionaries were present. The chiefs, convention. being determined to encourage the American missionaries, desired to know from the commander of the frigate whether they were to be thwarted by British officials; having reference, no doubt, to the already ascertained hostility of Richard Carlton, H. B. M. Consul-general for the Society and Sandwich Islands, who had arrived at Honolulu in the interval between the reception of the tidings of the king's death and the arrival of the *Blonde.* After being informed what were the objects and relations of the mission, Lord Byron declared his approbation of them; and his whole influence while at the Islands was gratefully acknowledged by the mission.

At this meeting, Kaahumanu recognized the hereditary rights of the land-holders, which Noble stand had not been properly regarded by Liholiho, of the chiefs. and declared her determination to restrain crime. Kapiolani, from the southern district of Hawaii, stated the success of herself and her husband Naihe,

4

in their efforts to prevent murder, infanticide, theft, Sabbath desecration, drunkenness, and licentiousness; and the regent commended her, and called on the other chiefs to do the same. Kuakini adverted to the errors of the late king, and urged the importance of guarding the young prince, now nine years old, from the influences which had proved so disastrous to his departed brother. Kuakini's proposal was, that he remain under the instruction of the missionaries, and in this there was a general concurrence. It was also decided, that the government remain in the hands of Kaahumanu and Kalanimoku, until the prince should be of age.

CHAPTER VIII.

THE RULERS CHRISTIANIZED.

1824–1828.

THE king embarked for England in November, 1823. In the following April, Kaahumanu held a convocation of the chiefs on the subject of reform, at which the missionaries were present by invitation. She then declared, for the first time, her determination to attend to the teachings of the missionaries, to observe God's laws, and to have her people instructed in letters and the new religion. Her prime minister, who was in advance of her in his attachment to the cause, then made a stirring address, contrasting the old religion with the new, and the former condition of the nation with the present. He declared his purpose to acquaint himself with the new religion, to keep the Sabbath, obey the law of Jehovah, and have his own people (meaning those living on his own lands) attend on the teachings of the missionaries. Appealing to the other chiefs, he asked whether they concurred with him; and their prompt reply was, "Ae." Kalanimoku added, that this would have been done before, but for the dissipation and distracting influence of the king, hurrying from place to place, and diverting the attention of the people. The rulers resolved at this meeting to discountenance every species of

Early stand for reform.

gambling; and so successful were they in this most important reform, — the schools taking for a time the place of the old immoral games, — that unfriendly foreigners accused the missionaries of depriving the natives of their amusements.

Kaahumanu was proud of her official station. *Improved character of the regent.* But her character had gradually become so modified by her religious knowledge, that on the fourth anniversary of the arrival of the mission, she was willing to take her place with her subjects as a learner. Five hundred pupils were present, and among them several high chiefs, besides the regent; and many of these showed good specimens of handwriting, ability to read, and some acquaintance with Christianity. An exercise in the schools of a joint and spirited cantilation of Scripture passages committed to memory, especially delighted the old queen.

Kaahumanu desired to receive baptism; but the *She desires baptism.* missionaries, connecting this rite, as applied to adults, with a public profession of faith in Christ, thought it proper to wait for more decisive evidence of her piety.

In May the house of worship at Honolulu was *New church at Honolulu.* consumed by fire. Kalanimoku immediately ordered timber to be brought from the mountains, and in a few weeks a larger and better house was finished and dedicated. Schools were in flourishing condition on several of the islands, and for their use three thousand copies of elementary lessons in spelling and reading were printed. At the end of the year there were fifty natives employed as teachers, and two thousand had learned to read.

The religion of the gospel was taking root in Kailua, the place where it was first pro- Kuakini at Kailua. claimed. The return of Mr. and Mrs. Thurston, in company with the king, has been mentioned. Kailua then contained about three thousand inhabitants, and within thirty miles were not less than thirty thousand clustered in villages. The governor, Kuakini, spoke the English language intelligibly, had tea and coffee served daily at his table, and was gaining in civilized habits. He had imported a framed dwelling-house from America; and had erected a church, sixty feet by thirty, within the ruins of a heathen temple where human Dedication of a new church. victims were formerly offered. At its dedication in the last month of the year, Mr. Thurston read a portion of Solomon's prayer at the dedication of the temple, translated into the Hawaiian language, after which the people sang the Jubilee Hymn, "*Pupuhi i ka pu oukou*," — "Blow ye the trumpet." The sermon was from Haggai i. 7, 8 : "Thus saith the Lord of hosts, consider your ways. Go up to the mountains and bring wood, and build the house, saith the Lord." Nothing could be more appropriate, for all the timbers for the church had been brought some distance from the mountains. In this church the usual attendance was from six hundred to a thousand persons, who listened with a good degree of seriousness. Kapiolani (of whom more in the sequel), with Naihe her husband, and their train, came repeatedly from Kaawaloa, a distance of sixteen miles. Kamakou, also, an aged chief residing at the same place, came An interesting old chief. with his train; and once he remained a week, that he might receive daily instruction. "He

expressed much satisfaction," says **Mr. Thurston,**
" in the truths which he heard, and longed to become
acquainted with the whole Word of God. The last
time he saw us, he appeared much animated. Everything he uttered, the very expression of his countenance, conveyed feelings that would warm the bosom
of angels. The morning of his return he called on
the governor, and, on being requested, readily engaged in prayer with him and his family. After
walking to the beach with his people, and before
stepping into his canoe, he kneeled down and offered
up a short prayer to God for protection on his way
home: ' A great minister,' says the governor, as he
stood reflecting on the prayers and conversation of
this man ; and seeing him sail away, he added, ' a
great missionary.' At his own place, he forbids his
people working or bathing on the Sabbath, and regu-
larly assembles them twice to pray and converse with
them on religious subjects. This has been his practice for many months past. Of late he has extended his exertions, crossing the bay, and there
meeting the people and conducting religious services. He has received but little instruction from
missionaries, yet there are few natives on the Islands who have more correct views on religious
subjects. He seems to have been searching for
truth as for hid treasure. · I once heard him pray in
his family, and I was much surprised at the simplicity, fervency, and apparent sincerity which were
manifested, as well as with the correctness of religious sentiment which the prayer contained." [1]

The gospel was introduced into Hilo and Puna,
Hilo and   on the opposite side of Hawaii, embracing
Puna.   eighty miles of seacoast, early in 1824.

1 *Missionary Herald,* 1825, p. 20.

Messrs. Ruggles and Goodrich were the pioneer missionaries. Touching at Lahaina, they had a striking
view of Mauna Kea, one of the two summits of the
great island, at the distance of one hundred and
twenty miles. They were accompanied by Dr. and
Mrs. Blatchley, for a temporary stay; by Messrs. Ellis
and Chamberlain, on a missionary excursion; and by
Mr. and Mrs. Ely, going to occupy Kaawaloa, in the
neighborhood of Kailua. Voyages from Tedious voy-
island to island in those days were often aging.
very trying. This company was nine days and nights
on board the small, crowded, uncomfortable vessel,
whose deck would probably have been swept had the
trade winds risen with a strength that is often experienced. Some of the missionary passengers preferred spending the whole time on deck, to occupying
berths below. On their arrival, they found none
to welcome them among the stupid natives, but
obtained shelter in a large thatched canoe-house,
which the Oahu chiefs had appropriated to their
use. Next day was the Sabbath, and Mr. First experi-
Ellis preached to a large number of people, ence in Hilo.
in another similar building, which the forethought
of Kaahumanu had secured for them. The service
was interrupted by the entrance of a large pet hog,
with huge tusks, belonging to Kaahumanu, and bearing her name. The animal had the privilege of
tabu, and the natives, not daring to resist its entrance, made a boisterous retreat; and it was not
until the keeper had succeeded in quieting the
brute that the congregation resumed their places,
and the preacher was able to proceed. In those days
Hawaiian females of the highest rank were not at
all fastidious in the choice of pets.

This being the windward side of the island, the
rains were frequent and abundant.   Of
The scenery.
course the arable lands all had a luxu-
riant growth, and the country being mountainous,
the landscape was beautiful and grand, as seen from
the bay of Waiakea.   Yet that region was not then
a favorite resort.   Not a civilized man, except the
missionaries, resided on that side of the mountains.

Schools were commenced, and native teachers
brought from other islands.   In two months
The gospel
in Hilo.
a house was erected for the families by
order of Kalanimoku, and a church finished in the
frail Hawaiian style.   This was the ninth church
erected on the Islands, in the first four years of
the mission.   A few years more, and Hilo became
the most interesting of all the Christian districts.

Kaahumanu's evidences of piety were not satisfactory until after the rebellion on the isl-
Rebellion on
Kauai.
and of Kauai, which occurred in the year
following Liholiho's departure for England.   As the
cause of that rebellion and its consequences had a
bearing on the mission, some account of it should
be given.

George, the son of Kaumualii, who accompanied
the mission from the United States, had never given
evidence of piety, nor was his conduct, after his return to the Islands, satisfactory to his father.   He
was allowed by the government, after his father's
decease, to return to Kauai, though not as a high
chief.   When subsequently visited by Mr. Bingham,
he was living with his wife, much in the native style,
and was disaffected towards the government.   The
island governor was a nephew of the prime minister,   •
but not equal to the emergency, and the general

dissatisfaction was manifested by various acts of insubordination. Kalanimoku came over, while Mr. Bingham was there, in the hope of quieting the people, but did not succeed. It was not long before the insurgents, headed by George, attempted a surprise of the fort at Waimea, near the missionary station. Had the fort been taken, the aged prime minister would doubtless have been slain. But the attack failed. The chief immediately sent the missionaries away for safety, in a vessel he despatched to the seat of government for reinforcements. On board that vessel was a hostile chief in bonds, who had been captured the night before. He was seen at the close of the day, but not the next morning. Some time in the night he had been killed, and thrown into the sea.

The principal chiefs were at Lahaina; and Hoapili, the governor of Maui, immediately collected a thousand men, and sailed with two vessels for Kauai, touching at Honolulu. *Successful measures for its suppression.* Before starting, and also at Honolulu, he took advice of the missionaries as to the manner of conducting the war; and it was urged upon him, as a Christian duty, that there be no unnecessary destruction of life, and that captives should be kindly treated. His army, after its arrival, though exposed to attack, rested on the Sabbath; and when his force was drawn up in presence of the enemy, Hoapili commanded silence until prayer should be *Prayer before a battle.* offered to the true God. He then addressed the soldiers, assuring them that God was on their side, and exhorting them to be of good courage, and to spare the captives, such being the advice of their teachers. They then rushed into battle, and their opponents, after a short resistance, fled in a panic. The commander had no longer control of his army; the spirit of heathenism ruled the hour, and humane teachings were forgotten.

The unhappy George, with his wife and infant Treatment of daughter, escaped to the mountains. The George. two latter were soon captured, and kindly treated. George eluded his pursuers for several weeks, subsisting on roots, till at length, nearly famished and naked, he delivered himself up to one of the victorious chiefs, who showed him mercy. When brought into the presence of Kalanimoku, the dignified chief, out of regard to his father, threw his own mantle over the shoulders of the misguided young man, in token of his safety. He was restored to his wife and child, and sent to Oahu, where he lived several years, until his death. The island of Kauai now became, if it was not before, an integral part of the kingdom.

When Hoapili and his troops had departed for Kaahu- Kauai, Kaahumanu proclaimed a fast, in manu's con- version. order to secure the blessing of God on the expedition. Having afterwards resolved to join Kalanimoku at the seat of the war, her thoughts took a still more serious turn, and she was seen to weep at a public lecture. Next day she sent for the missionaries, and requested them to pray with her before her departure. She expressed great affection for them, saying, "What we have is yours." Puaaiki, the blind preacher, was overjoyed in view of this new exhibition, and seemed ready to kiss the feet of the queen, because he thought she was taking a stand on the Lord's side. Arriving at Honolulu, where she received tidings of the victory, she

repaired, with her attendants, to the sanctuary, to
unite in public thanksgiving for the restoration of
peace to the nation. On arriving at Kauai, she put
herself in communication with Mr. Whitney, and
rendered him valuable service ; and soon after she
wrote a letter to Honolulu, expressing her desire for
the reformation and eternal salvation of her people,
and declaring her own strong attachment to the
Christian cause. After her return to Honolulu, she
attended a religious meeting of females, and gave
vent to her feelings in tears.

The aid which had been so opportunely received
from the Society Islands ceased in 1824. The foreign
Auna, the Tahitian deacon, returned to his ̲aid̲ ̲with-̲
̲drawn.̲
own country, on account of the health of his wife;
and in September, Mr. Ellis accepted the offer of a
passage to the United States, a change of climate
being thought indispensable to the preservation of
Mrs. Ellis's life. The information he was able to
give to the Prudential Committee and officers of the
Board, while in the United States, was invaluable;
and he greatly interested and animated the Tribute to
people of God by his statements, in many Mr. Ellis.
parts of the Northern and Middle States, concerning the missions in the Society and Sandwich Islands.
The health of his wife not permitting their return
to the Pacific, Mr. Ellis was employed as Secretary
of the London Missionary Society until his own
health failed. Afterwards he performed important
services to the mission of his Society on the island
of Madagascar; and lately he has still more endeared
himself to the missionaries at the Sandwich Islands,
and to their patrons, by a masterly refutation of
charges brought against the mission by Bishop

Staley.   Few men in modern times have been more
useful to the cause of missions.

We now enter the year 1825.   More than a hun-
dred natives of both sexes at Honolulu, had offered themselves as candidates for
Christian baptism.   Among these were Kaahumanu,
Kalanimoku, Kalakua or Hoapiliwahine, Namahana,
Laanui her husband, and others less known to the
reader.   Most of them had been four or five years
under instruction, and they had generally given good
evidence of piety.   It was deemed best, however, to
defer their baptism and consequent admission to
the church somewhat longer; but after a further
delay of six months, all of them, except two, were
received into the church at Honolulu.   The two exceptions were Kalakua, who made her public profession at Lahaina, and Kapiolani, who did the same at
Kaawaloa.   Kaahumanu received the name of Elizabeth, and Namahana of Lydia.

One of the important events of this year was the
institution of a prayer-meeting at Honolulu, by the prime minister and several others.
It was of the nature of an association, and was called
by the natives a "tabu meeting," since none were admitted who did not engage to live sober and correct
lives, and to attend to the external duties of religion.
The meetings were held every Friday afternoon, and
it was customary to discuss in them subjects of a
practical nature.   Similar societies, male and female,
were formed at other stations, and members were
soon numbered by thousands.   For a time they were
useful; but they began at length to encroach upon
the offices of the divinely instituted local church,
and it was deemed necessary to take measures for

their suppression. A female prayer-meeting, instituted by native females at Honolulu, is said to have
continued in existence a score of years.

What may perhaps be called the first awakening
on the Islands, was at Lahaina, early in the The first
year 1825. Mr. Richards thought that in awakening.
April there were in that place as many as fifty homes
where were family prayers morning and evening;
and scarcely an hour of the day passed in which he
had not calls from persons anxious to know what
they must do to be saved. In the morning when he
awoke, he often found persons waiting anxiously at
the door to see him. Six months before, he had not
expected to witness, for a whole generation, such an
interest among that people in the concerns of eternity. There was a similar experience at Kailua, on
Hawaii. At Hilo, on the other side of the island,
at least two thousand habitually attended on public
worship.

Late in 1825 and early in 1826, Mr. Bishop performed a preaching-tour of three hundred Preaching-
miles around Hawaii, starting from Kailua, Hawaii.
and going northward. The population of the island
he estimated at 60,000. The stations then and subsequently occupied by the mission, were all embraced
in this route. The exceedingly varied and picturesque scenes through which he passed, many of which
came, long afterwards, under the eyes of the writer,
cannot be here described. Now he was in a frail
canoe beneath a tall cliff overhanging the sea; then
climbing dangerous steeps; then descending into
deep and lovely valleys filled with native hamlets;
now crossing dark ravines, then confused masses of
rough scoria; and so on, for the space of a month.

He had frequent opportunities for addressing assembled natives; and was surprised to find, where there were schools, that every kind of work and diversion was laid aside on the Sabbath; and that wherever there was a teacher capable of taking charge of a meeting, the people assembled freely for Growth of   prayer.   In his whole tour, he saw but one temperance. man intoxicated; whereas, only two years before, in his tour with Mr. Ellis on nearly the same route, it was common to see whole villages given up to intoxication.

The superstition connected with Pele, the supposed goddess of volcanoes, was not easily eradicated. On the death of Keopuolani, Hoapili, the governor of Maui, was married to Kalakua, a sister of Kaahumanu and Kuakini, better known as Hoapiliwahine. She possessed the characteristic decision and energy Inroad of a of her family.   In the summer of 1824, a prophetess of Pele.   pseudo-prophetess came to Maui from Kilauea, the great crater on Hawaii, and made no little stir among the people by claiming to be herself the goddess. The people were variously affected; a part of them expecting her to make some terrible display of power, should the chiefs not yield to her demands. She was followed by an immense crowd, and marched with haughty step, her long, black, disheveled hair hanging about her shoulders, and her countenance The recep- fierce and savage.   On coming near the tion at La- haina. chiefs she exclaimed, " I have come; " to which Hoapiliwahine replied, " We are all here." " Good will to you all," said the prophetess. " Yes," said Hoapiliwahine, " good will, perhaps."   " I have now come to speak to you," said the impostor. " Whence are you? " responded the chief.   " From

Tahiti — from England — from America—whither I have been to attend your king." Indignant at this falsehood, Hoapiliwahine said, "Come not here to tell us your lies; what have you in your hands?" "I have the spear of Pele, and her kahilis." "Lay them down," said the chief. The command was repeated before it was obeyed. The chief continued: "Do not come here to tell us you are Pele. There are volcanoes in other parts of the world. The great God in heaven governs them all. You are a woman, like us, and there is one God, who made you and us. Once we thought you a god. Light is now shining upon us, and we have cast off all our false gods. Go back to Hawaii, plant potatoes, make tapa, catch fish,, fatten hogs, and then eat; and not go about saying to the people, 'Give this or give that to Pele.' Go to school and learn the *palapala*. Now answer me honestly; have you always been lying to the people, or have you not?" The impostor confesses confessed, "I have been lying, but will lie her imposture. no more." At the suggestion of Kaikioewa, a prayer was offered to Jehovah. She then threw her flags into the fire, and the people exclaimed, "Strong is the *palapala*."

CHAPTER IX.

WICKED men have their reasons for opposing the
Cause of the opposition. progress of the gospel. Their opposition
at the Sandwich Islands, in the days of
Kaahumanu, arose from the fact that the introduction of Christianity interfered with their unlawful
gains and sinful pleasures. In the first years of the
mission, the Islands were regarded by not a few seamen and traders who visited them, and by the foreign residents viciously disposed, as so far out of the
world, that they felt it safe for them to act without
regard to public sentiment in Britain or America.
Whatever they might do that was abusive to the native government and people, or to the missionaries,
or in violation of their duty to God, they expected
no report of it to reach their relatives and friends
at home.

It was with this expectation, as afterwards ap-
Outrage at Lahaina. peared, that Captain Buckle, of the British
whale-ship *Daniel*, while at Lahaina in Oc-
tober, 1825, finding native females prohibited from
going on board his vessel for immoral purposes, as
aforetime, encouraged his men to charge Mr. Richards with being the author of the law, and to demand of him its repeal. The sailors who came with

the first demand retired after hearing from Mr.
Richards that he was not the author, and that he
could procure its repeal only by telling the chiefs
and people that the law was opposed to the law of
God, which they well knew he could not do. Next
came a large company, and forced their way into the
inclosure, venting their rage through the open door
and windows. One of them, more bold than his fel-
lows, faced the missionary and threatened, in the
presence of his sick wife and children, first the destruction of his property, then of his life, and then
of the lives of his family. The missionary A brave re-
replied, that he had devoted his life to the sistance.
salvation of the heathen, and should expose his breast
to their knives rather than do what they demanded.
The wife, nerved by the grace of God, then said : "I
have none to look to for protection but my husband
and my God. I might hope, in my helpless situation,
that I should have the compassion of all who are
from a Christian country. But if you are without
compassion, or if it can be exercised only in the way
you propose, then I wish you all to understand, that
I am ready to share the fate of my husband, and
will by no means consent to live upon the terms you
offer." The mob did not venture, after this, to use
personal violence, but retired, uttering horrid oaths
and threats. That night, the house was guarded
by natives. Next day, Mr. Richards wrote to Captain Buckle, who replied that all his men were
ashore, determined not to return without women,
and that it would be best for Mr. Richards to give
his assent, after which there would be peace. The
following morning, a boat put off from the ship
with a black flag, and fifteen or twenty sailors landed

5

from it armed with knives, and two of them with pistols. They found a native guard at the gate.

Missionaries defended by natives. Pressing upon the guard, they made their way to the door, when a company of natives, armed with clubs, rushed in through every window, and obliged the mob to disperse.

Mr. Stewart, being about to leave the Islands, because of the failure of Mrs. Stewart's health, came from Honolulu to Lahaina the night following, on a farewell visit to his former associate. He landed at midnight, and was surprised to be challenged by a sentinel, and to find the house occupied by an armed native force. This protection was continued until the departure of the *Daniel*.

The next outrage was the worst of all, besides being a source of mortification to every well-disposed citizen of the United States. In January, 1826, the United States armed schooner *Dolphin*, commanded by Lieut. John Percival, arrived at Honolulu, and remained there about four months. This was the first public vessel from their native land, and the missionaries had a right to expect civil treatment, if not kind offices, from those on board. They were lamentably disappointed. The whole stay of the *Dolphin* was very unfavorable to the interests of religion and morality, and exceedingly oppressive and odious to the natives.

The commander lost no time in expressing his regret at the existence of a law prohibiting females from visiting ships on an infamous errand. He next insisted on the release of four prostitutes, then in the custody of the government for a violation of the law. This demand was repeatedly urged, until at last it was partially successful.

Meanwhile the high chiefs were much troubled by threats, which they understood the commander of the *Dolphin* to have uttered, His threats. that he would shoot Mr. Bingham should he appear as interpreter in the council of the chiefs, when he (the commander) was transacting business with them; and that, unless the law against prostitutes was repealed, he would tear down the houses of the missionaries; and they asked their missionary friends what they should do in case of the apprehended violence. The reply was, that such threats would not be executed; and the natives were desired Advice of the at any rate not to resort to violence in missionaries. their defense. It was no doubt this mild advice which prevented bloodshed in the subsequent affray.

Three thousand people were present at the morning worship, on Sabbath, February 26. It was in the open air, the roof of the great church having fallen in consequence of a copious rain. In the afternoon the state of the weather prevented a meeting. Towards night, Mr. Bingham went to the house of Kalanimoku, who was sick. He had not been long there, when six or seven sailors from the Assault upon *Dolphin*, armed with clubs, entered the the government. upper room, where the sick chief was lying on his couch with his friends around him, and demanded a repeal of the law, threatening, in case of refusal, to tear down the houses. Confusion ensued, and before the rioters could be expelled from the house and yard, they had broken all the windows in front. Meanwhile their number increased, and they directed their course to the house of Mr. Bingham. Escape of Mr. Bing-Seeing the danger to his family, he has- ham. tened home by another way, hoping to arrive before them. Failing in this, he fell into their hands. When they were about to strike him with their clubs, the natives, who had borne the whole with wonderful forbearance, laid hold on the sailors, and the missionary escaped. He was pursued by small parties; one aimed a blow at him with a club, and another sought to stab him with a knife; but by the timely interposition of the natives, he reached his house unharmed. A new company came soon after and broke the windows. But while two of these were striving to force the door, one of them, in a manner unaccountable, turned suddenly round, and struck the other with a club, so that he fell, and was carried off as dead.

In the midst of this tumult and outrage, the Forbearance of the natives. chiefs cried out earnestly to the people: "Do not kill the foreigners; hold them fast; handle them carefully;" — to which one or two responded: "How can we? They are armed with knives and clubs." One of the *Dolphin's* crew received dangerous cuts from a sabre in the hands of a native. Some of the principal chiefs said, and it was the general opinion, that but for the advice of the missionaries, the seamen engaged in the affray would all have been killed.

Lieutenant Percival waited on the chiefs on the Disgraceful conduct. evening of that day, not to express regret for what had occurred, but to renew his request for the repeal of the obnoxious law. He then declared, in the presence of the chiefs, that the prohibition should come off; that he would not leave the Islands until it was removed. Three of the missionaries were present at this interview.

It was rumored next day, that some of the chiefs,

wearied by importunity and terrified by threats, had
intimated, that should females resort to _{The result.}
their old practices, it would not be very
strictly inquired into. A considerable number repaired on board the ships; and when the first boat,
in the dusk of evening, passed along the harbor of
Honolulu, a shout ran from deck to deck, as if a
victory had been gained.

When Kalanimoku was informed of the permission thus given, he was very indignant, and called
the offending chiefs before him. They quailed under
his severe rebuke; but the fatal deed had been done.
The flood-gates of immorality had been opened, and
a deluge of pollution could no longer be prevented.
Had the prime minister been in health, there is
much reason. to believe that so terrible a calamity
would not have occurred. It should also be said,
that the chiefs seriously believed the lives of the
missionaries to be in danger; nor did they know
to what extent they might themselves carry their
internal regulations, without giving offense to the
United States and Great Britain. And in how
many places in Christian countries, at the close of
a similar struggle, might a better result have been
expected? The law had been three months in operation before the arrival of the *Dolphin,* and the incessant efforts to procure its repeal were resisted for
seven weeks after that arrival.

When it became known that the law was pros-
trate, Lieutenant Percival called on the chiefs to express his gratification; and he then declared his intention to visit Maui and Hawaii, where the law was
still enforced, and compel the chiefs of those islands
to rescind it. So great a calamity Divine Provi-

dence was pleased to avert, and Honolulu alone was
tainted by a visit from the *Dolphin.* It is painfully
significant, that even the common people were ac-
What the customed to apply to this vessel and her
natives
thought of it. commander, interchangeably, the appella-
tion of the " mischief-making man-of-war."

The opposition of foreigners, which had received
such an impulse, raged with violence for some months
after the *Dolphin's* departure. Mr. Bingham being
the only ordained missionary at the place, and
preaching constantly in the native language, was
the object of peculiar hostility, and his life was generally thought to be in danger. Not that all visitors
to the Islands, nor all the residents, were enemies of
moral improvement, or of the mission. Some, though
friendly, overawed by the noise and violence of the
profane, were silent; but there were others of a
more decided character, who took the part of the
missionaries, and defended them. The steadfast-
ness of the native population was remarkable.
When it is considered that Honolulu was visited
by more than a hundred ships, and by two thousand
Their confi- seamen, during the years 1826 and 1827,
dence in the
missionaries. and that every species of falsehood and the
most vulgar abuse were heaped upon the mission,
and how easily uncivilized people are made to dis-
trust their benefactors, it is matter of great surprise that none of the chiefs or people, for many
months, appear to have had their confidence in the
missionaries shaken.

Our attention is again called to Lahaina. While
Mr. Richards and Hoapili, the governor, were absent,
Another out- the crews of English and American ships
rage at La-
haina. committed great outrages upon the peace

and property of the inhabitants there. The sailors attacked the house of Mr. Richards, with the declared purpose of killing him, but found it guarded by faithful natives. The females had all fled to the mountains, by command of Hoapiliwahine, the governess.

These pernicious influences were in some degree checked by the U. S. sloop-of-war *Peacock,* A seasonable Captain Thomas Ap Catesby Jones, which arrival. arrived at Honolulu in October, 1826, and remained there till the following January. A circular had been prepared by the missionaries at their general meeting in that month, in which they stated the course they had pursued, denied the charges made against them, and challenged an investigation. The circular was printed, and circulated among the foreign residents and visitors. After a month, the missionaries at Honolulu were informed, by a letter with the signatures of a number of foreigners, that their challenge for investigation was accepted. Accordingly word was sent to the different missionary stations, and the greater portion of the missionaries were assembled at Honolulu early in December. The mission-A meeting for the investigation was held aries put on trial. at the house of Boki, and the parties were present, with many others, including Captain Jones and several of his officers. The missionaries demanded that their accusers should bring definite charges in writing, and produce their evidence in support of them. Richard Charlton, the British Consul, who was the leader of the opposers, refused to bring such charges, or to have anything written down as a charge, which he was to support by proof. Captain Jones listened in silence until he perceived the whole

ground of dispute, and then gave his opinion, that
the burden of proof rested on those who
had accepted the challenge. Whereupon
some one of them moved an adjournment.

Defeat of their adversaries.

When about to leave the Islands, Captain Jones
wrote an affectionate farewell to the missionaries, in which he bore a decided testimony to the good effects of the missionary labors, as
they had fallen under his observation at the Sandwich and Society Islands. The written testimony
of the principal chiefs, given at this time, is of the
most positive and favorable nature.[1]

Testimony of Captain Jones.

The executive officers of the Board now believed
it to be their duty to secure the missionaries from a renewal of these shameful
outrages, by arraigning the authors of the more fla-
grant of them before the tribunal of public opinion
in their native lands. They accordingly published,
early in 1827, Mr. Richards' statement of the case of
Captain Buckle, and it was copied into newspapers
and extensively circulated. The published statement
arrived at Honolulu near the close of the year; and
it so happened that Captain Buckle was there at that
time. A great excitement followed. The
discovery that men could no longer wallow
there in the lowest depths of moral pollution, and
return home with untarnished reputations, was more
than the vicious could bear. The British Consul,
the most exceptionable of the foreign residents, took
the lead; affirming, that the Hawaiian rulers had no
right to make laws without the concurrence of Great
Britain, and threatening the vengeance of his nation
should they presume to make laws for themselves,

*A new tribu-
nal for the
wicked.*

Its effect.

[1] See *Missionary Herald*, 1827, p. 248.

as they were believed to be on the point of doing.
In their rage they threatened to proceed to Lahaina
and kill Mr. Richards. Fuel was added to the flames
by the arrival, just then, from Lahaina, of The John
the English ship *John Palmer*, Captain Palmer.
Clark, the commander of which had been detained
on shore at Lahaina by Hoapili, the governor, until
he should deliver up certain immoral native women,
who were on board his vessel in violation of law, and
he had been permitted to go on board his ship only
on a promise of releasing them, but had sailed the
next morning for Oahu with the women still on
board. The British Consul now demanded satisfaction from the government, for the constraint imposed on Captain Clark at Lahaina.

So great was the tumult, that Kaahumanu deemed
it expedient to order the principal chiefs The mission-
and the missionaries at Lahaina to come to aries summoned to
Honolulu. A council was then held to Honolulu.
investigate the complaints against the missionaries,
and the disaffected foreigners attended. Their chief
complaints were founded on Mr. Richards' letter,
but they refused to make their charges in writing.
After some hours had been uselessly consumed, the
chiefs sent for Mr. Richards. On hearing Their ac-
that he was coming, the complainants rose cusers dare
not face
immediately, and hastily retired. The them.
chiefs described them as "jumping up like persons
seized by the colic." Mr. Richards acknowledged
to the chiefs that he wrote the letter in question.
Hoapili said, they all knew the letter to be true;
and the council agreed, that it could be of no use to
pay any further attention to the matter. Hoapili
thought proper, however, to ship a supply of cannon

to Lahaina, to be used in defense against a future attack, like the one from Captain Clark.

The arrest and detention of Captain Clark by Governor Hoapili, with the avowed and single purpose of compelling him to deliver up the native females, who were on board his ship contrary to the laws, is strictly defensible on the most obvious and acknowledged principles of government. Hoapili enforced his claim by an argument from a reciprocity of rights and duties; since deserters from the ships, when application was made for them to the government, were immediately given up. It was a serious aggravation of Captain Clark's offense, that his crew — as was believed with his consent, if not at his suggestion — opened a fire upon the town, throwing five cannon-balls into it, all in the direction of the mission-house.

Nor had Captain Buckle any just reason to complain of Mr. Richards' letter, or of its publication. The disgraceful facts it contained were never denied, nor could they be. The efficacy of the press, as an instrument for restraining and punishing crimes which the civil law will not reach, was evinced in the fact, that there was no similar scene of outrageous wickedness at the islands, subsequently to this period.

CHAPTER X.

1827-1829.

KALANIMOKU did not live to witness all the painful scenes just narrated, but finished his earthly career early in 1827. As one of the greatest reformers and benefactors of his nation, he is entitled to a special memorial.

His birthplace was in East Maui, whence his parents were driven by war to Hawaii. On reaching manhood, he joined himself to Kamehameha, by whom his valor and counsels, and his energy and despatch in business, were so appreciated that he rose to high distinction. *Early life of the prime minister.*

His civil position after the departure of Liholiho for England, was next to that of the regent; he was her prime minister. We find him among the first to appreciate the value of the instruction brought by the mission. As early as 1823 he said: "I am growing old. My eyes are dim. I may soon be blind. I must learn in haste, or never know the right way. Come, therefore, to my house daily and teach me, for soon my eyes will see no more." He early became a firm friend of the missionaries, and of the religion they inculcated. The high chiefs, for obvious reasons, were all kept a considerable time on probation, before admission to *His early appreciation of the gospel.*

the full communion of the church. Kalanimoku was received with others at the close of 1825, and appears ever to have honored his Christian profession.

He suffered from dropsy through 1826, and the disease became alarming in the following year. Withdrawing from public life, he thankfully re-
His religious ceived the attentions of his missionary
experience. friends, which they were most happy to render. They deemed it worth some painstaking to see the old warrior and statesman, so lately a heathen, receiving comfort from texts of Scripture and stanzas of hymns, translated for his benefit. He greatly desired to die at Kailua, his former residence, which was endeared to him by many recollections and important transactions. When the day came for his departure from Honolulu for that place he waited some time for the arrival of a missionary to pray with him, — a thing he seemed unwilling to dispense with before bidding a final adieu to the shores of Oahu. This exercise being closed, he walked with feeble and trembling steps towards the shore, supported on either side by the arm of a friend, and was attended to the boat by a large concourse of people, who pressed around him to view, for the last time, their venerated chief, the "Iron Cable" of their country, and to receive his parting aloha.

Four or five days were spent at Lahaina, where
At Lahaina. nearly the whole population was assembled
on the beach at his landing. While there, the sacrament of the Lord's Supper was administered, and the occasion was one of special interest to him, for the young princess Nahienaena, daugh-

ter of Keopuolani, was that day admitted to membership in the church. He regarded her with the
affection of a father, and she afterwards, at the request of the other chiefs, invited him to spend the
residue of his days with them. His reply was
beautiful: " He could not deny so polite and affectionate a request, if persisted in. But, as he had
given notice that he was going to Kailua, it was
still his wish, if they would consent, to proceed.
And if the Lord would hold him back from the
grave for a little time, he would return and leave
his remains beside those of Keopuolani." To this
the princess and her advisers consented.

He proceeded to Kailua with comparative comfort;
but shortly after his arrival he failed under
the operation of tapping, and in a few hours _{His death.}
expired, February 8, 1827. Not long before, he
said : "This world is full of sorrow, but there is
none in heaven; there it is good—light—happiness."

The cheerful conformity of Kalanimoku to what
he understood to be the requirements of _{His charac-}
God's Word, his steady adherence to Chris- _{ter.}
tian principles, his uniform friendship towards the
missionaries, his earnest endeavors to promote the
instruction and religious improvement of the people,
his readiness to attend on the worship of God, his
faithfulness in reproving sin, his patience in suffering, his calm and steady hope of heaven through
the atonement by Christ, whom he regarded as the
only Saviour, and to whom as he said, he had given
his heart, soul, and body, — all combine to authorize
the confident belief, that on finishing his earthly
course, he was graciously admitted to the rest which

remaineth for the people of God. A competent education would have made him an accomplished statesman. He was an honor to his nation, and deserves
a place among the good and honorable men of his
time.

The missionaries all felt his loss; but to none was
His loss   his death more affecting than to the re-
greatly felt. gent, who hastened to Kailua on learning
of his departure. Her grief under this bereavement is supposed to have affected her health, and
shortened her career. Especially must she have felt
the need of his sustaining and guiding presence in
the subsequent tumult of passion among the lawless
foreigners at Honolulu (already described), when they
discovered how responsible they were henceforward
to be held to the public sentiment of the Christian
world; and still more, in the later troubles, of a
more domestic nature — hereafter to receive a brief
notice, — which grew out of the unprincipled ambition of Boki, brother of the lamented chief, and his
wife, a daughter of the loyal Hoapili.

Namahana, sister to Kaahumanu and Kuakini,
Death and   known also under the names of Opiia and
character of
Namahana.   Piia, has been repeatedly mentioned. Her
death occurred at Honolulu in September, 1829.
She was one of the earliest, most constant, most
efficient friends of the mission. As early as 1822,
she and her husband Laanui had morning and evening prayers in their family, generally assisted by
Auna, the Tahitian teacher. They were then dili-
gently learning to read and write. Three years
later, we find her at a prayer-meeting composed
chiefly of native females; where, at the request of

Mrs. Bingham, she selected and read a hymn, made a serious address, and offered an appropriate prayer. She was deeply concerned for the reformation and improvement of her own people, and urged the governor of Oahu to promote the establishment of schools in different parts of the island. Her special interest, however, was for the district of Waialua, owned by herself, which afterwards became a favored missionary station. As a ruler, she had the decision of her family. An aggrieved native husband once requested her interposition, alleging that his wife was disposed to leave him for a foreigner, who sought to entice her away. Namahana explained to the wife what was her duty, and said: " Return to your husband, and if you forsake him I will put you in irons." Money was offered her by the paramour as a bribe, but her reply was, " No, I desire not your money." She was regarded as a pillar of the church at Honolulu.

When stricken with her last sickness, in the summer of 1829, her sister, the regent, sent a note to Mr. Bingham, requesting him to hasten to his sick friend. Coming with Mrs. Bingham, he found her mind unclouded, and her soul relying on the grace of the Lord Jesus. Repeating his visit, on a second summons received past midnight, he found the hand of death upon her. The once vigorous arm was paralyzed. At the break of day, she was heard to whisper, " Praise." It was her last word. A note of wailing from the numerous company around announced her death, but this was soon hushed that they might listen to the voice of prayer. Her funeral in the church naturally called together a great assembly.

CHAPTER XI.

1826–1828.

NOT long after the visit of the *Dolphin*, Kaahumanu made a tour through Oahu, in order
to counteract the pernicious influence exerted by that vessel. The distance travelled was
about a hundred miles, She was accompanied by
Mr. Bingham; and the regent and missionary had
thus an opportunity to address a large portion of
the inhabitants of that island, who naturally gathered about them in their progress. Mr. Bingham
daily read and explained portions of the Gospel of
Matthew, which he had translated. The company
numbered between two and three hundred, and most
of them travelled on foot. It was a sort of
travelling school. Numbers carried their
books; as many as fifty had slates and pencils. Such
as were able wrote out the text of every sermon
they heard, and committed it to memory. The more
advanced received daily instruction, and putting their
acquisitions to use, urged the duty of repentance
upon the villagers, as they passed along. Kaahumanu insisted on God's right to give laws to
his creatures, and to punish the violators
of his laws; while his mercy had provided for the
pardon of the penitent and believing. She main-

Marginal notes: The regent's tour on Oahu. Her retinue a travelling school. Her influence.

tained the right of rulers to make and execute laws. She also expressed her apprehension that the people, because of the hardness of their hearts, would not receive the gospel message, as presented by the missionary.

One of the scenes in this tour had a peculiar interest. The valley of Waimea, on the north side of the island, is almost environed by mountains, rising on three sides and forming a picturesque amphitheatre, containing hamlets, trees, and plantations. It was in this valley that Lieutenant Hergest and the astronomer Gooch, while on shore from an English vessel, were murdered by the natives of a previous generation. Here the gospel of the Lord Jesus was now proclaimed to a peaceable and listening multitude, "while the hills seemed to leap for joy at what the King of Zion was then doing for the nation." Beautiful scenery.

Subsequently the regent made repeated tours on other islands, addressing the people in the different villages, prohibiting immoral acts, enjoining a due observance of the Sabbath, encouraging them to learn to read, and exhorting them to love and obey the Saviour of sinners. Mildness and affection characterized these addresses, but they were of course regarded, more or less, as coming with authority. The people were accustomed to obey their high chiefs without hesitation. "The chiefs gave orders to the people to erect houses of worship, to build school-houses, and to learn to read, — they readily did so; to listen to the instructions of the missionaries, — they at once came in crowds for that purpose; to forsake sin and turn to the Lord, — they put on, without hesitation, the Tours on other islands. Great influence of the chiefs.

6

forms of religion at least, and exhibited an external
reformation. Not that they did these things solely
out of regard to the authority and wishes of these
chiefs, but that authority and those wishes had necessarily great influence, and the Holy Spirit made
use of that influence to accomplish immense results." [1] The regent was specially successful in her
reforming influence, not only because of the weight
of her authority, but also from the force of her example and character. The proclamations of Liholiho
against immoral acts, and in favor of the Sabbath,
had the countervailing influence of his own dissolute .
life. But the old queen was in earnest, and her life
showed that she was.

In the year 1826, Kaikioewa, formerly governor
Tour of Kai-
kioewa. of Oahu and guardian of the young prince,
and then governor of Kauai, made a tour
around that island, accompanied by Mr. Whitney;
and in every village he urged the people to forsake their sins and turn to the Lord. An apparent
timidity was observed in the demeanor of the common people while listening to the governor, but
that disappeared when the missionary rose to address
them. At one place they encountered a man, who
had formerly been employed by pagan chiefs to seize
human victims for sacrifices, and had so trained
himself that he could spring, like a tiger, on his
unguarded prey, and break his bones. This caterer
for the bloody gods of the last generation was now
willing to shake hands with a Christian missionary,
and listen to his warnings and invitations. The
The govern-
or's wife. governor's wife accompanied him, and seems
to have been the better Christian of the

---

[1] Dibble's *History*, p. 205.

two. She said she wanted to hear him say more
about Jesus Christ and his cross, and less about the
young prince. Indeed, it was not until some time
after this that the governor's evidence of piety became entirely satisfactory. The missionary said to
the wife on this tour, " I am tired of your smoking;"
to which she pleasantly replied, "Is it forbidden in
the Scriptures ? " " You make it a sin," said the missionary, "by using it to excess." Whereupon she
handed him her pipe with a smile, saying, "I will
smoke no more." Her example was followed by
others.

An influential meeting was held at Kailua in October, 1826. The regent was there, with National
many of the chiefs, and most of the mis- at Kailua.
sionaries. Kuakini had promoted the new order of
things with his characteristic energy. Early in the
year he sent people to the mountains to cut and
draw down timber for a large church, the first having
become altogether too small. Some thousands of
his people were employed for weeks during the summer in erecting and thatching this new building.
Its dimensions were one hundred and eighty feet by
seventy-eight, and it would contain an audience of
about four thousand. It was now ready to Dedication of
be dedicated, and this was the immediate a church.
occasion of the gathering of the chiefs and missionaries. The dedication sermon was preached by Mr.
Ely of Kaawaloa. Including the pupils and teachers
from forty schools, there were more than four thousand persons present. It was such a day of rejoicing
as had not before been witnessed on that island;
and the older missionaries were impressed by the
contrast, as they compared the crowds then assem-

bled with those at the same place on the arrival of
the mission, only six and a half years before.

The next day, the people were addressed by Kaa-
Remarkable humanu, Kuakini, Hoapiliwahine, Kapio-
declarations. lani, and Naihe, who declared their determination to govern according to the precepts of the
gospel. At this meeting the missionaries also re-
affirmed their purpose to refrain from interference
with the political concerns of the nation; while, as
missionaries, they would declare the whole word of
God, whatever might be its bearings on the former
customs and existing usages and proceedings of the
government and people.

After this convocation Mr. Bishop visited Kawai-
A vast con- hae, some distance north of Kailua, where
gregation. the inhabitants of the districts of Kohala
and Hamakua were assembling to meet the regent
and other chiefs. He there preached twice to a
congregation of more than ten thousand people, —
the largest audience, it is believed, that ever assembled on those Islands for Christian worship.

The *Missionary Packet* arrived in October, 1827.
The Mission- This was a small vessel sent out by the
ary Packet. Board to the mission, under the care of
that early and valued friend, the late James Hunnewell, Esq., which proved a great convenience.[1]

The missionary force on the Islands, in the opening
Missionary of the year 1828, was as follows: Messrs.
force on the
Islands. Thurston and Bishop were stationed at
Kailua, Messrs. Goodrich and Ruggles at Hilo, and
Mr. Ely at Kaawaloa, all on Hawaii; Messrs. Rich-

---

[1] Mr. Hunnewell was first mate of the brig *Thaddeus*, which took the
original company of missionaries to the Sandwich Islands. He died
recently at his home in Charlestown, Mass.

ards and Whitney were at Lahaina, on Maui; and
Messrs. Bingham and Chamberlain were at Honolulu. Mr. Whitney soon resumed his station at
Waimea, on Kauai, greatly to the delight of the old
governor, who was one of Kamehameha's veterans.

A second reinforcement arrived in the spring of
1828; consisting of the Rev. Messrs. An- Second rein-
drews, Green, Gulick, and Clark, Dr. Judd, forcement.
and Mr. Shepard, a printer, with their wives; and
Misses Ogden, Stone, Ward, and Patten, unmarried
female assistant missionaries, who were to reside in
different families of the mission. Mr. Loomis, the
former printer, having gone home on account of his
health, the arrival of a new printer gave an impulse
to the printing department. Four natives had also
become so far proficients in the art as to be employed in the office. The four Gospels had Translating
been translated, and twenty thousand copies and printing.
of Luke were printed at Honolulu. The other Gospels were printed in the United States, under the
superintendence of Mr. Loomis — fifteen thousand
copies of one at the expense of the Bible Society, the
others at the expense of the Board. In the autumn
of this year, Mr. and Mrs. Ely were constrained by
failing health to return home.

During the summer the mission made tours of
inspection around Maui, and the small isl- Extent of
school in-
ands of Molokai, Lanai, and Kahulawe. struction.
The population of Molokai was ascertained to be
about five thousand. Although no missionary had
been upon that island, except a mere landing by Mr.
Chamberlain, they found there a thousand learners,
a large portion of whom were able to read. Upon
the four islands above named, the visiting brethren

examined two hundred and twenty-five schools, in which were present five thousand males and five thousand two hundred females, or ten thousand two hundred in all; more than six thousand of these could read, and more than a thousand could write. The estimated population on these islands was thirty-seven thousand. The impulse given by this visit raised the number of pupils to more than eighteen thousand. About a fifth of the learners were under fourteen years of age, and some were sixty and upwards.

In this year, religious instruction seemed to take Attendance a stronger hold on the people than ever at prayer-meetings. before. The attendance at Lahaina on the stated prayer-meeting was seldom less than a thousand; in the autumn, it was considerably more. At a score of places on Maui, these meetings were conducted by native teachers; and the same may be said of as many more on Molokai and Lanai. The time was occupied in reading and teaching the various Scripture tracts and other books, and the meeting was closed with prayer.

The teachers, it must be believed, having so lately been heathen, could not have had a very adequate conception of the true nature of religion. To many of them, it perhaps seemed to consist chiefly in external observances. Yet there was doubtless a good degree of honesty in most, and not a few acted according to the best idea of the new religion they had been able to gain. There is something remarkable in the extent to which this outward conformity was Outward religious conformity. sometimes carried. It became known, about this time, that some natives in an interior district, with no one to instruct them, having ascertained which day was observed as Sabbath by the missionaries, kept their own reckoning, and when the day came, washed themselves, put on their best clothes (if they had any best), lay down in their huts, and went to sleep. Yet even this ignorant obedience may have rendered them more accessible to the gospel when once it was proclaimed in their hearing; and who, save the Omniscient, can tell whether sometimes it had not the germ of true piety?

At Kailua, there was a special attention to religion through the year 1828. The spacious church was often filled to overflowing on Sabbath morning. People came the distance of seven or eight miles, and returned the same day. The canoes belonging to the neighboring villages were all put in requisition, and when drawn up together during the service along the beach, they reminded the missionaries of the rows of vehicles so often witnessed on the Sabbath at the country churches of their native land. The first converts were received into the church in March and November, — fourteen men and twelve women, — several of them persons of distinction and influence. Among them was Keona, wife of Kuakini the governor, and a chief of the first rank in the Islands. They had all given satisfactory evidence of piety for a full year, many of them much longer.

The experience of these converts, as described by their spiritual guides, was strongly analogous to that in the congregations of Christian lands. There was substantially the same view of human nature, of dependence on the aids of the Holy Spirit, of the guilt and desert of sin, and of the adaptation of gospel provisions to the wants of

ruined sinners; the same frank and humble confes-
sion of sinfulness, and the same repentance and faith.
The instruction was simple, and as far as possible in
the words of Scripture; it being found that those
words carried with them an incomparable authority
and conviction. Through their influence on the conscience and heart, revelations were made of the depravity that before pervaded the masses, of which
the details would be too shocking to relate. Such,
in the language of the missionaries, were once those
of whom we have been speaking. But now they had
been washed, they had been sanctified by the Holy
Spirit. Mutual love and confidence had succeeded
to hatred and disgust. The savage had become the
humble follower of the Lamb. The dishonest, bru-
talized, libidinous son of earth had become the peaceful citizen, the zealous promoter of order, sobriety,
and Christian morality.

This was said concerning the people of Kailua at
the time. Thirty-five years later, it was the
writer's privilege to spend a Sabbath at
that place, on the forty-third anniversary of the
planting of the mission. Only one of the *lunas*, or
principal men of the church, who met me on the
morning of that day in Mr. Thurston's study, remembered the landing of that excellent missionary,
and he was then the main pillar of the church. It
was the day for the celebration of the Lord's Supper.
On my way to the church, — a large stone building
erected by Kuakini, — in company with Mr. Paris,
horses were seen fastened to the rough lava surface
in every direction. Mr. Paris thought there were
as many as five hundred. Horses had then nearly
superseded the use of canoes. The congregation

of that day was estimated at a thousand, and the communicants at six hundred. The twenty-six original members of the church had all gone from earth, and Mr. Thurston himself, worn out with years and labors, was then absent,—his work done, as it afterwards appeared,—and here was his large flourishing church, then made up from the second and third generations. I was never more conscious of being in active fellowship with the people of God, than while aiding them in commemorating the Lord's death.

We have a remarkable illustration of the power of Christian principle, in one of the first fruits at Kailua. She was the sister of Naihe, and was one of the wives of Taraiopu, the reigning king when Cook discovered the Islands. She was eighty years old. Her character, in the days of paganism, is said to have been as bad as that of a full-bred heathen could be. Yet, at the time of which I am now writing, she was a conscientious and devoted Christian. From the first, she attracted Mr. Thurston's notice by the fixed attention she paid to his words, and her friendly manner. Soon after the establishing of a school at Kailua, she came, with several of her people, and placed herself among the pupils. But being old and slow of apprehension, she appeared a most unpromising scholar. It was with the utmost difficulty, and after a long time, that she was able to remember her alphabet. Often she was advised to give up the thought of learning in her old age; but so great was her desire to be able to read the Word of God, that she persevered. She chose one of her female attendants, who had become expert in reading, to be her teacher; her book was her daily companion, at home and abroad; and at length,

after two or three years, she was able to spell out
her words without a prompter, and finally able to
read a chapter with tolerable facility. She was a
remarkable instance of one in old age, whose habits,
disposition, and character had undergone a total
revolution; and the Christian graces shone forth in
her as naturally, as if they had grown with her
growth, and strengthened with her strength.

The first Romish missionaries arrived in 1827.
Arrival of papal priests. The occasion of this mission was one John
Rives, a French adventurer, who had shown
peculiar hostility to the American mission. He was
refused permission to accompany the king, as one
of his suite, but stole on board the vessel as it was
leaving the harbor, and so accomplished his main
object. After the king's death, he went to France,
and boasted of his wealth and influence at the Islands,
which the fact of his having accompanied the king
rendered probable. His application for priests was
favorably received. Three were appointed, — one
designated by the Pope as prefect of the Sandwich Islands, and one an Irishman educated in
France, — and they arrived at Honolulu, in July, in
a French ship, the captain of which landed them
privately, and refused to take them away, though
ordered so to do by the regent. Rives did not
return to the Islands, and nothing more was heard
of him, or his possessions. The English consul insisted successfully on the Irishman's right to remain
as an English subject.

CHAPTER XII.

1829–1831.

In October, 1829, the chiefs enacted a criminal code against murder, theft, licentiousness, retailing ardent spirits, Sabbath-breaking, and gambling, professedly based on the divine law; and *Foreigners resist the laws.* declared that these laws would be enforced against foreign residents, as well as against natives. Englishmen and Americans had habitually claimed to be independent of Hawaiian law, and had threatened the vengeance of their respective governments should they be punished for violating it. The English Consul went so far as to warn the chiefs of the wrathful intervention of Great Britain, should they presume to proclaim laws without first obtaining for them the sanction of the British monarch. The regent and her advisers were not to be thus intimidated; yet it perhaps required more energy and firmness than the chiefs possessed, to execute the laws in their fullest extent. Divine Providence, as heretofore, brought the needful succor.

On the 14th of October, just one week after the laws had been proclaimed, the United States sloop of war *Vincennes*, Capt. W. C. Bolton Finch, *The government sustained by the United States.* arrived at Honolulu, bringing presents from the government of the United States, and a

letter written by direction of John Quincy Adams,
the President. The Rev. Charles S. Stewart, whose
return to the United States on account of the failure of his wife's health will be remembered, was
chaplain of the ship. The letter from the President
contained some very opportune and important statements. After congratulations upon the progress
at the Islands of " a knowledge of letters and of
the true religion, the religion of the Christian's
Bible," the letter proceeded to say : " The President
anxiously hopes that peace and kindness and justice
will prevail between your people and those citizens
of the United States who visit your Islands, and that
the regulations of your government will be such as
to enforce them upon all. Our citizens, who violate
your laws, or interfere with your regulations, violate at the same time their duty to their own government and country, and merit censure and punishment. We have heard with pain that this has
sometimes been the case, and we have sought to
know and to punish those who are guilty."

These suggestions were the more appropriate
Significance
of the visit   and timely, since they were evidently
of the Vin-   intended — as doubtless was the visit of the
cennes
Vincennes — to counteract the injuries inflicted by the
Dolphin. It was during the administration of President Adams that the outrages had been committed
by the commander of that vessel; and it was by his
order that a court of inquiry sat upon the case of
Lieutenant Percival. The nature of the punishment
inflicted was never made public ; but it was stated at
the Islands, on the authority of an officer of the
United States Navy, that Lieutenant Percival was
reprimanded by the President. The chiefs were thus

encouraged in the position they had taken, and soon gained resolution and strength for executing their laws on offending foreigners, as well as upon their own people.

The greatest apparent danger to the Islands, and to the cause of morality and religion, Disloyalty of Boki. after the death of Kalanimoku, was from the ambitious and disloyal machinations of his brother Boki. Boki was in the suite of the king on his visit to England, and received more attention after his return on this account than was due to his rank or abilities. For a time, both he and his wife seemed disposed to help the people forward in their religious progress. Kaikioewa, guardian of the young prince, being made governor of Kauai, and Boki resuming the office of governor of Oahu, and being popular, Kaahumanu committed to him the immediate care of the youthful prince, — a measure she soon had occasion deeply to regret.

Boki's regard for religion soon vanished. He became greedy of gain; countenanced, for that purpose, grog-shops and houses of ill fame; fell into intemperate habits; made efforts to revive the heathen sports and vile practices of former times; became the dupe of malicious and designing foreigners; opposed the missionaries; and did everything in his power to overthrow the government of Kaahumanu. He soon contracted heavy debts, and to pay the interest of these, he imposed oppressive taxes on the people, particularly in sandal-wood. Moreover, he was several times detected in collecting soldiers, guns, and ammunition, to make war upon the regent. At length Kaahumanu endeavored to separate the young prince from his company, and

to take him under her own immediate care. But it
was too late. Not only was Boki tenacious of his
claim, but the young prince, having acquired a taste
for such pleasures as the house of Boki afforded, was
not willing to exchange them for the household of
the serious Kaahumanu. Kalanimoku was then living, and the conduct of his brother was a sore trial
to the aged chief, but his remonstrances had no
effect. The wayward governor, having the heir to
the throne under his influence, was able to occasion
much solicitude even to so energetic a ruler as
Kaahumanu. Providence, however, disconcerted his
seditious plans, and suddenly cut short his career.

Boki's debts pressed hard upon him, and he was
His wretch- ashamed to meet the reproving eyes of the
ed end.   well-disposed chieftains, by whom he had
so often been detected in acts of sedition. He was
ready for any wild and reckless enterprise. Being
informed by traders that an abundance of sandal-
wood might be found on a certain island of the
South Pacific, he, in the absence of Kaahumanu,
hastily and imperfectly equipped the man-of-war
brig *Kamehameha*, and a smaller vessel, and sailed
on the 2d of December, 1829. The procedure indicated a mind given up to infatuation. Boki embarked in the larger vessel, with three hundred
men; and Manuai, an agent of his in all his plans,
had charge of the other vessel, with one hundred
and seventy-nine men; embracing, together, a large
portion of the company of opposers. Suffice it to
say, that the *Kamehameha* and Boki were never
again heard from; and that the smaller vessel, after
the most painful sufferings by those who sailed in
it, returned to Honolulu in August of the following

year, without its commander, and with only twenty-
seven persons on board. The destruction was like
that of Korah and his company.

Yet the spirit of sedition was not entirely removed.
Liliha, the wife of Boki, shared in his spirit, <small>Disloyalty of Liliha, the</small>
and had been left by him in the govern- <small>wife of Boki.</small>
ment of Oahu. The Romish priests were among
her partisans; they put her forward, and even
declared her, in their published letters to their
patrons in Europe, to have succeeded to the
regency. The regent had now regained her ascend-
ency over the prince, and they together spent most
of the year subsequent to May 1830 on the islands
of Maui and Hawaii; and it was this opportunity
Liliha took to mature her conspiracy against the
government. The laws against immorality were not
enforced by her. Restraint was removed from tippling shops, drunkenness, gambling, and their at-
tendant vices. Preparations were made for war, for
which no lawful reasons could be assigned. The
alarm was increased among the people by a reported
threat of Mr. Charlton, the British Consul, that
with five hundred men, whom he claimed to have
under his command, he would seize the prince and
his sister, and revolutionize the government.

It was now time for the regent to act decisively.
She appointed her brother, Kuakini, temporary
governor of Oahu, and ordered him at once to quell
the insurrection. He put Naihe in his place as
governor of Hawaii, landed troops unexpectedly on
several parts of Oahu, took possession of <small>Vigorous</small>
the fort and military stores at Honolulu, <small>proceedings.</small>
established an armed police in the streets of that
town, suppressed the tippling shops and gaming
houses, and rigidly enforced the laws for the sup-

pression of immoralities. Attempts were made to
evade the laws, such as selling coffee and giving
away rum, but the new governor was not to be trifled
with. To the request for permission to sell to
foreigners, though not to natives, his reply was:
" To horses, cattle, and hogs you may sell rum ; but
to real men you must not, on these shores." Kaahumanu now joined her brother, bringing the prince
with her ; and Liliha accompanied her father Hoapili
on his return to Lahaina, of course divested of all
authority.

The government regarded the Romish priests as
Romish priests implicated.
leaders in this conspiracy; and as such they
were ordered to leave the Islands in three
months. At length, when all other measures for
getting them away proved ineffectual, the government fitted out one of its own vessels, formerly the
brig *Waverley* of Boston, and employed Captain Sumner, an Englishman, to take them to California, then
under a Roman Catholic government. The American
Consul had written to the Governor-general of California, to learn whether he would receive them, if
they should be sent away from the Islands, and
letters had been received from him and from the
prefect of the Roman Catholic missions there, urg-
Their conse- ing them to come to their aid, as their
quent ban-
ishment. services were greatly needed. On the 7th
of December, 1831, Kaahumanu issued her proclamation, stating that they were to be sent away,
because the chiefs had never assented to their residing there, and because they had led some of the
people into seditious practices. Toward the last of
that month, they were put on board, and on the
28th of January, arrived at San Pedro in California.[1]

1 Tracy's *History*, p. 259.

CHAPTER XIII.

CHRISTIAN INFLUENCES.

1829–1835.

THE Rev. Jonathan S. Green, in compliance with instructions from the Prudential Commit- Exploration of the north-west coast. tee, spent a part of the year 1829 on a tour of exploration along a considerable portion of the northwest coast of America, but found no place which it seemed expedient, at that time, for the American Board to occupy.

An attempt was made, three years later, to institute a branch of the Hawaiian mission The Washington Islands. on the Washington Islands, a division of the cluster usually denominated the Marquesas Islands; but it was found that the time had not come for such a mission. It was subsequently ascertained by the Prudential Committee, that the London Missionary Society regarded those islands as within its appropriate field.

About this time, arrangements were made for completing the translation of the Scrip- Translating the Scrip-tures. tures. It was also recommended that each station form a class from the more promising pupils, to be educated for teachers, and ultimately for preachers of the gospel. Though Education of teachers. every part of the Sandwich Islands is healthful, so many of the missionaries suffered from

7

the liver complaint, that the formation of a health
A health station was deemed expedient. One was
station. accordingly commenced at Waimea, on
Hawaii, at an elevation of two thousand feet above
the sea. Kuakini, governor of Hawaii, had been
received into the church in the previous year; and
he now gave such prompt and generous aid that, in
less than three months, five good native houses were
erected, and the whole inclosed by a fence. Several
missionaries resorted to this place, with their families, and received essential benefit. It ultimately
became the permanent abode of Mr. Lyons. For
some reason the demand for a sanitarium has long
since ceased.

The attendance on public worship was everywhere
Attendance well sustained. Tolerable buildings for
on public
worship. worship were now to be found in every
considerable village on Maui, and in not a few of
the villages on the other islands.

There was no abatement of the religious interest
Prevalence in the next year. In many districts the
of religious
practices. practice of family prayer and of asking the
divine blessing at meals, had become almost universal. It must be admitted that along with this
was often a degree of ignorance and levity, if not of
habitual immorality, which made it but little better
than a mere form; and it was necessary to exercise
extreme caution in admissions to the church.

The number of places occupied by resident mis-
Places occu- sionaries, that were of frequent resort by
pied by mis-
sionaries. natives, should be considered. Such were
Kailua, Kaawaloa, Waimea, and Hilo, on Hawaii;
Lahaina, Lahainaluna, Wailuku, and Haiku, on
Maui; Kaluaaha, on Molokai; Honolulu, Ewa,

Waialua, and Kaneohe, on Oahu; and Waimea, Koloa, and Waioli, on Kauai. In the year 1835 there were at these sixteen stations twenty-four ordained missionaries, and forty-two assistant missionaries, male and female. The great object of all these, at their stations and in their tours, was to make known the gospel, and urge sinners to immediate repentance.

Nor must I omit to notice the aid derived from the common schools and the press. Owing to Influence of the number of schools, and in part to the the press. schools and very great simplicity of the Hawaiian alphabet, the learners, in 1834, exceeded fifty thousand; and about one third of these were able to read with a good degree of ease. Many could write, and a few had some knowledge of arithmetic and geography. More than five sixths of the pupils were over ten years of age. An early and wide efficiency was thus imparted to printed religious sheets and school books in the native language, such as is not possible in the more elaborated and difficult languages of heathendom.

The manner of propagating the schools during the first twelve or fourteen years of the Manner of mission, is worthy of special consideration. schools. propagating. It conformed to the political and social condition of the times. The first schools were mostly in the numerous trains of the chiefs. As the chiefs began to take an interest in the diffusion of Christian knowledge, they sent teachers into the districts which they held by a sort of feudal tenure, and which, for political reasons, were singularly scattered in the different islands. The head-man of the district was required by his chief to furnish the teacher with a house to dwell in, a school-house, kapas, and food. Thus Kaahumanu sent teachers, not only into different parts of Oahu, where was her principal residence, but to Hawaii, Maui, Molokai, Lanai, Kauai, and Niihau; and teachers, sent by Kalanimoku, Namahana, Kuakini, Hoapili, and other high chiefs, were found on most of the islands. As soon as these had taught a number to read, they were expected to divide their districts, and thus to multiply the schools, until at length the land became full of them. It should be added, that the inhabitants of these districts, old and young, were all required to attend the schools, and many old and gray-headed men thus learned to read the Word of God. True, the teachers knew but little, yet they knew much Value of the more than the people at large, and what Instruction. they taught was invaluable to the learners as a means for acquiring knowledge. In the year 1832 there were nine hundred schools. Not a few of the teachers gave their pupils correct views of the gospel method of salvation.

It has been stated that the native language was so Amount of far reduced to writing at the close of the the printing. second year of the mission, as to allow the press to commence its operations in January, 1822. From that time until March, 1830, twenty-two books were printed in the Hawaiian language, amounting to 387,000 copies and 10,287,800 pages. Besides this, 3,345,000 pages were printed in the United States. Had these books been distributed gratuitously among the fifty thousand learners, the cost for each learner would have been thirty cents. As the supply of books was almost the only expense to which the Board was subjected on account of schools, each of the nine hundred schools would have cost only about fifteen dollars. But the mission deemed it best for the natives to pay for their books, The books and they were able and willing to pay in natives. products of the Islands, or in labor. It was only the want of a circulating medium among the natives, that prevented the printing establishment from supporting itself. In some of the islands, native cloth was offered for books; in others, wood; in all, meat, fish, vegetables, and labor. These were often valuable to the missionaries, but were often of little use, and the system of barter had many disadvantages.

The school system ceased at length to be a power in the land, such as it had been. The five The school or six hundred teachers had taught their system at length exhausted. pupils to read and write, and perhaps a little more, but had now exhausted their stock of knowledge, and the system was coming to a dead stand. The mission therefore resolved to establish a high-school at Lahainaluna, on Maui, A high-with the special object of educating teach-teachers. ers. The school was opened in September, with the Rev. Lorrin Andrews as principal, and twenty-five young men as pupils. Before the close of the year, the pupils increased to sixty-seven. The course of study was to embrace four years, and was liberal for so youthful a nation. Teacher and pupils entered upon their work with much enthusiasm. School-house and lodging rooms were to be built, and food was to be raised. The site of the institution was on the gradual slope of the mountain north of Lahaina, a mile and a half from the town, by the side of a water-course, affording beds for cultivating the *taro*.

The timber was far away on the mountains, and was all to be cut by the students, hewed to the proper thickness, since there were no saw-mills on the island, and then dragged along the ground, there being no teams to aid in the work. Coral for lime had to be carried from the sea-shore; and the wood for burning the lime, and for writing-tables, benches, window-shutters, and doors, must be brought from the mountains. While the American Board could not prevent the necessity for such manual labors at the outset, it afterwards did much towards the needful buildings, library, and apparatus.

Christian marriage had now made considerable Christian progress on the Islands. I have already marriages. mentioned the marriage of Hoapili and Kalekua or Hoapiliwahine, at Lahaina, in 1823; but their example was not immediately followed. In 1826, Hoapili forbade marriages in the old form, on the island of Maui; and Mr. Richards, previous to April, 1828, had solemnized more than one thousand according to the new or Christian form. He regarded violations of the marriage law as very few, and says that such offenses were invariably punished. It was no uncommon thing for persons, after they had lived together for years, to request to be married in a Christian manner. At Kaawaloa, on Hawaii, Naihe and Kapiolani ordained, in 1827, that thereafter no marriage should be accounted valid, unless solemnized by a minister of the gospel. The number of marriages at seven stations, up to 1830, exceeded two thousand. The progress thus indicated of good morals and domestic happiness, from the time when every matrimonial tie could be sundered by the will of the parties, must have been very great.

We should not fail to recognize the progress of temperance in the use of intoxicating drinks. Progress of temperance. The mission found the Sandwich Islanders a nation of drunkards. The king and his principal chiefs were addicted to the grossest intemperance; and it was no uncommon thing for the missionaries to find whole villages in a state of beastly intoxication. For some years after their arrival, the tendency was sadly in this direction. I have already stated how it was at Honolulu, under the demoralizing rule of Boki, and how decidedly Kuakini opposed himself to the progress of the evil. Under his administration as governor of Oahu, a temperance society was formed at Honolulu in the year 1831, having about a thousand members, with the following significant pledges:—

1. We will not drink ardent spirits for pleasure.

2. We will not deal in ardent spirits for the sake of gain.

3. We will not engage in distilling ardent spirits.

4. We will not treat our relatives, acquaintances, or strangers with ardent spirits.

5. We will not give ardent spirits to workmen on account of their labor.

This was nearly forty years ago, and almost in advance of the great temperance reform in the United States.

The mission received its third reinforcement in the summer of 1831, consisting of the Rev. Third reinforcement. Messrs. Baldwin, Tinker, and Dibble, and Mr. Johnstone, all married men. They brought a letter to Kaahumanu from Jeremiah Evarts, Esq., the Corresponding Secretary of the American Board, one of the last letters which that great and good man lived to write. The reply of the regent will be interesting to the reader.

OAHU, *September* 11, 1831.

" Love to you, Mr. Evarts, the director of mis-
_{Letter from} sionaries, my first brother in Christ Jesus.
_{Kaahumanu.} This is my thought for you, and my joy. I now abide by the voice of the Saviour, Jesus Christ, who hath redeemed me from death. I was dwelling in the eyeball of death, I was clothed and adorned in the glory and likeness of death. When I heard the voice of Jesus as it sounded in my ear, it was refreshing to my bosom, saying thus : ' Come unto me, all ye that labor and are heavy laden, and I will give you rest.' Again the voice of him said, ' Whosoever is athirst, let him come, and drink of the water of life.' Therefore I arose, and came, and prostrated myself beneath the shade of his feet, with great trembling. Therefore do I bear his yoke, with this thought concerning myself, that I am not able to put forth strength adequate to carry his yoke, but of him is the ability [to bear it], his aid to me by night and by day ; there am I continually abiding by his righteousness [excellence or glory] and his love to me. There do I set my love and my desire, and the thoughts of my heart, and there on Jesus do I leave my soul. There shall my mouth and my tongue give praise continually during the life which I now live, till entering into his everlasting glory. Such is the thought of mine for you.

" This is another thought of mine for you. I praise [or admire] the kindness of our Lord Jesus Christ in aiding us by several new teachers. They have arrived. We have seen their eyes and their cheeks,

we have met with them in the presence of God, and
in our own presence also, with praise to our common
Lord, for his preserving them on the ocean till they
arrived here at Hawaii.   Now we wait while they
study the language of Hawaii.   When that is clear
to them, then they will sow in the fields the good
seed of eternal salvation.   Then my former brethren,
with these more recent, and my brethren and my
sisters of my own country, will all of us together
take up the desire of Christ (or what Christ wills
or wishes), on this cluster of Islands, with prayer to
him for his aid, that the rough places may by him
be made plain, by his power through all these lands
from Hawaii to Kauai.

"I and he whom I have brought up have indeed
carried the word of our Lord through from Hawaii
to Kauai; with the love of the heart towards God,
was our journeying to proclaim to the people his
love, and his word, and his law, and to tell the people to observe them.

" Thus was our proclaiming not according to our
own will, but according to the will of God did we
undertake it.   Such is this thought of mine for you.

" This is one more thought to make known to
you.   Make known my love to the brethren in Christ,
and to my beloved sisters in Christ Jesus.   This is
my salutation to you all.   Pray ye all to God for all
the lands of dark hearts, and for the residue of all
lands of enlightened hearts, and for you also.   Thus
shall we and you unitedly call upon our common
Lord, that the nations may in peace follow him,
that his kingdom may be smooth and uninterrupted
even to the ends of the earth; that all men may
turn to him without dissent, and praise his ever-

lasting name. That is my sentiment of love to you all.

"Great love to thee. Our bodies will not meet in this world, but our thoughts do meet in this world, and hereafter our souls will meet in the glory of the kingdom of our Lord Jesus Christ, thy Saviour and mine. This ends my communication to you.

"Elizabeth Kaahumanu."

CHAPTER XIV.

LIFE, DEATH, AND CHARACTER OF KAAHUMANU.

1821–1832.

THE regency of Kaahumanu extended from the departure of the king in 1823 to 1832, the Duration of year in which she died. In point of fact, her regency. she was scarcely less than regent from the death of her husband, Kamehameha, in 1819. She was a remarkable person, and some special notice will now be taken of her life and character.

In her days of heathenism, she was imperious and cruel. No subject, whatever his station, Her days of cared to face her frown. Mr. Jarves and heathenism. Mr. Dibble both bear testimony, in works published at the Islands, that many suffered death in her moments of anger; and that, though really friendly to the missionaries, her deportment towards them, in the first years of their residence, was lofty and disdainful. But her decision, energy, and ability, in connection with similar high qualities in Kalanimoku, extricated the nation from difficulties, in which it had become involved by the follies and extravagance of Liholiho. After the king had gone from the Islands, and they both came into friendly and active coöperation with the mission, there is no estimating the value of their united influence. It was just what was needed by the nation. The prophet asks, "Shall a nation be born at once?" Humanly speaking, the spiritual import of this question could be realized only by a hearty union, such as now occurred, between national rulers having absolute sway, and a pervading evangelical influence.

Not until this haughty ruler had been brought Is softened low by sickness, at the close of 1821, when by sickness. Mr. Bingham was called in as her spiritual adviser, was there evidence of her coming under the influence of the gospel. Her heart was then in some measure touched, and from that time there was a noticeable change in her demeanor towards the missionaries. Her husband, the former king of Kauai, no doubt contributed to this result. So also, we may suppose, did the marked courteousness towards the members of the mission of Commodore Vasciliett, of the Russian Exploring Squadron, whose physicians aided materially in her recovery. She was now past the age of fifty; and considering her age, habits, and the demands upon her time, it seemed doubtful whether she would ever learn to read and write. Yet, after two years, under the Learns to combined sense of duty and interest, she read at fifty. became a learner; and on the fourth anniversary of the mission, she placed herself among the pupils at a school examination, and wrote the following, which she presented for inspection : " This is my word. I am making myself strong. I declare, in the presence of God, that I repent of my sins, and believe in God our Father."

The desire she expressed for baptism at this time Evidences of was not encouraged, there not being sather conver- isfactory evidence of her conversion. Yet sion. her course ever after was onward. In the general alarm created by the rebellion on Kauai, she proclaimed a fast; and when the rebellion was subdued, she united with others in a public thanksgiving. Hauteur in the presence of her Christian teachers gave place to affectionate expressions of confidence. She became, and continued till the close of life, a decided reformer, and sought to render her own daily life conformable to the will of God. This gave weight to her exhortations. Her addresses to the people, in her official tours, had, as they must needs have had, the air of authority; but we have the best evidence that they were characterized by mildness, affection, and Christian love.

I have elsewhere spoken of the value of these services; and it was in them, and in the spirit they manifested, that she secured the confidence of her spiritual guides as to the soundness of her conversion. This was in the year 1825, which therefore forms an era in the mission. The people wondered at the change in the regent's demeanor, and it was surprising to the missionaries. Going to Hilo in the frigate which had brought the bodies of the king and queen from England, she sent for Mr. Ruggles, then the resident missionary, to come to her. Such had been his experience of her heathenish and imperious deportment when he was residing on the island of Kauai, that he declined. She had not been formally recognized as a Christian, and he did not believe that she was one. She sent again and entreated him. He came, and found he had misjudged. She met him in tears, threw her arms around his neck, and assured him, not only of her friendship, but of her submission to Christ, and her determination to support his cause. While there, she was so earnest in promoting the schools and religion, that the people called her, "Kaahumanu ho-u," the "new Kaahumanu." For one born and nurtured in heathenism, so long familiarized with its superstitions and abominations, with her disposition, and after a proud and absolute sovereignty of thirty years, the change was certainly remarkable.

Her tour, on this occasion, was extended to Kaa-
Her changed manner. waloa. Here, her condescending and affectionate manner towards all who approached her, was not less a matter of surprise than of joy to her subjects. The feeling of awe, as she extended her hand and gave them her aloha, was softened at once into the most cordial attachment. To see their once haughty queen now going from rank to rank to salute her people, drew tears from many a hardy, sunburnt face, and her affectionate and pious addresses to all classes were listened to with great attention.

The death of Kalanimoku, her prime minister, in
Her love for the missionaries. 1827, occurred when her government was environed with difficulties and dangers. In one of the most trying cases, when the lives of those whom she regarded as the best friends of her people were threatened, she directed the most obnoxious of them to come to the seat of government, for a public investigation in the presence of their accusers. "When we landed," says one of them, "there stood the tall, portly, and beloved Kaahumanu, ready to welcome and shield us, having armed men on either hand. She saluted us cordially and with tears; then stepping forward, led us through the fort, and out at the northern gate, and thence onward half a mile, to the mission establishment,

at the eastern extremity of the village. Giving
her hand, she then said: 'I have seen you safe
to your house, and will now return to my own, and
see the chiefs recently arrived. The body has been
made strong by the love of the heart." At evening
it was found that the mission premises were guarded
by armed natives.

It has been made a point against her, that she
punished her Roman Catholic subjects. Not a perse-
Mr. Bingham remonstrated with her for cutor.
this, and said, "You have no law that will apply."
She replied, "The law respecting idolatry, for
their worship is like that we have forsaken." She
referred to a law in 1819, before the arrival of the
missionaries, by which idolatry was abolished, and
subject to punishment. Their application of this to
the Romish worship was then new to the missionary, and was the result of their own observations
and reflections. The adult Sandwich Islanders had
themselves taken part in idolatrous worship, and
some of them had been priests; and it was natural,
perhaps unavoidable, for them to look upon the
worship performed by the Romish priests as the
same in nature with the old idolatry of the Islands.
When fully informed by the missionaries as to the
Christian method of treating religious errors, the
punishment ceased.

Violations of the fourth commandment in the dec-
alogue, received no countenance from her. Reply to a
A trader, fond of riding for amusement on breaker.
the Sabbath, once said to her, that he knew of no
divine law against it. "Indeed you know there is
one," said the queen. "Where is it?" he demanded. She calmly and promptly replied, "Remember the Sabbath day to keep it holy."

Kaahumanu was too ill to be present at the formal reception of the fourth reinforcement
to the mission, which arrived in May, 1832,
consisting of Rev. Messrs. Alexander, Armstrong,
Lyman, Emerson, Spaulding, Forbes, Hitchcock,
and Lyons, and their wives, Dr. Chapin and wife,
and Mr. Rogers, a printer. She received them in
her own room, neatly attired, and seated in her arm-
chair, and gave her hand affectionately to each.
Such were her emotions, when expressing her satisfaction in view of their arrival, that she covered her
face with her handkerchief and wept.

Her illness increasing, she sought retirement in
her valley of Manoa, among the mountains, three
miles beyond where the Oahu College now stands.
She was carried thither on a litter by her servants.
Here the two missionary physicians and their wives
did what they could for her relief and comfort. She
was visited also by most of the missionaries, and was
grateful for their attentions. The printing of the
New Testament in the Hawaiian language
was completed after her removal to this
place, and a copy of it, neatly ·bound in
morocco, was put in her hands. She examined it
attentively, inside and out, pronounced it "*maikai*,"
"excellent," wrapped it in her handkerchief, and
laid it in her bosom; then clasping her hands, she
cast her eyes gratefully upward, as if giving thanks
for so precious a gift.

Even in her paroxysms of· distress, she listened
to the reading of Scripture, and to the exercises of
devotion.

Though solicitous for the health of her beloved
spiritual guide, she desired him to be near in her

dying struggles. After a severe paroxysm he said
to her, "Elizabeth, this perhaps is your
departure; stay yourself on Jesus, your
Saviour." Her reply was, "I shall go to Him, and
shall be comforted." A little before the failure of
her powers of utterance, she ejaculated two lines of
a favorite Hawaiian hymn, which may be translated
thus : —

> "Lo, here I am, O Jesus,
> Grant me thy gracious smile."

Perceiving herself to be dying, she called Mr.
Bingham. As he took her cold hand, she said, "Is
this Biname?" On being told that it was, she
said, "I am going now." These were her last
words; and after a few minutes she ceased to
breathe, dying just before the dawn of day, June 5th,
1832. Her age was fifty-eight.

At the announcement of the regent's death, there
were some bursts of wailing among the
people, but for the most part Christian solemnity and order prevailed. An appropriate sermon was preached in the great church to the royal
family, and to as many as could gain an entrance;
after which the remains of the deceased were placed
in the repository provided for persons of her rank.
The contrast is affecting between this Christian
burial, and the confusion and untold abominations,
which in their heathen state invariably attended the
death of a distinguished chief.

. Kaahumanu entered the service of Christ late in
life, yet it is the lot of few to fight in so
many battles with the workers of iniquity,
as she did in the short space of eight years. She
was bold and energetic when the cause of Christ

8 .

was assailed, or needed her support; but humble and retiring when her own honor or emolument merely was in question. She suffered reproach and abuse with meekness, and few have left brighter evidence of exchanging earth for heaven, and worldly rank and distinction for glory everlasting.

Viewed in any light, Kaahumanu must be regarded as a remarkable person. She was one of those characters which Christian historians feel bound to regard as providential creations for extraordinary exigencies. Her sphere was indeed viewed by the world as narrow and humble, and she had none of the advantages of early education; but in strength of mind and will, and in some of the qualities of her disposition, she resembled Queen Elizabeth of England. After her conversion, however, of which so many proofs have been given in this history, the two would not be thought of in connection. She became a nursing mother to the church. Frederick of Saxony was not more interested for the safety of Luther, and for the success of the Reformation, than was Kaahumanu for the endangered life of the missionary at the seat of her government, and for the triumph of the gospel, among her people. The testimony of Mr. James Jackson Jarves is very emphatic, and above suspicion: "After the conversion of Kaahumanu," he says, "her violent passions were checked, the cold and contemptuous behavior gave way before the strong, natural flow of affection. To the missionaries she became warmly attached; and among her own people, and even foreigners, her character was so entirely altered, and her deportment so consistent with the principles of her faith, that none could doubt her sincerity. 'The new and good Kaahumanu,' passed into a proverb."[1]

She was nearly fifty years in heathenism, and began the Christian life under all the disadvantages of such a training, aggravated greatly by the fact that, during many of those years, irresponsible power was in her hands. Her personal presence was commanding. She was tall and portly, with a swarthy complexion, black hair, dark commanding eyes, deliberate enunciation, a dignified and measured step, and, before her conversion, a queenlike but heathenish hauteur. Christian affection character- ized her addresses to the people ever after she took her place among the followers of Christ.

She must be regarded as an instrument of divine Providence, for conducting the Hawaiian nation through the perilous exigencies of the inter- regnum following the death of Liholiho; and to strengthen it for the scarcely less perilous reaction following her own death, and the accession of Kaui- keouli to the throne, until the universal outpouring of the Holy Spirit, in the years 1838 to 1840, which Christianized the nation.

[1] Jarves' *History*, Honolulu ed. 1847, p. 125.

CHAPTER XV.

1832–1834.

PRINCE KAU-I-KE-A-OU-LI was too young to be invested with royal authority. His half-sister,
Kinau, succeeded Kaahumanu as regent.
She had been the wife of Kahalaia, but he died
shortly after their marriage. She then married
Kekuanaoa. Though smaller than the chiefs generally, she had a good figure, was dignified, and her
Christian character had a remarkable combination
of modesty and firmness. She was exemplary in
her dress, manners, and habits, and excelled her
predecessors in courteous attentions to respectable
strangers. While at the Islands, in 1863, I frequently saw Kekuanaoa, who survived her
many years, and thought his person was
probably one of the best developed upon the Islands.
She was his superior in birth, station, education, and
piety; but is said ever to have manifested a com-
placency in him, and a satisfaction in his honorable
and gentlemanly deportment. Though young for
the station, Kinau enjoyed the confidence of the
prince, and of the chief men; and she entered upon
her duties with the feeling that her success de-
pended on the blessing of God, and the prevalence
of the Christian religion among the people. She

Kinau as regent.

Kekuanaoa, her husband.

early took occasion to declare publicly her intention to pursue the policy, and carry out the measures, of her predecessor.

While Kaahumanu lived, the authority of the government was freely employed to main- Church and tain religious order and influence. The state. mission was not responsible for this; it grew out of the fact that the supreme power in a despotic government was wonderfully united with piety in the rulers. It was somewhat analogous to what existed in the palmy days of the Israelitish nation, and in the Puritan age of New England. Perhaps it was well for the Sandwich Islands, that this union of church and state was dissolved before the government had begun to use it for secular and unhallowed purposes.

Kinau was well disposed, but her influence was inferior to that of her predecessor. Num- Growth of bers of influential persons, in the younger immorality. class, were impatient under the restraints of Christianity. Most of the personal followers of the young prince were of this class, and some of them went so far as to advocate a system of loose morals and heathenish sports. The most zealous and influential of these was Kaomi, the son of a naturalized Tahitian by a Hawaiian mother. He possessed considerable shrewdness, and early manifested a desire for instruction, made good progress for a time, and became a teacher and exhorter. After several years, he desired baptism, but it was not granted. He soon showed that he was not a fit subject. His personal affairs becoming embarrassed, he attached himself to the immoral, denied the inspiration of the Scriptures, and declared that he had tried religion and found nothing in it, and would again try the pleasures of the world. He became a favorite with the dissolute young men about the prince, and with the prince himself, who made him his counselor. The infidel party, under Kaomi's lead, coincided with the libertinism of influential foreigners ; and the newly formed party entered boldly on a course, which created some alarm for the peace of the nation, and even for the safety of Kinau and her friends. Kuakini came up from Kailua, and Hoapili from Lahaina, to see what they could do to save the nation from confusion and disaster.

They were but partially successful. The young 1888. prince, then scarcely eighteen years old, had been thwarted by Kinau in a favorite scheme, involving more expense to the deeply indebted nation than she thought it able to bear, and was determined to reign as king. The high chiefs demurred, supposing his intention was to set aside Kinau, to abrogate the existing laws, and promote Liliha or the plebeian Kaomi to the second rank in the kingdom. There was no small agitation. Intoxication and licentiousness increased. But a kind Providence continued to watch over the nation. The prince summoned the chiefs and people to hear what was his pleasure. The community was perplexed by conflicting rumors. At the time for the meeting, many of the praying women assembled, and besought divine interposition. The convocation Accession of the young prince. was held in the open air, and Kinau, with dignified step, walked calmly into the crowd, and saluted her brother. He announced his majority, and his claim to rule as supreme sovereign. It was for him to say who should be next

to him in rank, in accordance with the usage of the
government, and great was the anxiety when he
lifted his hand to designate which of the three candidates then standing about him, should be the premier; and there was no small relief and A wise
satisfaction when he named Kinau. It choice.
was afterwards conceded by him that no measure
of the government would be constitutional without
her concurrence, though this was questioned at
first.

The king's proceeding disappointed the infidel
party; and when they inquired why he Disappoint-
had done thus, his reply was, "The king- infidel party.
dom of God is strong." He attended church next
day, and afterwards requested a supply of Hawaiian New Testaments for his personal attendants.

The restraints upon the manufacture, sale, and
use of intoxicating liquors, were now re- Increased
laxed; though Kinau, Kuakini, Hoapili, tion
and Kaikioewa refused to grant licenses. Kaomi
and a large class of foreigners favored the opposite
policy; and the king was led to believe that his
revenues would be augmented by encouraging the
traffic. Of course there were men ready to bring to
the Islands as much of the poisonous liquid as could
find a profitable sale. Among those who bought
were some of the king's agents. Certain places, devoted to the old saturnalia, were for a time exempted
from the laws of order; but it was not so over the
largest portion of the Islands, and Sabbath riding
for amusement could not gain popularity even at
Honolulu. The agitation was of course unfavorable
to the schools, and diverted attention from the "one
thing needful."

Yet it is a question, whether all this was not Restoration of order. finally overruled by divine Providence, so as to be productive of more good than evil. Kaomi soon fell into neglect, and died, and none mourned the loss of the infidel despiser of revealed religion. In the year of his apparent triumph, ending with June, 1834, the additions to the churches had been one hundred and twenty-four, and there were only five excommunications. The readers in the schools were reputed to be twenty thousand, and the number of Christian marriages was eleven hundred. At Honolulu, the seat of this agitation, the Sabbath congregation was about two thousand, and half of the congregation were learning a verse daily in the Scriptures.

It was in this year that special efforts began to Efforts for seamen. be made for improving the moral and religious condition of the foreign residents and seamen; first by setting apart a member of the mission for that purpose; and then by the arrival of the Rev. Mr. Diell, as a chaplain of the American Seamen's Friend's Society, — a most useful agency, which has been kept up since that time. It should Improvement of the king. be gratefully acknowledged, also, that the young monarch gained in experience and character as he advanced in years; and though never regarded as a man of piety, he deserves and will ever have an honorable place in the history of this nation.

CHAPTER XVI.

PREPARATION FOR THE GREAT AWAKENING.

1833–1837.

THE attention of the Board at home was now directed to the question, how to bring the evangelical agency to bear, in the shortest possible time, upon the entire people of the Sandwich Islands; and thus, should the divine blessing attend the effort, afford an impressive illustration of the renovating influence of Christian missions. The Hawaiian nation presented the best field for such an experiment within reach of the Board.[1] Accordingly, in the year 1833, the Committee directed a large number of inquiries to be addressed to the mission. The answers to these inquiries covered more than three hundred pages of letter paper, and contained a full account of the religious condition and prospects of the Islands. A very condensed view of the facts thus presented will suffice to prepare the way for an intelligent account of the Great Awakening, which may be regarded as having had its commencement in the year 1836.

The total population of the Islands, at that time, was believed to be about one hundred and thirty thousand, of whom but little more than one half

A new and interesting question.

Inquiries proposed to the mission.

The responses.

[1] See this first stated in the *Annual Report of the Board*, 1837, p. 97.

might be properly regarded as accessible to the mis-
Additional laborers needed. sion, as it then was. To supply the defi-
ciency, the mission requested an increase of
eighteen ordained missionaries, two physicians, and
twenty-one lay teachers. It was clearly stated how
these additional laborers should be distributed among
the people, so that their labors might prepare the
way for a general outpouring of the Holy Spirit,
should such be the divine pleasure. Moreover, as an
important fact bearing on the same great end, it was
shown how the native church members, then some-
Degree of preparation for them. what more than eight hundred in number,
had been providentially distributed over
the Islands; and to what extent there was a capacity to read among the people, and how far reading matter of the right sort had been provided.

The decline of the common schools, in conse-
Schools for teachers. quence of their teachers having exhausted
their stock of knowledge, was the occasion
of commencing the high-school at Lahainaluna, on
the island of Maui, as a remedy for this evil. To
hasten the result, members of the mission, male and
female, gave a part of their time to school instruction; and thus not less than a thousand native men
and women received a higher education than had
been possible in the common schools. Sabbath-
schools also contained more than two thousand pupils, Bible classes nearly a thousand, and singing
schools two hundred, all taught by missionaries. The
common schools, in their highest prosperity, contained as many as fifty-two thousand pupils, or considerably more than one third of the island popula-
Results of the schools. tion. At the time now under consideration,
the readers were estimated at twenty-three

thousand; and the number who had been taught to read so as to derive benefit from the perusal of books, was somewhat over thirty thousand.

Up to this time, the native teachers had derived their support from the chiefs, the people, and their own manual labors on the soil; and the school system, though necessarily imperfect, had been better adapted to the condition and wants of the people, than if it had been supported by the mission. It also filled a place, which nothing else could have filled; and, to some extent, it had given form and order to society, where, in these early years of the mission, there must otherwise have been a mere chaos of humanity.

The good influence of the mission upon the sea-men frequenting the Pacific Ocean, was now becoming apparent. A large number Efforts for seamen. of whaling vessels resorted to Lahaina for their annual refit, because Hoapili, the excellent governor, had put the island under a strict prohibitory law, and banished thence the means of intoxication; while at Honolulu the traffic in ardent spirits was but imperfectly suppressed. At one time, fourteen captains of vessels and one hundred and fifty seamen were at public worship; and upon occasion of a vessel coming from Honolulu with rum for sale, not fewer than eighteen shipmasters petitioned the governor to send her immediately away, which he did. About the same time, a petition was presented to the king at Honolulu, praying him to Petition for a prohibitory law. put an end to the distillation and sale of ardent spirits. This was signed by the highest chiefs, by nearly two thousand people in the Hono-lulu district, and by nearly a thousand in other parts of the island; and thousands on other islands united their influence to secure this object. The effort was so far successful, as to detach the government from the deleterious traffic.

A fifth reinforcement, consisting of Rev. Messrs. L. Smith and B. W. Parker, and their wives, and Mr. Fuller, a printer, arrived in the year 1833; and in 1835, a sixth, consisting of the Rev. Mr. Coan, and Messrs. Dimond, a bookbinder, and Hall, a printer, with their wives; and Misses Hitchcock and Brown.

New mission-aries.

Miss Brown's object was to teach the native women to card, spin, knit, and weave. She was to introduce the domestic wheel and loom, for the manufacture of cotton grown on the Islands. Her first class of six young women at Wailuku, on Maui, learned readily, and within about five months ninety yards of cloth were woven. Later, five hundred yards were reported. Successive classes were taught there, and on other islands. Governor Kuakini became so interested as to plant cotton, and introduced spinning and weaving into his own family. His young wife and others were instructed in these arts; but perhaps the same reasons that have driven such healthful employments from farmers' families in more civilized lands prevented the ultimate success of the experiment at the Sandwich Islands.

Introduction of domestic manufactures.

The years 1836 and 1837 were in some respects remarkable. Though the Prudential Committee were not able to make all the additions to the force at the Islands which the mission had requested, yet, on the 14th of December, 1836, the largest reinforcement embarked that has

Reason for a large accession of missionaries.

ever been sent by the Board to any one of its missions. It was so large, I may say once more, because the field was accessible in every part, and the
best within reach of the Board for an effort to do
the work up decisively and soon. It was Seventh re-
composed of the Rev. Messrs. Bliss, Conde, inforcement.
Ives, and Lafon, Dr. Andrews, and Messrs. Castle,
Bailey, Cooke, Johnson, Knapp, Locke, McDonald,
Munn, Van Duzee, and Wilcox, with their wives;
and two Misses Smith, — in all thirty-two. Subsequent experience showed, that the cost of lay
teachers is as great, in the foreign missions, The lay ele-
as that of ordained missionaries, and that ment.
it might have been better to make up the reinforcement more largely of ordained missionaries. But
they could not be obtained. The harvest was plenteous; the laborers were few. Years afterwards, in
the process of bringing the mission to a close,
several of these lay helpers proved invaluable accessions to the Christian community then forming on
the Islands. The arrival of so great a company of
Christian laborers, just in time to take The season-
their positions and acquire the language, able arrival.
before the wonderful outpouring of the Holy Spirit,
soon to be experienced, was another of the singular
providential interpositions, of which there were so
many. Of course, neither the committee, in calling
for the information which gave rise to this large
accession, nor the mission, in taking so much pains
to give that information, could have distinctly fore-
seen the exigency. The voyage of the reinforcement to the Islands was unusually prosperous. The
religious services on board ship were well attended,
and about half the crew appeared to become pious

during the voyage. Six of them, including two of the officers, were received into the mission church at Honolulu.

These years were further distinguished by three communications of a peculiar nature from the Islands, but all bearing on the cause of missions.

The first was a memorial from the mission, addressed to the members of the American Board and other philanthropists, on the importance of increased efforts to cultivate the useful arts among the Hawaiian people, as auxiliary to the permanent establishment of Christian institutions.[1] The memorial went largely into the subject, and made specific propositions; but as the Board, when the subject came before it, was clearly of the opinion that the whole lay beyond its province, as a missionary institution, I need not occupy the space necessary to state its purport.

Memorial from the mission.

Another memorial, of nearly the same date, and probably the immediate occasion of the former, was addressed by the king and chiefs to the American Board. It was dated at Lahaina, August 23, 1836, a little more than sixteen years after the arrival of the mission, and was as follows : —

Memorial from the government.

"Love to you, our obliging friends in America. This is our sentiment as to promoting the order and prosperity of these Hawaiian Islands. Give us additional teachers, like the teachers who dwell in your own country. These are the teachers whom we would specify: a carpenter, tailor, mason, shoemaker, wheelwright, paper-maker, type-founder;

[1] For the Memorial, see Bingham's *History,* pp. 490–495.

agriculturists skilled in raising sugar-cane, cotton, and silk, and in making sugar; cloth manufacturers, and makers of machinery to work on a large scale; and a teacher of the chiefs in what pertains to the land, according to the practice of enlightened countries; and if there be any other teacher that could be serviceable in these matters, such teachers also.

"Should you assent to our request, and send hither these specified teachers, then we will protect them, and grant facilities for their occupations, and we will back up their works that they may succeed well."

This was signed by the king, the princess, the regent, the governors of Oahu, Hawaii, and Maui, and the other high chiefs who were then at Lahaina.

The other document was an earnest and powerful appeal of the missionaries, sent home in a printed pamphlet, calling upon the friends of Christ to engage, in far larger numbers, and with far greater zeal, in spreading the gospel through the world. It was brought to this country by Mr. Richards in the year 1837, a year distinguished beyond almost all others for the severe commercial distress which pervaded the United States. The appeal was based on the assumption, that consecrated men were mainly wanted, rather than money; so that it failed, in the peculiar circumstances of the times, in that effect upon the Board, and upon the Christian community, which the mission had expected. This was a source of painful disappointment at the Islands. The appeal was, however, a very striking evidence of the revived state of religious feeling among the members of the

mission, and was one of the most noticeable pre-
cursors of the great awakening that soon afterwards attracted the attention of the religious world.

The princess Nahienaena, sister to the king, and
The young   a year older than he, was long a favorite in
princess.   the mission, and sanguine hopes were entertained concerning her. It will be remembered, that
she was admitted to the church at Lahaina, in 1827,
during the visit of the venerable prime minister,
when on his way to Kailua, where he died shortly
afterwards. In the year 1833, six years later, at the
age of nineteen, she had lost somewhat of her vivac-
ity, and of her interest in schools, though still taking the lead in most of the branches to which she
had given attention. Few read as well, few wrote
better, and none excelled her in arithmetic. She had
gained considerable knowledge of geography, and
was skillful in drawing and painting maps. She
could repeat most of the Scripture historical catechism, and was accustomed to commit the verse for
the day, according to the verse-a-day system. To
most of the outward forms of religion she was attentive, and in her public acts and addresses she
espoused the cause, not only of morality and good
order, but also of piety. She most evidently knew,
and sometimes gave evidence of her belief, that
members of the mission were her best friends and
benefactors. She was, however, less docile than formerly, and did not often engage readily in conversation on the subject of religion; but when drawn into
it by her teachers, she often manifested strong feeling, and spoke as if she knew the inward conflicts
of the Christian. She never avowed a confident hope
of heaven, and often spoke doubtfully as to her pros-

pects after death, and was far from exhibiting a proper solicitude on that subject. Naturally volatile, and surrounded by vain and trifling persons, she was regarded by her missionary friends as in constant danger of falling. Rank and riches were no more favorable to piety at the Sandwich Islands, than they are in more civilized portions of the Christian world. Her brother had begun to develop an un- Laudable influence on favorable side to his character, and had her brother. then asserted his supremacy in the government, and she was alarmed by the dangers which beset him, and made great exertions to restrain him. Her home was at Lahaina, and twice she visited Oahu for this express purpose. At one time, she hung upon his arm until it was wrested from her, and then followed him through threats and insults; and when she could no longer approach him privately, she begged him, in the most public manner, to listen to the better informed counsels of the older chiefs. She was often seen to weep for him on account of the course he was pursuing; but still was not aware that she was herself exposed, and eminently so, to an equally dreadful vortex.

She fell in the way that had been so common among her countrymen; and it was found necessary for the Lahaina church to separate her from its communion. In this the public sentiment acquiesced, though she was heir-presumptive to the throne; thus evincing the power of religious principle at that time on the Islands.

She sickened at Honolulu in the latter part of 1836 and died before its close, confessing Her death. her sin and folly, and giving faint evidence of repentance. The tears and lamentations of her friends testified to the interest they felt in her case.

The effect on her brother, the king, was salutary. After the customary solemnities at royal funerals, including a religious service at the church, he had the body conveyed to Lahaina, and placed by the side of her venerated mother, Keopuolani.

On the 17th of April, while the king was absent on this mournful errand, the Romish priests returned to Honolulu from their banishment in California. They came in the brig *Clementine*, wearing English colors, but the property of Jules Dudoit, a Frenchman. To secure their permanent residence, no small amount of deception and threatened violence was practiced on the government by Messrs. Charlton and Dudoit, the British and French consuls, aided by Captain Belcher, of the British sloop-of-war *Sulphur*, and by Captain Dupetit Thouars, of the French frigate *La Venus*, especially the former. There is reason to believe, that Captain Bruce, of the British ship-of-war *Imogene*, which arrived two months later, advised the government in the exercise of a more friendly feeling. The king was not to be persuaded or intimidated, and issued a proclamation, declaring "the rejection of these men perpetual;" and on the 18th of December, he published "an ordinance, rejecting the Catholic religion." The preamble mentioned the seditious movement in the time of Kaahumanu, the banishment of the priests for the part they took in those movements, and the "increased trouble, on account of those who follow the Pope," which had been suffered, all showing the tendency of the Romish faith "to set man against man" in the kingdom.

The ordinance therefore forbade all persons, natives or foreigners, to teach or assist in teaching that faith in any part of the kingdom. It also forbade the landing of any teacher of that faith, except in cases of absolute necessity. In such case, a priest would be "permitted, in writing, to dwell for a season on shore, on his giving bonds and security for the protection of the kingdom." It also prescribed the mode of enforcing this law, and the penalties for transgression. The American missionaries have been accused of procuring the passage of this ordinance, but the falsehood of that charge has been abundantly shown.[1] However impolitic sending away these Romish priests may be regarded, yet all must see that, as an act of self-defense, it came within the legitimate province of the Hawaiian government.

[1] See Tracy's *History*, pp. 357 and 405, and the Appendix to the Annual Report of the Board for the year 1841.

CHAPTER XVII.

1830–1839.

THE preparation for the great awakening was

Nature of the preparation. more in the mental and social condition of the people, than in the visible signs of civilization. Some indeed, who resided near the mis-

In domestic life. sionary stations, had built or were building comfortable houses, with several rooms, and with pleasant yards; and not a few of the women, in different parts of the Islands, sought to keep their houses clean, and make them agreeable to their visitors. Some learned the use of tools by seeing foreigners use them; and their own native ingenuity enabled them to make useful articles, when the pattern was before them, such as doors, chairs, chests, tables, bedsteads, and cupboards. The women were so far taught, by females in the mission, how to braid and sew hats and bonnets from the cocoa-nut and palm-leaf, that these came into general use. Females employed in the mission families learned to wash and iron clothes, and to perform the different branches of domestic labor according to the usages of civilized life; and these, in their turn, taught others; so that in many families there was an air of neatness and comfort, to which they once were entire strangers. The first attempts at imitation

were of course rude, but perseverance made them
more successful. In the opinion of some of the
older missionaries, converted natives needed only
example, motive, and means properly before them
to overcome their idle and sluggish habits. Of
course in the interior districts, the social life retained much of the rudeness of olden times. Yet
in all parts of the group, there was a growth of religious knowledge and principle, and a preparation
to act more from conviction of duty than from obedience to the chiefs.

The schools were in a process of improvement.
Graduates from the seminary at Lahaina- In schools
and religious
luna were scattered as teachers through knowledge.
the Islands, and proved themselves more competent
than had been expected ; and there were not a few
good teachers raised up in the mission schools already mentioned. At Hilo there was a boarding-
school with ninety pupils, many of them preparing
to be teachers; though its leading object was to
prepare scholars to enter the seminary at Lahainaluna. As a further advance, youths began to take
the place of adults in the high-school. A boarding-
school for girls was also opened at Hilo by Mrs.
Coan ; and there was a larger one at Wailuku, on
the island of Maui, where a stone building had been
erected for it. In proportion as more competent
teachers were multiplied, the schools bcame interesting, and not a few adult schools were revived.
Aided by small appropriations from the mission, the
natives in many places erected better school-houses,
and began of their own accord to contribute for
the support of schools. The number of pupils in
1837 under this higher instruction, cannot have
been less than fourteen thousand.

In addition to the meeting-houses already mentioned, Kuakini had completed one of stone
at Kailua, one hundred and twenty feet
long, forty-eight broad, and twenty-seven high, with
gallery, shingled roof, steeple, and bell. The great
stone church, now the glory of Honolulu, was commenced about this time; the king giving $3,000 at
the outset, and the chiefs and people $2,350, to-
wards its erection. Houses for worship, of clay hardened in the sun, were built at Ewa, on Oahu; at
Kaanapoli and Oloalu, on Maui, and at Koloa on
Kauai; and one of grass was built on the island of
Lanai, opposite Lahaina. These houses had thatched
roofs, verandas, glass windows, and pulpits.

In the year 1837, there were seventeen missionary
stations, seventeen churches, and twenty-
seven ordained missionaries. The missionary helpers, male and female, including married females, were sixty. The plenteous harvest which soon
after covered the fields, was the consequence in part
of the multiplication of laborers, and of the great
extent to which good seed had been and was being
sowed. Messrs. Bingham, Thurston, and Whitney,
the pioneer missionaries, were still on the ground;
and the whole body of missionary laborers must have
had free use of the native language. Kaahumanu,
that noble mother in Israel, had now been sometime
dead, but while living she had performed a most important preparatory work; and Kinau, her worthy
successor, was in power. The heroic Kapiolani,
and the eloquent blind preacher, lived through the
season of special interest. More than a thousand
Christian marriages were solemnized in the year
above mentioned. At least a fourth of the popula-

tion had learned to read, and much religious and
secular information existed in books. The national
mind was so far educated and awakened, that the
mass of the people must have had at least glimpses,
and very many of them distinct apprehensions, of
the fundamental doctrines of the gospel.

The translation of the whole Bible into the Hawaiian language, was completed on the 25th Translation
of February, 1839, a few days short of nine- of the Scrip-
teen years from the time when the mountains of tures
Hawaii were first seen from the deck of the *Thaddeus*. The translators of the New Testament were
Messrs. Bingham, Thurston, Richards, Bishop, and
Andrews; of the Old Testament, Messrs. Bingham,
Thurston, Richards, Bishop, Clark, Green, Dibble,
and Andrews. Large portions of the Old Testament
had previously been printed in separate editions, and
several editions of the New Testament.

About this time the king and chiefs made great
improvements in the laws. Originally, the Improve-
only law known on the Islands was the ment in the laws.
temporary and changing "thought of the chief."
Every chief regarded himself as the absolute master
of his own people, and the king was the absolute
master of both chiefs and people. Since the introduction of Christianity, several laws had been proclaimed, forbidding certain gross vices, but the
relations between the rulers and people remained
unchanged. As knowledge and civilization advanced,
the chiefs saw the necessity of a change in the structure of their government, and in the year 1836 they
applied to the American Board to send Application of
them a teacher in jurisprudence. The the government for aid.
Board very properly decided, that this did not come

within its legitimate province. On learning this
decision, the chiefs, two years later, requested Mr.
Richards to become their chaplain, teacher, and
interpreter, and engaged to provide for his support.

Mr. Richards As they had no other resort, Mr. Richards
made coun- was released from his connection with the
selor to the
government. Board, and complied with their request.
Though he had not received a legal education, he
was endowed with excellent common sense, and had
graduated with honor in a New England college, and
subsequently in the oldest of the New England theological seminaries. He entered at once on his new
and responsible duties.

At this time, the graduates and students of the
seminary at Lahainaluna had begun to discuss the
subject of law-making in the " Kumu Hawaii," a native newspaper edited and published at that institution. It would seem that, without special reference
to Mr. Richards, the king directed one of the grad-
New code of uates to draw up a code of laws. When it
laws.   was prepared, he and some of the chiefs
spent several hours a day, for five days, in discussing
it. The code was then recommitted to the graduate,
with instructions to supply certain deficiencies, and
correct certain errors. This having been done, a
longer time was devoted to revision, and it was again
recommitted with instructions. After the third reading, the king asked the chiefs if they approved it,
and their answer being in the affirmative, the king
said, " I also approve," and he affixed his signature,
June 7, 1839.

The introduction, which was a Bill of Rights,
reads thus, translated into English: " God hath made
of one blood all nations of men, to dwell on the face

of the earth in unity and blessedness. God has also bestowed certain rights alike on all men, and all chiefs and all people, of all lands.

"These are some of the rights, which he has given alike to every man, and every chief; namely, life, limb, liberty, the labor of his hands, and productions of his mind.

"God has also established governments and rulers for the purposes of peace; but, in making laws for a nation, it is by no means proper to enact laws for the protection of rulers only, without also providing protection for their subjects; neither is it proper to enact laws to enrich the chiefs only, without regard to the enriching of their subjects also; and hereafter there shall by no means be any law enacted, which is inconsistent with what is above expressed; neither shall any tax be assessed, nor any service or labor required of any man in a manner at variance with the above sentiments.

"These sentiments are hereby proclaimed for the purpose of protecting alike both the people and the chiefs of all these Islands; that no chief may be able to oppress any subject, but that chiefs and people may enjoy the same protection under one and the same law.

"Protection is hereby secured to the persons of all the people, together with their lands, their building lots, and all their property; and nothing whatever shall be taken from any individual, except by express provision of the laws. Whatever chief shall perseveringly act in violation of this constitution, shall no longer remain a chief of the Sandwich Islands; and the same shall be true of the governors, officers, and all land agents."

The laws regulated the poll tax, the rent of lands,
the fisheries, and the amount of labor
Advance thus made. which the king and chiefs might require.
They secured to landholders the permanent possession of their lands on paying their rent, the amount
of which was prescribed. Labor for the king and
chiefs might be commuted by a payment, which
was in no case to exceed nine dollars. Parents having four children living with them, were freed from
all labor for the chiefs; and if there were five children, the parents were not liable to taxation. Local legislation was forbidden to individual chiefs.
The authors of new and valuable inventions were
to be rewarded, and the descent of property was
regulated. These were the more important items
in the code, which was to take effect six months
after its promulgation. The chiefs were to meet
annually, in the month of April, to enact laws and
transact the business of the kingdom.

This is perhaps the first recorded instance of a
An example for despotic governments. hereditary despotic government voluntarily
setting limits to its own power for the
good of the subjects. Only twenty years before,
the king, chiefs, and people were idolatrous, immoral, unlettered pagans.

Kinau, the premier, died in April, 1839; and
Death of Kinau. Kaikioewa, the aged governor of Kauai, on
the tenth of the same month. The loss
thus experienced by the nation was doubtless un-
speakable gain to the departed. Kinau was succeeded in the premiership by Kekauluohi, her half-
sister. The latter held office six years, until June,
1845, when she died at the age of fifty-one.

Kinau left no equal in stability of character.

Ever wakeful to the interests of the nation, she showed no ordinary skill in managing Her charac-ter. its concerns, even in the most troublous times. She set her face against the prevailing immoralities, and gave satisfactory evidence of a readiness to make personal sacrifices for promoting Christian morals and the best interests of the people. So much was she esteemed by all classes, and so much relied on by all, that her sudden death had an almost paralyzing influence.

CHAPTER XVIII.

1836–1838.

THE awakening influences of the Holy Spirit, in
their more striking form, were first seen,
in the mission itself, at its annual meeting

<small>Commence-
ment of the
awakening.</small>

in March, 1836. And it is worthy of special note,
as showing how good men are often most effectually
roused for local efforts, that the desire then pre-
dominating in the hearts of the missionaries, was
for the conversion of the whole world. Every mind
appears to have been fully occupied with that mo-
mentous topic, and under its influence there was
the utmost harmony and love among the brethren.
The impression was general and strong, that the
measure of prayer and exertion among Christians
came far short of what was needed to usher in the
millennial day; and that they themselves, and all
God's people, were called to enter at once upon a
broader sphere of action. This they embodied in the
printed appeal of great power already mentioned,
which they sent to the churches at home.

The state of feeling now described continued
through the year, but there was nowhere any very
special outpouring of the Holy Spirit. The same
interest in the world's conversion appeared in the
general meeting of the following year, but it was now

connected with much feeling and mutual exhortations with respect to the field they occupied. This feeling was providentially chasteued and intensified by bereavements in several families, but most of all by the sudden removal of one of the youngest of their number, and one of the most promising as to health and usefulness. The Holy Spirit evidently applied the admonition especially to the afflicted husband, who returned home to Waimea on Hawaii, with his motherless child, to witness at his station the commencement of the great awakening. Soon, a similar state of inquiry appeared at Wailuku on Maui, and indeed at most of the stations. The moving power was evidently from above, The moving power from above. for there was then in the United States such a season of rebuke and darkness, as has rarely been seen, — a partial insolvency prevailing throughout the land, such as obliged the Prudential Committee of the Board to curtail their remittances almost universally.

The presence of the Holy Spirit became more marked in the autumn. Of this there was abundant and heart-cheering evidence in the improved spiritual condition of the native churches. The standard of piety in them was so raised that the mission bore testimony, concerning not a few of the church members that, "for their ardent feelings and uniform activity in religion, they would be ornaments to any church in the United States." Hitherto the churches had been composed chiefly of the aged and middle aged, but the work now in progress embraced all ages, many children and youth being among the hopefully converted.

Still more apparent was the divine influence early

in 1838. It was so at nearly all the stations,
and at some the work was truly wonderful. Stupid natives became good hearers, the imbecile began to think, the groveling sensualist with a dead conscience showed signs of deep feeling.

The means employed were those commonly used during times of revival in the United States, such as preaching, the prayers of the church, protracted meetings, and conversing with individuals, or small companies. The protracted meetings were conducted in a very simple manner, and were found to be adapted to the character and circumstances of the people, much of the time being given to the plain preaching of revealed truth, with prayer in the intervals. The topics of discourse were such as these: the gospel a savor of life or death; the danger of delaying repentance; the servant who knew his Lord's will and did it not; sinners not willing that Christ should reign over them; halting between two opinions; the balm of Gilead; the sinner hardening his neck; God not willing that any should perish. The topic most insisted on, was the sin and danger of refusing an offered Saviour.

In respect to measures adopted, Mr. Armstrong's course at Wailuku may be taken as an illustration of that pursued by the larger number of the brethren. He resorted to no special measures, except calling upon those who had chosen Christ to separate themselves, that they might be instructed in classes and carefully watched over, so as to learn what manner of spirit they were of. He kept a book, in which he wrote the names of individuals who appeared to be

serious, and then classed them by neighborhoods or
villages, and met them every week for instruction,
conversation, prayer, etc. When satisfied with any
one, he baptized him forthwith.

While it is true that at most of the stations
there were no special efforts to excite the feelings,
aside from plain, simple preaching, it was to be
expected that there would be some exceptions among
so many laborers, and at a time of so great interest.
The Rev. Sheldon Dibble, in a work published at the
Islands in 1843, soon after this remarkable season,
makes the following statement : " The special
measures used to operate upon the feelings of the
congregation, were not probably so much designed,
as naturally incident to a kind of uncontrollable
state of tumultuous feeling, both on the part of
the pastor and the people. The pastor, in some
instances, descended from the pulpit, and paced
through the midst of the congregation, preaching
and gesticulating with intense emotion. Sometimes
all the members of a large congregation were permitted to pray aloud at once. And again, at times,
many expressed their fears and sense of guilt by
audible groans and loud cries. Feelings were not
restrained. Ignorant heathen are not accustomed
to restrain their feelings, but to manifest their
emotions by outward signs, more so by far than
people who are intelligent and cultivated. Perhaps
their feelings were too intense to be restrained, and
necessarily burst forth in shrieks and loud lamentations." [1] But such measures and indications of feeling were confined almost entirely to two or three
districts on Hawaii. As a general thing very little

[1] Dibble's *History*, p. 848.

use was made of special means. The missionaries aimed, with simplicity and plainness, to impart correct conceptions of the character of God, the nature of sin, the plan of salvation, the work of the Spirit, the nature of true religion, and especially the sin and danger of rejecting an offered Saviour. The hearts of the people were tender, and under such truths, the house of worship was often a scene of sighing and of weeping.

Some of the congregations were immense. That Immense as-sembliea. at Ewa was about four thousand in number. Honolulu had two congregations, one of two thousand five hundred, the other between three thousand and four thousand. At Wailuku the congregation was one thousand eight hundred; at Lahaina, it was generally two thousand; and at Hilo, it was estimated to number at times more than five thousand.

The congregation at Lahaina was in an interest-All classes aroused. ing state. All classes crowded to the place of worship. The children thrust themselves in where they could find a little vacancy. Old, hardened transgressors, who had scarcely been to the house of God for the fifteen years that the gospel had been preached there, were seen in tears, melting under the omnipotent power of truth. The blind, who had not been in the house of God before, were now led thither, sometimes by a parent, sometimes by a child, sometimes by a grandchild. Cripples labored hard to enjoy the privilege of hearing. Two crawled on their hands and feet to every meeting. One, whom none of the missionaries had ever seen before, and whom none of the pious people had known, gave reason to hope, that in soul at least, like the cripple who sat at the gate called Beautiful, he had been made whole.

There was a remarkable prayer-meeting of native females in the same place, under the super- A female prayer-meeting. vision of Mrs. Baldwin. "It was some- times literally a Bochim. We have often noticed it as a trait of character among the people, that they could attend to but one thing at a time; or to express the matter more correctly, that they could not easily change from one kind of business to another the same day. This trait was remarkably exempli- fied in their prayers, and in all they did to Character- istics of the promote the work. Those whose hearts work. were interested in it went at the work with their whole souls, and gave it their undivided attention. It was pleasing to see their singleness of purpose. They had seen, in several particulars, the reality and the power of God's working among them. They saw a universal moving among the people ; they saw some old transgressors, that had resisted all means hitherto, now melting down with scarcely any means at all; they saw, and they wondered as they saw, some iniquities, which had heretofore resisted the power of the law of the land and all the force of persuasion, now dissipated as chaff before the wind ; and that, too, while such sins were perhaps not even named by us in public or private. This was partic- ularly the case with tobacco smoking, which is a great evil in this land. One of the earliest effects witnessed of the operations of the Spirit here was, that old, inveterate smokers were abandoning their pipes, and flocking to the house of God."

The interest awakened among the children of La- haina, was almost universal. They had been as

10

thoroughly taught in iniquity as perhaps any in
the Islands, for they saw not only the sins of
native growth, but the place was then more
frequented by ships, during one half of the year,
than any other in the group. The common saying
among the pious people at the close of the meeting was, that there were no longer children to
make a noise along the beach. Parents were aston-
ished to find their little ones not only more docile
and ready to listen to them, but to find them often
alone praying to God to save their souls. For a
long time, one could scarcely go in any direction,
in the sugar-cane or banana groves, without finding
these little ones praying and weeping before God.
Mr. Baldwin had himself turned out of his way to
avoid disturbing them.

Among the children.

At Kaneohe, the congregation on the Sabbath
was about a thousand. There was, moreover, a good
degree of interest in Sabbath-schools, Bible classes,
and other meetings. The influence of the gospel
had greatly improved the condition of the
people. They were better clothed and
housed, more neat in their persons and dwellings,
and provided better for their children. More than
thirty new houses were built near Mr. Parker, the
missionary, within the space of six months, chiefly
by persons who had lived in remote parts of the
districts, that they might enjoy the privileges of
schools and other means of instruction. Not a few
in the congregation took notes of the discourses, on
which they were afterwards questioned.

Effect on the condition of the people.

At Kaluaaha, on the island of Molokai, Mr.
Hitchcock's first intimation of a gracious
influence among his people, aside from

Great inter- est on Molo- kai.

the state of his own feelings, was the fact that a
number were in the habit of rising an hour before
light, and resorting to the school-house to pray for
the coming of the Holy Spirit. This meeting increased in numbers, and there was unusual solemnity. The weekly meetings were all numerously
attended, and the Sabbath congregation filled the
house of worship. This was in the spring of 1838.
A protracted meeting was held, with help from
the brethren at Lahaina. The prevailing characteristic was a profound solemnity. Church members had wonderful enlargement and assistance in
prayer. Missionaries declare that they had never
witnessed more earnest, humble, persevering wrest-
ling in prayer, than was exhibited by some of the
native Christians at this time; and that they had
reason to bless God for being so greatly edified, comforted, and assisted by their earnest supplications.
At one time, the native Christians were so overcome
with a sense of the divine presence and love, that
they could do nothing but weep, and their meeting strongly suggested the Pentecostal scenes.

Several of these brethren, going to outstations,
were surprised to find that the awakening influence
had preceded them, and their visits had a very beneficial result. The children became specially interested. In every previous religious excitement, they
had been unmoved, but now no effort seemed necessary to fix their attention, and there was hope of
the conversion of not a few. Protracted meetings
were held at two outposts, twelve and twenty miles
from the station. In congregations averaging from
three to four hundred, the seriousness was almost

universal; and so intense was the anxiety for religious conversation, that the missionaries did not easily find time for sleep. The meeting-house being near, the voice of prayer was often heard there long before it was light.

CHAPTER XIX.

1838–1841.

THE statistics of all the island churches, at this time, were necessarily somewhat confused. *Results of the great* In May, 1841, there were eighteen churches, *awakening.* and the number admitted to these churches, in the years 1839–41, respectively, were five thousand four hundred and three, ten thousand seven hundred and fifteen, and four thousand one hundred and seventy-nine; or twenty thousand two hundred and ninety-seven in all. The admissions at Waimea, on Hawaii, in the first year of the awakening, were two thousand and six hundred, and nearly as many more in the second, which must. have been a large part of the adult population of that district. It is due to Mr. Lyons, the pious and very laborious missionary at Waimea, and the "sweet singer" of their *At Waimea,* Israel, to say, that these admissions were *on Hawaii.* the result of conviction, after free personal inter-course with the candidates at their homes and at the station, that they were truly converted persons. A subsequent experience of thirty years, including more than one generation, during all which time he has been the resident missionary, shows that he must have had more reason for his belief, than was supposed at the time by many of his brethren. Nor would it be strange if there was au excess of caution at some of the other stations.

At Hilo, Mr. Coan admitted five thousand to the church in one year, and fifteen hundred in the next; and the number of members in his church in 1841, was seven thousand one hundred and sixty-three. The facts were so extraordinary, and attracted at that time so much attention among the patrons of the mission, that pains were taken to draw from him a statement of his labors in the districts of Hilo and Puna, and of his manner of ascertaining the Christian character of the thousands added to his church. The results of these inquiries I will give as concisely as may be.

Many of the more discreet, prayerful, active, and intelligent of the church members were stationed at important posts throughout the two districts, with instructions to hold conference and prayer meetings, conduct Sabbath-schools, and watch over the people. Some of these native helpers were men full of faith and of the Holy Ghost, and their influence was happy. They often succeeded in persuading the wild and uncultivated to attend to instruction, and were the means of turning many to the Lord. Other members of the church were sent forth, two and two, into every village and place of the people, at times when it was not convenient for the missionary to be absent from the station. The men went everywhere preaching the Word. They visited the villages, climbed the mountains, traversed the forests, explored the glens. These measures, while they were blessed to those engaged in them, prepared the way for the missionary in his succeeding tours.

As to measures for ascertaining the character of candidates for admission to the church, no labor was spared in selecting, examining, watching, and teaching them; and though the admissions were numerous, they were designed and believed to be not hasty or indiscriminate. Every effort the nature of the case would admit, was made to ascertain the true character of the candidates; and while the injunction, "Preach the Word, be instant in season and out of season," was not forgotten, the searching out, gathering, guiding, and feeding of the sheep and the lambs, were objects of ceaseless anxiety and of incessant toil.

It was the habit of the missionary, both at the station and on his tours, to write down the names of those who professed to be anxious for their souls. The persons thus recorded were in this manner kept under his eye, though unconsciously to themselves, and their lives were made the subjects of scrutinizing observation. After the lapse of three, six, nine, or twelve months, selections were made from the list of names for examination. Some were found to have gone back to their old sins; others were stupid, or gave but too doubtful evidence; while many were found to have stood fast, and run well. Thus, from a list of a hundred names, ten or twenty, and from a thousand names, one or two hundred, more or less, were selected; while the doubtful cases were deferred for a more full development, or to be more effectually wrought upon by the continued influence of the gospel.

Thus many who came into the church were converts of two years' standing, at the time of their baptism. A still larger class were of one year's

standing. Another large class had been hopefully
converted for from six to nine months ; and the cases
received after a shorter period than three or four
months were exceptions to the general rule.

Most of those who were received from the distant
parts of Hilo and Puna, left their villages, and spent
some time at the station previous to their union
with the church. They were there instructed from
week to week and from day to day. They were examined and reëxamined personally, often five or six
times. In this way they were sifted and re-sifted,
with every effort to separate the precious from the
vile. The church and the world, friends and enemies,
were also called upon and solemnly charged to testify,
without concealment, if they knew aught against
any of the candidates. To this charge a great multitude in the church were faithful, being afraid, as
they said, to conceal the sins even of their nearest
friends. It was therefore difficult for any one to
practice outward sin for any length of time without
detection.

Much care was also taken to instruct the young
Instruction converts on the nature and evidences of
given. union to Christ, on the import and design
of the ordinances of the church, on Christian doctrines, and on the practical and active duties of life.
It is admitted that, notwithstanding these precau-
tions and many others, some gave painful evidence,
in later years, that they did not enter by the door
into the sheepfold; it not being possible for any one,
except the omniscient Shepherd, fully to distinguish
the sheep from the goats.

The aged, the infirm, the sick, and those whose
circumstances rendered it impossible or improper for

them to come to the station, were admitted to the
church by the missionary in his tours through the
districts.

Inquiries were made as to the character of the
church members. They were represented _{Character of church members.}
as babes in knowledge and Christian expe-
rience, encompassed with infirmities, and beset by
temptations; but very few were convicted of scanda-
lous offenses, and scarcely any, when under censure,
exhibited the distinctive marks of apostasy. A great
majority of the cases which called for the discipline
of the church, were for intoxication occasioned by
smoking tobacco. Some were separated from the
church for levity of manners, for neglecting schools,
meetings, etc., and for general stupidity and indifference to instruction. A few were guilty of theft and
adultery. The proportion of those under church
censure was about one to sixty.

The watch and care in the church appears to
have been strict. At each successive tour _{Watch and care exercised.}
through Hilo and Puna, special attention
was paid to the members of the church. They were
visited in their respective villages; their names were
called; each one was seen face to face; the wanderers were sought for; the stupid were aroused; the
afflicted were comforted; the feeble were strengthened; and all were warned, reproved, exhorted, or
encouraged, as the case might require. Thus the
location, the life, and the feelings of every individual
of that numerous flock were frequently brought into
review, and became the subjects of examination, so
far as was possible for a single shepherd.

Inquiry was made, how the missionary could become acquainted with so many thousands of converts,

so as to be able to judge of their characters in the
space of two or three years. The response was,
that he could not be so fully acquainted with them
as was desirable, or as he longed to be.   But he had
a multitude of souls committed to his charge, for
every one of whom he felt no small degree of responsibility ; and he must do what he could for all.
Should he neglect to gather converts into the church
till he had a close and intimate knowledge of their
feelings, conversation, and actions, as developed in
their family retirement and in their every-day duties
and intercourse with each other, the great mass of
them might never come within the visible fold of
Christ, and might wander in darkness, unknown and
unrecognized as the sheep and lambs of the Lord
Jesus, and in danger from the great enemy of souls.
By dividing the people into sections and classes; by
attending to each class separately, systematically,
and at a given time, and by a careful examination
and a frequent review of every individual in each
respective class ; by keeping a faithful note-book always at hand to refresh the memory; by the help of
many faithful members of the church, and by various
other collateral helps, the missionary believed himself to have gained a tolerable knowledge of the
individuals of his flock.

The documents furnishing the basis for the preceding statements were written in June, 1839, when
the government proclaimed its code of laws, and only
a month before the outrages committed by Captain
Laplace, of the French frigate *l'Artemise*, to be described in the next chapter.

It was perhaps unavoidable, that such extraordinary excitements should be followed by reaction and coldness. Returning from the

Season of
reaction.

general meeting of the mission at Honolulu in 1841, after an absence of seven weeks, Mr. Coan made a tour through Hilo and Puna, and found a greater degree of stupidity among the people than he had seen since 1836. Many, who had been zealous and active in the work of God, then seemed cold and indifferent. Meetings were more thinly attended, and a considerable number of the church had fallen into sin. Though the great multitude of the disciples still maintained their standing as Christians, and avoided all disciplinable offenses, yet there was a falling off in their moral energy, an apathy in their feelings, and a want of vitality and unction in their prayers. In some villages considerable numbers had indulged in some besetting sin. The appar- The apparent causes of this decline were, the absence ent causes. of their spiritual guide, the fall of several chiefs, the breaking down of the bulwarks of temperance and virtue by the French, and the promulgation of the new code of laws. Though these laws were good, yet so great were the changes made by them, so numerous, and (to the people) so complex and difficult were the little earthly interests to be adjusted, so unskilled and often unfaithful were the new officers appointed to execute the laws, and so ignorant and blindly attached to old customs were the people, that it is not wonderful they should, for a time, be absorbed in temporal things, to the neglect of the eternal.

Yet the external condition of the church was prosperous throughout the Islands. During the New houses time under review, a stone meeting-house for worship. was erected at Wailuku, on Maui, one hundred feet by fifty-three, with a gallery; another at Haiku, fourteen miles from Wailuku, ninety feet by forty-two; another at Waimea on Hawaii, one hundred and twenty feet by fifty; and another at Kealekekua, on the same island, one hundred and twenty feet by fifty-four. At Hilo a grass meeting-house was built spacious enough to hold three thousand people; and six others were built by the people in different parts of the districts of Hilo and Puna, of sufficient capacity to accommodate from one or two thousand each. The school-houses erected on the Islands were too numerous to mention. The contributions of the people in two years, in addition to the building of churches and school-houses, amounted to $12,000.

CHAPTER XX.

A PAPAL INVASION. — SCHOOL FOR YOUNG CHIEFS.

1839.

DIVINE PROVIDENCE was pleased to permit a naval outrage of the grossest character to occur in the midst of this great work of grace. Captain Laplace, of the French frigate *l'Artemise*, arrived at Honolulu in July, 1839. He came professedly in the interest of the Romish mission, and his proceedings while there would seem to have an adequate explanation only in a statement made not long after by a French naval officer to a member of the mission of the American Board at the Gaboon, in West Africa. He represented the queen of Louis Philippe as very religious, and as much interested in the missions of her church; and said it was well understood among the higher officers in the navy, that the most hopeful means of their promotion was in efforts to advance the Roman Catholic missions. Laplace declared on his arrival, that he had come by command of the French king to put an end to the ill treatment the French had suffered at the Islands. He asserted that to persecute the Catholic religion, to tarnish it with the name of idolatry, and to expel the French (meaning French missionaries) from the Islands, was to offer an insult to France and to its sovereign. With a singular disregard of truth, he also asserted that there was no civilized nation which did not permit in its territory the free toleration of all religions.   He demanded —

1. That the Catholic worship be declared free throughout all the dominions subject to the king of the Sandwich Islands, and that the members of this religious faith enjoy in them all the privileges granted to Protestants.

His demands.

2. That a site for a Catholic church be given by the government of Honolulu, a port frequented by the French, and that this church be ministered to by priests of their nation.

3. That all Catholics, imprisoned on account of religion since the last persecutions extended to the French missionaries, be immediately set at liberty.

4. That the king of the Sandwich Islands deposit in the hands of the captain of *l'Artemise* the sum of twenty thousand dollars, as a guarantee of his future conduct towards France, which sum the government will restore to him when it shall consider that the accompanying treaty will be faithfully complied with.

5. That the treaty signed by the king of the Sandwich Islands, as well as the sum above mentioned, be conveyed on board the frigate *l'Artemise* by one of the principal chiefs of the country, and also that the batteries of Honolulu salute the French flag with twenty-one guns, which will be returned by the frigate.

If these conditions were not complied with, and the treaty signed which accompanied the manifesto, Captain Laplace declared his intention to make immediate war upon the Islands.   He addressed letters to the English and American consuls, informing

them of his intention to commence hostilities on
the 12th of July, at noon, against the king of the
Islands, should he refuse to accede to the conditions
of the treaty, the clauses of which were explained,
as he informed them, in the manifesto, of which he
sent them a copy; at the same time offering an asylum on board the frigate to the citizens of the two
nations, who in case of war should apprehend danger to their persons or property. But in the letter
to the American consul, there was this important
addition, —

"I do not include in this class the individuals,
who, although born, it is said, in the United States, make a part of the Protes- *His hostility to the mission.*
tant clergy of this archipelago, direct the counsels
of the king, influence his conduct, and are the true
authors of the insults given by him to France. For
me they compose a part of the native population,
and must undergo the unhappy consequences of a
war, which they shall have brought on this country."

He referred of course to the American missionaries, who, for the reasons alleged, were not to be
recognized and treated as American citizens.

The king being at Maui, a vessel was sent for
him, and the time for commencing hostilities was,
at the request of Kekauluohi, the regent, deferred to
the 15th of the month. On Saturday, the 13th, the
acting governor of Oahu delivered on board the frigate the $20,000 demanded by Captain Laplace, and
also the treaty signed by the regent and himself in
behalf of their sovereign. The king arrived the
next day at nine o'clock in the morning. At eleven
o'clock a military mass was celebrated on shore, in

a house belonging to the king, attended by Captain Laplace, who was escorted by a company of one hundred and fifty men with fixed bayonets and martial music. The treaty was brought to the king for signature on Tuesday, the 16th, at five o'clock P. M., and he was told that if it was not signed by a prescribed *Indignity of-* hour the next morning, the French gov- *fered to the* *king.* ernment would send a larger force, and take possession of the Islands. The king requested time to advise with his chiefs, but the threat was repeated, and he was induced without longer delay to sign the document.

One of the articles of this treaty provides, that French wines and brandy shall not be prohibited, and shall pay a duty of only five per cent. on the value. The frigate sailed on the 20th of July.

It was well understood by all parties at the time, *Real object* that the real object of the treaty dictated *of Laplace.* by Laplace to the Hawaiian government, was to secure, by intimidation and force, a free access for the Romish priests to the Sandwich Islands. Indeed, the only object gained by these dishonorable proceedings, except removing obstacles from the sale of intoxicating liquors, was the introduction of those priests against the wishes of the islanders. The French trader had really as much liberty before the visit of Laplace, not only to reside at the Islands, but for every traffic there except in wine and brandy, as he has had since, and he was as secure in person and property. Nor were the American missionaries the authors of the proceedings of the government towards the papists, otherwise than by having been the means of the general adoption of the Protestant evangelical religion.

The French consul, having obtained a treaty according to his mind, engaged largely in Results of the sale of intoxicating drinks. The Eng- ceedings. lish consul had before succeeded in retaining one of the Romish priests, named Walsh, at the Islands, on the plea of his Irish nativity, and consequent right to receive British protection. This man, emboldened by the late proceedings, made no longer a secret of his profession, and exerted himself to proselyte the natives. He denounced the Hawaiian Bible, and told the people that their marriages, solemnized by Protestants, were invalid, and that the missionaries themselves were living in adultery. He encouraged the use of wine, brandy, and tobacco; which last was so used by the natives as to produce a pernicious intoxication. At first, there was a rush to his place of worship, but the attendance soon began to fall off. The native Romanists were zealous. They even renewed the old incantations over the sick, and pretended to work miracles. By such means, a considerable Romanist party was raised on Oahu, including, among its most zealous members, those who had always been foremost in every outbreak of the old idolatry. Yet the influence of Romanism, down to the end of the year, was almost wholly confined to Oahu, and even there only a few church members were drawn away, and there were fewer converts among the people than had been expected. In the minds of the natives, the outrages by Laplace, war, brandy, the robbery of $20,000, and popery, were all closely associated; and the people were little disposed then, and it has been so ever since, to favor a religion which had been forced upon them at the cannon's

11

mouth, and the whole tendency of which was so evidently demoralizing.[1]

The United States East India squadron, under Commodore Read, arrived in the October following, remained about a month, and an account of the French outrage, drawn up by Mr. Castle, was published at Honolulu at the expense of sixteen officers of the squadron.

Visit of an American squadron.

In this year a school was instituted for the young chiefs. It grew out of the fact that the old chiefs were rapidly disappearing, and that, in the change of times, the nation could no longer be ruled by ignorant men, whatever their rank. It was obvious to the chiefs themselves, that their children must be educated, or not inherit the consideration and authority of their fathers. Heretofore the chief men had not been willing to have their children deprived of that train of attendants, which they had regarded as essential for persons of their standing. But they now saw the necessity of a good education, and of dispensing with this train, even in the case of children belonging to the highest rank. They therefore assented to the plan of having their children taken into the family of a missionary; and Mr. and Mrs. Cooke were the persons of their choice. A suitable house was erected, and the late Hon. John Ii, an intelligent and faithful member of the native church — since a judge in the Supreme Court of the Islands, and more recently, and till the close of his life, acting pastor of the church at Ewa, — was appointed assistant guardian, to be aided by his wife, a person of like character. The school was liked by the parents. The king, on one

School for the young chiefs.

[1] Tracy's *History*, p. 408.

occasion, when surveying the happy group of pupils, and noticing their improvement, said to them : " I wish my lot had been like yours. I deeply regret the foolish manner in which I spent the years of my youth." The government at length assumed the support of the school, which contained fourteen young chiefs of both sexes. Two of them _{Who were educated there.} have since reigned as kings, and one (Emma) as queen ; the education of those three royal persons having been obtained at this school.

When at the Islands in 1863, I saw no ladies more accomplished than Queen Emma, and another lady, also educated at this institution, then the wife of a highly respectable American resident at Honolulu. But the circumstances of the pupils were not favorable to permanent religious impressions.

CHAPTER XXI.

REMARKABLE GROWTH OF THE CHURCHES.

1825–1870.

FROM the year 1837 till the author's official visit
to the Islands in 1863, — when the large
mission churches began to be divided into
smaller ones, with the expectation of placing each
under a native pastor, — the mission was accustomed
to send to the Missionary House annual tabular
views of the several churches. These furnish a
striking illustration of the power of divine grace on
those Islands; and I have thought it worth while to
bring the facts therein contained into a single tabular view. Without some such exhibition of the
growth of the churches through the entire
period, we cannot properly estimate the
extent and value of the religious influence exerted
on the Sandwich Islands, nor the degree of discretion exercised by our missionary brethren. The table
will show that, if the great awakening did not ex-
tend in its more active form beyond the year 1840,
the fruits of it were largely gathered after that time,
and also that religion was frequently revived in subsequent years. There is probably no great district
of our own country that, for so long a time, has had
such accessions to its churches in proportion to the
population.

The table gives the number admitted to each of
the station churches, in each year from
1837 to 1863 inclusive; that is, for twenty-

(marginal notes: Sources of information. Reasons for a tabular view. Description of the table.)

six years. The first column states the admissions during the twelve years preceding 1838; and the last shows (according to a careful revision made in 1863), what was the whole number received into each of the churches, and the grand total down to that time. To this the footing up of the yearly admissions, as they are given in the table, nearly agrees. The sum total of admissions to 1863, was fifty thousand eight hundred and eighty-one; and through fifty years to 1870, it was fifty-five thousand three hundred.[1]

It hence appears, that in the twelve years preceding 1838, one thousand one hundred and sixty-eight hopeful converts were gathered into thirteen churches. The number received into twenty churches in the twenty-six years following 1837, was forty-nine thousand seven hundred and thirteen, which is an annual average of about nineteen hundred. The average in the last twelve of these years exceeds a thousand. The reader will see reason to believe, that very many of the converts of 1838 and 1839 — as at Kohala, Kailua, Kaawaloa, Kau, Wailuku, Kaluaaha, and Honolulu — were kept on probation one, two, or three years.

(margin note: Results of the tabular view.)

---

[1] The footing of the reported admissions each year to 1863, is . 51,146
The corrected estimate is 50,881

Excess 265

The actual excess must have been somewhat larger, since it appears from the tables, that some of the churches occasionally failed to report their admissions. The yearly additions, subsequent to 1863, were as follows: for 1864, 384; for 1865, 347; for 1866, 583; for 1867, 735; for 1868, 827; for 1869, 884; for 1870, 689; or 4,449; making a total of 55,300. The report of the Evangelical Association for 1870, states the number of church members at 14,850. This was after a careful revision, at that time, by the pastors. The reduction had been going on for several years, and is one of the indications of decline in the Hawaiian population of the Islands.

ADMISSIONS TO THE CHURCHES.

		1825–1837.	1838.	1839.	1840.	1841.	1842.	1843.	1844.	1845, 1846.	1847.	1848.	1849.	1850.	1851.
HAWAII	Hilo	84	639	5244	1499	154	273	381	306	553	117	186	265	164	169
	Waimea	25	2600	2300	419	40	170	322	55	62	–	61	96	50	82
	Kohala	–	629	149	80	15	124	467	297	–	24	68	26	8	–
	Kailua	208	68	92	373	175	501	739	28	12	7	137	–	2	53
	Kaawaloa	49	81	262	385	337	289	919	58	11	8	8	–	4	13
	Kau	–	–	–	–	–	72	845	8	–	39	99	97	38	58
MAUI	Lahaina	248	2	151	134	86	54	105	2	263	68	12	90	6	57
	Wailuku	16	208	200	192	179	62	148	90	213	124	11	55	31	19
	Kaanapali	–	–	–	–	36	31	20	19	21	96	22	–	–	–
	Hana	–	–	62	58	88	95	170	–	54	259	40	–	9	–
MOLOKAI	Kaluaaha	28	14	59	59	32	24	319	69	174	–	162	276	–	145
OAHU	Honolulu, 1st	281	134	390	275	92	70	394	102	48	113	98	306	369	19
	Honolulu, 2d	–	49	672	436	115	184	360	–	99	31	47	126	63	–
	Ewa	10	329	742	174	89	151	8	17	93	411	132	10	2	47
	Waianae	–	–	–	–	–	20	6	2	9	155	58	5	–	–
	Waialua	38	127	202	–	4	112	20	–	1	5	66	151	24	58
	Kaneohe	–	–	85	–	–	–	–	20	2	46	–	36	38	48
KAUAI	Waimea	104	18	69	20	9	68	54	31	20	–	1	7	–	48
	Koloa	55	–	57	15	6	57	1	7	10	9	11	8	20	10
	Waioli	22	38	9	–	16	27	68	–	25	14	33	40	33	82
	Total	1168	4930	10,725	4118	1473	2384	5296	1111	1670	1518	1243	1594	861	800

ADMISSIONS TO THE CHURCHES (Continued).

		1852.	1853.	1854.	1855.	1856.	1857.	1858.	1859.	1860.	1861.	1862.	1863.	Number from beginning.
HAWAII	Hilo	192	442	176	95	88	105	81	48	51	106	72	57	11,491
	Waimea	–	99	137	53	57	114	128	176	64	167	43	40	7,267
	Kohala	24	28	66	–	32	–	39	17	23	35	81	17	2,269
	Kailua	111	273	56	–	9	263	90	3	9	7	117	–	3,325
	Kaawaloa	195	112	64	85	44	84	57	53	55	–	45	52	3,443
	Kau	–	64	52	–	–	8	–	10	–	15	–	5	1,477
MAUI	Lahaina	–	45	41	80	5	23	–	103	33	14	27	6	1,543
	Wailuku	64	74	306	58	7	1	6	2	–	39	54	–	1,597
	Kaanapali	61	–	98	228	6	–	–	–	–	4	8	–	885
	Hana	58	–	–	–	73	401	–	14	–	–	–	21	–
MOLOKAI	Kaluaaha	81	–	210	–	–	92	–	–	103	54	8	12	2,104
OAHU	Honolulu, 1st	279	331	176	118	99	–	189	77	5	323	90	12	4,427
	Honolulu, 2d	31	83	35	26	7	15	116	23	–	240	41	–	2,765
	Ewa	–	65	52	6	44	11	–	–	5	99	11	1	2,568
	Waianae	7	14	21	–	6	–	–	–	–	78	–	–	582
	Waialua	11	63	124	15	26	17	12	12	27	84	8	1	1,067
	Kaneohe and Hanaka	84	–	–	21	18	18	1	4	143	75	18	1	923
KAUAI	Waimea	88	124	–	56	90	53	36	25	–	2	–	–	963
	Koloa	61	22	20	35	80	13	39	1	30	102	45	2	758
	Waioli	57	96	67	26	13	1	3	19	22	21	160	18	777
	Total	1404	1880	1701	852	488	1169	803	587	570	1465	828	244	50,881

The number admitted to the churches in 1843, was five thousand two hundred and ninety-six, a greater number than in any preceding year save 1839.

Up to the time of this awakening, the churches Conversion contained very few young people, but of the young. nearly six hundred children and youth were reported as converts in the year 1838, and the steady accessions to the churches during many subsequent years render it very probable that the children received, in one way and another, what may be regarded, under the circumstances, as a Christian education.

The accessions to the local churches, in the last fifAdmissions teen years embraced in the tabular view, are to particular churches. worthy of special note. On the island of Hawaii, we may instance Hilo, which received four hundred and forty-two in 1853; Kailua, two hundred and seventy-three in the same year; and Kaawaloa, one hundred and ninety-five in the year preceding. On Maui, Hana received two hundred and fifty-nine in 1847; Wailuku, three hundred and six in 1854; Kaanapali, two hundred and forty-eight in 1855; Lahaina, one hundred and three in 1859; and Kaluaaha, on Molokai, one hundred and sixty-two in 1848. On Oahu, Ewa received four hundred and eleven in 1847; Waialua, one hundred and twenty-four in 1854; and Honolulu, five hundred and sixty-three in 1861. On Kauai, Koloa received one hundred and two in 1861; Waioli, one hundred and sixty in 1862; and Waimea, one hundred and twenty-four in 1853.

The church members in 1863, were nineteen thouLosses by excommunica- sand six hundred and seventy-nine, and tion and otherwise. eighteen thousand eight hundred and fortyeight had then died in the fellowship of the church.

If we subtract the sum of these two numbers from the grand total of admissions, it leaves as many as twelve thousand somehow lost to the churches. Of these almost three thousand were from the church at Waimea, on Hawaii, which had still one thousand seven hundred and fifty-six members in regular standing. The church at Hilo, previous to the year 1863, had received eleven thousand four hundred and ninety-one on profession of faith, but had excommunicated less than five hundred. That church had lost six thousand five hundred and thirty-five by death, and then had four thousand three hundred and eighty-three members in regular standing. Discipline in most of the churches, was very strict. Abating the large number at Waimea on Hawaii, the losses by excommunication and otherwise do not exceed what might reasonably have been expected, averaged for so many years, in so many and such large churches; considering, moreover, the anxiety of the natives to become members of the church, and their ignorance, fickleness, and deceptive character.

It was a question difficult to resolve satisfactorily, whether the people of the Sandwich Islands might be represented as nationally Was the nation Christianized? Christianized at the close of the great awakening. There was not then, nor was there for a score of years afterwards, a well defined opinion in the Christian community at home as to what constitutes a national conversion to Christianity. Yet it was true of the Islands at that time, that the constitution, laws, institutions, and religious professions were as decidedly Christian as in any of the older nations of Christendom. There was no other acknowledged religion, no other acknowledged worship. They had the Sabbath, Christian churches, and a Christian ministry; and their literature, so far as they had any, was almost wholly Christian. Theirs were some of the largest churches in the world, and as great a proportion of the people attending the Sabbath worship, as in any Christian nation. On the other hand, the people as a body, including the greater part of the church-members, had only a partial engrafting of civilization upon their Christianity. They were rude in their dwellings and their social habits, and were sadly wanting in industry and thrift, in judgment and decision of character, and were yet painfully liable to the national sin, which was still wasting them as a people.

We must probably admit, that whatever right the

Not fully entitled to take rank in Christendom

Hawaiian churches of 1841 might claim to the Christian name, — and they, doubtless, were fully entitled to it, — the nation, as such, could not properly be allowed to take rank in Christendom as a Christian nation. Scarcely twenty years had passed since they were barbarous pagans. Their moral, social, and civil elevation was not yet sufficient to entitle them to such a recognition. Nor were the churches at home prepared to admit it. At the annual meeting of the American Board in Cin-

The Board slow to recognize the national conversion.

cinnati, as late as 1853, the Prudential Committee ventured upon a somewhat jubilant announcement, that the Sandwich Islands had been Christianized; but so unprepared was even the Board, at that time, for appreciating and receiving such intelligence, that the announcement awakened no apparent interest; nor does the fact seem to have been generally credited by the Board until ten years later.

The island churches were in their primitive condition as late as 1863. All their centres were at the missionary stations, missionaries were, for the most part, the pastors, and but few natives were professedly training for the pastoral office. The important discovery had scarcely then been made, that self-governed, self-reliant churches are hardly a possibility among the heathen, without pastors of the same race. Nor was it till quite recently, that the missionaries were fully prepared to enter on a vigorous course of measures for putting the native churches on an independent footing. Churches formed as those at the Islands had been, and so much under the direction of missionaries as they were, could do comparatively little to educate the nation for self-government in its civil departments; except only as they inculcated the principles of justice, equity, and mercy.

CHAPTER XXII.

GROWTH OF THE CIVIL COMMUNITY.

1838–1842.

MR. RICHARDS, soon after entering upon his
A constitu- official duties, delivered a course of lec-
tion adopted. tures to the chiefs on political economy
and the general science of government. From the
ideas thus obtained, a constitution was drawn up,
based upon their old forms, and published in 1840. It
is an interesting fact that, although this constitution
greatly restricts the power of both king and chiefs,
it was adopted unanimously. In comparison with
the past, the progress of the nation was now more
rapid. The liberal policy of other nations, and whatever of their forms could with propriety be transplanted, were embodied in the constitution and laws,
but on a scale commensurate with the feebleness and
youth of the nation. The penal code was greatly
improved; primary courts and courts of appeal were
established; the jury system was adopted. Sufficient
was done to benefit greatly the position of natives
and foreigners. Taxation was rendered more equal,
and lighter; encouragement was proffered to industry, and to the increase of population; an enlightened public school system was organized. Imperfect
as the system may appear to the critical eyes of a
superior civilization, it was yet in advance of the

condition of the people. Wherever it operated fairly and systematically, much good was effected, and it served to prepare the way for more important changes.[1]

The common people could now become owners of land in fee-simple. But their extreme pov- *Property in* erty and want of skill were in the way of *the lands.* their becoming purchasers. So far as was possible, they received the counsel and aid of their missionary fathers. In one year, through the agency of a single missionary, seven thousand acres of pasture, and several hundred acres of arable land, were secured to a great number of poor people in the northern district of Oahu. A commission was appointed by the government to settle land titles; and, before the close of 1852, the claims of nearly all the people of the Islands had been investigated. The titles thus obtained were never to be questioned, even by the highest courts; and would invest the people with rights before unknown on any of the Islands, scarcely even by the highest chiefs. An impulse was thus given to the erection of better dwellings, and to a better cultivation of the soil, as was soon manifested throughout the Islands.

An impressive lesson, teaching the people that the laws were more than mere recommenda- *Enforcement* tions, was the execution of a chief for the *of law.* murder of his wife. He was put on trial, pronounced guilty by a native jury, and suffered the full penalty of the law, which was death by hanging. A similar lesson was taught to foreigners, by a fine imposed on the English consul for riotous conduct.

The Laplace treaty had proved so injurious to the

[1] Jarves's *History*, p. 171.

cause of temperance, that a movement to arrest the
evil was simultaneously made among the
chiefs, without concert, at Honolulu and
at Lahaina. The king was at the latter place, and
he and the chiefs who were with him formed a temperance society. On putting his name to the pledge,
he said: "I am one who wish to sign this pledge.
Not, however, on account of the address we have
just heard (referring to an address by Mr. Baldwin),
but I thought of it before, and the evil of drinking
rum was clear to me. Here is the reason why I
thought it an evil. I am constituted a father to the
people and the kingdom, and it belongs to me to
regulate all the other chiefs. I have therefore become
really ashamed, and I can no longer persist in rum-
drinking. This is the reason why I subscribe my
name to this pledge."

Two days previous to this, a large temperance
meeting was held at Honolulu, and Governor Kekaunaoa, and several other chiefs,
with some hundreds of the common people, took the
pledge. In addition to this, about seven hundred
children belonging to the first parish in Honolulu,
then under the care of Dr. Armstrong, formed a
"cold-water army," and took the pledge as teeto-
talers, with much zeal for the cause. Their motto
was, "Water only; away with that which intoxi-
cates." The restraints of law having been weakened
by French interference, it was deemed the more
necessary to create a public sentiment. This was in
March, 1842. Writing from Honolulu in the October following, Dr. Armstrong declares, that he had
known only three cases of drunkenness among the
natives since April, and it was then as much as a

(marginal notes:) The king and temperance.

General tem-
perance
movement.

native's character was worth to be seen drinking a glass of rum. He also represents the king as frequently addressing temperance meetings.

Hoapili, the aged governor of Maui, and the highest among the living male chiefs, next to the king, died in the first month of 1840. He was among the earliest converts on Maui, and was a striking monument of the grace of God. He excelled all his compeers in his humble faith, his attachment to the word and house of God, and his patriotic devotion to the interests of his country, both as a magistrate and a citizen of Zion. Those who saw him while awaiting the summons of death, were affected by the interest he manifested in his prospects beyond the grave. His hopes rested humbly but confidently on the righteousness of the Lord Jesus, his all-sufficient Saviour. Ten days before his death, he requested to be carried to the house of God, a privilege he longed once more to enjoy. His last interview with the king was tender and affecting. After conversing in a dignified manner concerning his own departure, and entreating the king to become a Christian man, he became much affected, and laying his hand on the lap of the king, burst into a flood of tears. He strictly prohibited wailing on the occasion of his death, and requested that his grave might be near that of Mr. McDonald, a member of the mission who had died in the previous year; and these injunctions were strictly complied with.

The time had now come to look for some reaction in the community; to expect those who had been affected in the great awakening, but not truly converted, to fall away; those who had counterfeited piety, to throw off the mask; and those Christians whose zeal had outrun their other graces, to relax their efforts, and become lukewarm and careless. The reaction was aided by the united power of popery and intemperance. There was more or less of revival, however, at all the stations on Hawaii, and at some places on the other islands.

Popery and intemperance rendered each other important aid. The priests aided the grog-shops, by teaching the lawfulness of alcoholic drinks: and the shops nourished an appetite which made people love such preaching, and follow the preachers. In some parts of Oahu, the natives began to manufacture a kind of whiskey. Fanaticism of the grossest form lent its aid. One man on Oahu pretended to be the Messiah, and obtained followers. Some pretended to be possessed of devils, and one to cast out devils by a variety of incantations. Universalism and infidelity showed themselves; heathen songs and sports were resumed. All these forms of error, folly, and vice belonged to one party, and composed a grand anti-protestant influence, of which popery was the exciter and leader. A bishop and three priests arrived early in the year, and three more priests and some lay assistants in November. They made vigorous efforts to obtain converts, especially on Oahu, and in the western and northern part of Hawaii; but were less successful than they expected to be, and indeed less than they thought they were. Hundreds of apparent converts left them before the end of the year. At Kailua, they were deliberately cheated. A large number of natives, acting in concert, joined under a fictitious name. Having

[marginal notes:]
Alliance of popery and intemperance.

Anti-protestant movement.

It is unsuccessful.

gratified their curiosity by seeing "the pope and the images" to the best advantage, they disappeared, and when the priests inquired for them, no such persons could be found. In all parts of the Islands, those who witnessed the Roman Catholic worship generally agreed that it was idolatry; a religion of the same kind, essentially, with that which they had practiced in the days of Kamehameha the Great. David Malo, one of the most intelligent of the natives, made the tour of Oahu for the purpose of lecturing on the subject, for which his intimate knowledge of the old idolatry admirably qualified him. When the priest insisted that their use of images was not exactly worship, the natives quoted from the second commandment, "Thou shalt not *bow down* unto them." The bowing down could neither be denied, nor explained away to the satisfaction of the people. But very few members of the churches became their followers. Even those who were under censure, very generally rejected them.[1]

The visit of the United States Exploring Squadron in September, 1840, under Commodore United States Wilkes, continued two months or more, Exploring Squadron. and was an advantage to the Islands. Captain Hudson was a pious man, and repeatedly addressed congregations of natives, and with good effect. The general deportment, both of the officers and the scientific corps, was such as to strengthen every good 'influence; and the "Narrative of the Exploring Expedition" by Commodore Wilkes, published after his return, contains much valuable information concerning the mission. An outlay, moreover, of sixty thousand dollars by the squadron, while at the Islands, for the

[1] Tracy's *History*, p. 439.

supply of its wants, did something to mitigate the embarrassment occasioned by Captain Laplace's oppressive levy on the government. The commodore set himself zealously against the late demoralizing influence of the French man-of-war; and, at his recommendation and that of his officers and the American consul, the king published a law, prohibiting his subjects from the manufacture and use of intoxicating drinks. The evil was thus greatly checked; though not until after there had been sad confirmation of the truth, that reformed drunkards do not easily resist the intoxicating cup, when it is pressed to their lips.

A prohibitory law.

The most effectual check, however, in the vicinity of Honolulu, was a new outpouring of the Holy Spirit at Ewa, after a day of humiliation and prayer. The house of God was again filled. Many backsliders returned to their duty, and many who had appeared hopeful during the late revival, and had afterwards lost their seriousness, were again awakened. Prayer-meetings were established in every neighborhood, and the study of the missionary was often thronged by persons desirous of conversing with him on the subject of religion.

Revival at Ewa.

A stop was thus put to the progress of drunkenness and other vices that were beginning to prevail, and great numbers were brought to the house of God, who had long neglected divine worship.

The elevation of the common schools by means of a supply of teachers from Lahainaluna, suffered an unexpected check from the operation of the new code of laws. These laws very properly made every native master of his own earnings, except so much as went to pay his taxes. One of

Unexpected result of good laws.

the first consequences of this freedom was, that the teachers began to fail of their support. To remedy this evil, a law was enacted requiring all children, over four and under fourteen years of age, to attend school five days every week; and a piece of land was set apart in each school district, for the support of the teacher. Upon this land every man was required to labor nine days in the year; three of the days to be taken from the king's time, three from that of the local chiefs, and three from his own. Under this law, the number of schools rapidly increased.

The decease of Hoapiliwahine occurred at Lahaina in the first month of 1842. She was the widow of Hoapili, who died just two years before, and a sister of Kaahumanu. She was indeed a mother in Israel. For fifteen years her heart and hand had been in every good work, and her name was precious to all on the Islands who loved the cause of Christ. Very many of the poor and needy mourned her loss as that of a parent; and the members of the mission felt bereaved of one who was always a tender-hearted friend. *Death of Hoapiliwahine.*

The eighth and ninth reinforcements arrived in the time now under review, consisting of the Rev. Messrs. Bond, Dole, Paris, Rowell, and J. W. Smith, and Mr. Rice, as teacher. The last named clergyman was also a physician. *New missionaries.*

I now give a summary view of the means employed in 1842 for educating the nation. *The national education.*

The seminary at Lahainaluna — opened as a self-supporting school for adults in 1831, and in 1837 made a boarding-school for children from seven to twelve, and for youth from twelve to twenty years of age — had been furnished with ample *Lahainaluna seminary.*

buildings by the American Board. The principal building had been enlarged and greatly improved, and furnished with apparatus, and houses had been erected for a printing-office, and for three ordained married teachers. These buildings, with dormitories for more than a hundred students, formed a village of some interest. There were one hundred and seven pupils. Of its graduates, one hundred and forty-four were then living; and of these one hundred and five were teachers, thirty-five were officers of government, seventy-three were church members in regular standing, and nine were officers of churches. There was a small theological class in the seminary.

The female boarding-school at Wailuku, on Maui, under the care of Mr. and Mrs. Bailey and Miss Ogden, had sixty pupils. They were instructed, not only in Christian truth, but in geography, mental and written arithmetic, moral philosophy, natural theology, reading, writing, drawing, composition, and various arts adapted to the station of Hawaiian females. At daylight the pupils repaired to their gardens, where they exercised till half past six, when they were called to prayers. They breakfasted at seven, and after that were employed for an hour in putting their rooms in order. From nine to eleven was spent in study and recitation. The next half hour they spent as they pleased. From half past eleven to twelve, they bathed and prepared their dinners. From dinner until two was at their own disposal, and much of it was spent in study. From two till four, they gave attention to spinning, weaving, sewing, knitting, making mats, etc., under the instruction of Miss Ogden. From four to five, they devoted

to exercise, had supper at five, and the remainder
of the day was at their own disposal. At the evening devotions they recited the "Daily Food" and
received such religious instruction as seemed appropriate. During the year, five of the girls were married to graduates of Lahainaluna.

There were two boarding-schools at Hilo, one
under the care of Mr. and Mrs. Lyman, Other board-
commenced in 1837, having from thirty ing-schools.
to sixty boys, preparing generally for the Lahainaluna seminary; the other for girls, commenced by
Mrs. Coan in 1839, taught by her, and sustained by
her, with such aid as she could obtain from the
pupils and their parents, and from other natives.
The annual expenses of this school were about four
hundred dollars. The scholars, of whom there were
twenty, were taught the common branches, and the
school was easily governed, and repeatedly enjoyed
the special influences of the Holy Spirit.

At Waialua, on the northern side of Oahu, was
a manual labor boarding-school for boys, Manual labor
with from fifteen to twenty pupils. It was school.
a successful experiment, but was brought to a close
after a few years by the lamented deaths of Mr. and
Mrs. Locke, with whom it originated.

At Waioli, on Kauai, there was a select school,
for educating teachers, under the care of School for
Mr. and Mrs. Johnson. This was partly teachers.
a manual labor school. The pupils numbered from
thirty-five to seventy-five, and many of them were
boarded by native church members.

Select schools were maintained at nearly all the
stations, to train teachers, and to show Select
how schools should be taught. Mr. and schools.

Mrs. Knapp were at the head of one such school at Honolulu, in a first-rate school-house built by the natives.

In 1841, the American Board opened a school for the children of missionaries at Punahou, about two miles from the harbor of Honolulu, and placed it under the care of Mr. and Mrs. Dole.

School for children of missionaries.

The number of common schools was three hundred and fifty-seven, and of pupils, eighteen thousand and thirty-four. They were languishing early in the year, from the fact that the rewards of labor in almost every other department of industry were becoming more sure to Hawaiians, with no corresponding increase in that of education. The teachers could not be expected to be uninfluenced by this state of things; many of them left their work, and at length government took the common schools under its support and direction, and provided by law for the attendance of the children, and for a more liberal and regular support of the teachers.

Common schools.

It should be added, that Sabbath-schools were taught at all the stations, and were attended by great numbers, both of adults and children. The care and instruction of these schools devolved chiefly on the missionaries; but they were aided by many of the more intelligent native church members, and in some instances these had the entire charge of large, successful schools.

Sabbath-schools.

CHAPTER XXIII.

KAPIOLANI, HEROINE OF THE VOLCANO.

1841.

KAAWALOA, the residence of Kapiolani, was on the northern shore of Kealakekua Bay, where Her resi-dence. Captain Cook was killed in 1779. Mr. Ely, and after him Mr. Ruggles, resided there; but Mr. Ruggles removed to a more desirable abode for a missionary and his family, about two miles back from the bay. The chiefs and people then made a road from thence to the bay, and erected there a convenient house of worship. The site is one of the pleasantest on the Islands, at least two thousand feet above the ocean, fanned by the sea breeze during the heat of the day, and by the land wind at night. The soil is fertile, and produces grapes, figs, pomegranates, oranges, guavas, coffee, and other tropical fruits.

Naihe died in November, 1831, nearly ten years before his wife. He belonged to the race Death and of chiefs, and sometimes was spoken of as Naihe. character of " the national orator;" why, I do not know. When Kuakini was sent to Oahu, early in 1831, to suppress the insurrectionary movements on that island, he made Naihe temporary governor of Hawaii, but near the close of the year he died suddenly of paralysis. Naihe had been more conservative than his

compeers, and slow to renounce the idolatry of his
ancestors, but refused to aid those who made war in
its defense. When Kapiolani, in her zeal for the
new religion, decided to invade the regions of Pele,
he advised against it, but left her free to act on
her own discretion. When Kaahumanu wished to
put the bones of the deified kings into coffins, and
bury them in the earth out of the way of the superstitious people, Naihe, a resident in that region, had no boards to spare for that purpose, but
his wife came promptly to her aid. , At length the
gospel appeared to gain the control of his heart, and
he became a firm and steady supporter of good
morals and religion. As a magistrate, he was firm
in executing the laws, which were enforced by his
example, as well as by his authority. The mission
pronounced him an affectionate brother, an able
counselor, and a valuable coadjutor in the support
of schools and other means of planting the institutions of the gospel.

Kapiolani was a descendant of one of the ancient
Early history Hawaiian kings. Her landed possessions
of Kapiolani. bordered on the beautiful waters of Kealakekua Bay, and rose into the woodlands of Mauna Loa.
In early life she is said to have been intemperate;
and, for a year or more after her first acquaintance
with the missionaries, she lived with two husbands,
according to the pagan custom with persons of her
rank. Following the example of Keopuolani, as
soon as she became similarly enlightened, she separated herself from the younger of the two. The
mission families were objects of curiosity to the
people from the time of their first landing at Kailua,
which was about sixteen miles north of Kaawaloa;

and many came to see them, even from more distant places. Kapiolani was among their more frequent visitors, coming with her husband, in their well manned double canoe. Even then, her sprightly, inquisitive mind made her interesting, and she soon seized upon the outlines of the gospel.

The removal of Mr. and Mrs. Thurston to Honolulu, already mentioned, in consequence of the withdrawal of the royal family from Kailua, induced Naihe and Kapiolani to remove also, and they remained at Honolulu till the spring Her residence at Honolulu. of 1823. While there, Kapiolani was much enlightened and benefited by her intercourse with the missionaries. When the first reinforcement arrived, she urged the claims, both of Kailua and of her own Kaawaloa, as stations; and great was her joy at the prospect that both places would soon be occupied.

In anticipation of this event, Kapiolani began, immediately on her return, to erect a thatched Reception of a missionary house of worship down on the shore, like one which Kuakini had erected at Kailua, and she became almost impatient at the unavoidable delay of Mr. and Mrs. Ely. Though her husband did not yet fully sympathize with her in these matters, he did not refuse coöperation; and the old chief Kamakau seems to have been more advanced in the Christian life than herself. The house of worship was dedicated on the last day of February, 1824. Mr. Thurston preaching on the occasion to a large and attentive audience. Mr. and Mrs. Ely arrived soon after, and found that a house had been built for their accommodation, and received also a pledge from the friendly chiefs of vegetables and fresh water, free of expense, which had to be brought from a distance.

In July, Kapiolani had a painful illness. When Mr. Ely expressed anxiety for her recovery, her reply was: "I wish to suffer the will of God patiently. If it be his will, I desire to depart and be with Christ. Then I shall be free from sin. Once I greatly feared death, but Christ has taken away its sting." From this sickness she recovered; and a call she made at Mr. Ely's soon afterward, will illustrate the character of her piety. She spoke with great interest of the state of man. "The heavens and earth," she said, "the sun, moon, and stars, the birds and fishes, the seas, mountains, valleys, and rocks, all combine to praise the Lord. But where is man, poor, sinful man? He is mute. God has given him a mouth and knowledge, but man refuses to praise Him." As she spoke, she wept. Then she added: "We are dreadfully depraved. We are justly the objects of God's displeasure. We shall stand speechless at the bar of God."

Not long after her recovery, Kapiolani made a visit of a month at Lahaina, where Mr. Richards was then residing. Her habit was to make a daily call on him and his wife. Her nature was eminently social, and seems to have been remarkably sanctified by grace. Speaking of public worship, one Sabbath evening, she said: "I love to go to the house of God, for there I forget the world. When among the chiefs, I hear so much about money, and cloth, and land, and ships, and bargains, that I wish to go where I can hear of God, and Christ, and heaven." She continued: "When I hear preaching about Jesus Christ, my spirit goes out to him; and when I hear about God, my spirit goes to God; and when I hear about heaven, my spirit goes up to heaven. It goes and comes, and then it goes again, and thus it continues to do." She then inquired, with earnestness, whether Mr. Richards did not think she had two souls, saying that it seemed to her she had one good soul, and one bad one. " One says God is very good, and it loves God, prays to Him, and loves Jesus Christ, and loves preaching, and loves to talk about good things. The other one says it does no good to pray to God, and to go to meeting, and keep the Sabbath."

" We shall long remember the last evening that we enjoyed her society," wrote Mr. Richards. " She was expecting soon to return to Hawaii, and I therefore invited her to take tea and spend the evening with us. She came with Keameamahi, who is also one of our best friends. Honorii and Pupuhi joined the circle. The evening was not spent in general conversation. Kapiolani was pleased with nothing that would not come home to the heart. Many enlightened Christians, after leaving a pious circle, would blush at their own coldness could they but have seen how anxious this chief was to spend her last evening in the best manner possible. At the close of the evening we sung the translation of the hymn, ' Wake, Isles of the South,' and then parted with prayer."

The visit of Kapiolani to the great crater of Kilauea at the close of 1825, while on her Visit to the volcano. way to the new missionary station at Hilo, deserves a special notice. The people living in sight

of this greatest of volcanoes, were more wedded to
their heathen superstitions than those whose idols
'had been destroyed, and who were in frequent intercourse with foreigners. They daily sacrificed to
Pele, the reputed goddess, supposed to have her
dwelling in the fiery abyss, and occasionally her
prophets wandered into more civilized districts, de-
nouncing an awful retribution for the general apostasy. The spell of this superstition was best
broken, perhaps, by a bold intervention on the part
of some native of rank and character, and Kapiolani
became the honored instrument for this purpose.

Hearing at Kaawaloa that missionaries had com-
Determines   menced a station at Hilo, Kapiolani re-
to brave the solved to visit them, though her visit in-
wrath of the
goddess.   volved a journey on foot of more than a
hundred miles, over a rough and most fatiguing
way. And as Kilauea was on the route, it was her
purpose, after reaching it, to give practical demon-
stration of her own belief, that Jehovah is the only
God of the volcano. In this act of Christian heroism, she rose far above the ideas and sentiments
of her countrymen, and indeed of her own husband
Naihe, who sought to dissuade her from what appeared to them all so rash an enterprise. The destruction of the tabu and the idols had not given
the people a new religion. On her way, she was
accosted by multitudes, and entreated not to proceed, lest the goddess of the volcano should be
provoked to destroy her. Her answer was: "If I
am destroyed, you may all believe in Pele; but if I
am not, then you must all turn to the *palapala*."
Is warned by In approaching the region of the volcano,
a prophetess
of Pele.   she was met by a prophetess of Pele, who

warned her not to proceed, lest the goddess should
come out against her. "And who are you?" said
Kapiolani. "One in whom the god dwells," was
the reply. "Then," said Kapiolani, "you are wise,
and can teach me; come, sit down." As she hesi-
tated, Kapiolani commanded, and she obeyed. Food
was offered her, but she said she was a god, and did
not eat. She held a piece of tapa in her hand,
which she said was a letter from Pele. "Read it,"
said Kapiolani. She was reluctant, but when forced
to comply, with unexpécted presence of mind she
held her cloth before her eyes, and poured forth a
torrent of unintelligible sounds, which she would
have them believe were in the dialect of the ancient
Pele.

Kapiolani then produced her Christian books, and
said to the impostor, "You have pretended to deliver a message from your god, which none of us can
understand; I too have a *palapala*, and will read
you a message from our God, which you can understand." She then read several passages, and called
her attention to the character, and works, and will
of the great Jehovah, the true God, and to Jesus
Christ, as the Saviour of the lost. The who is
prophetess held down her head, and said silenced.
the god had left her, and she could make no reply.
Being again invited to eat, she no longer refused.

Kapiolani was met by Mr. Goodrich at the crater,
who had heard of her intended visit to the volcano,
and had come from Hilo, about thirty miles distant.
She was glad to see him, and, with her com- Descends in-
pany of about eighty, and Mr. Goodrich, to the crater.
she descended some hundreds of feet to the black
ledge in the crater, and there, amid some of the

most terrible natural phenomena on the earth's surface, which had ever been appalling to
her countrymen, she ate the berries consecrated to Pele, and threw stones into the seething
mass.   Then she calmly addressed her company:
" Jehovah," she said, " is my God. He kindled these
fires. I fear not Pele. Should I perish by her anger,
then you may fear her power. But if Jehovah save
me, when breaking her *tabus*, then must you fear
and serve Jehovah.   The gods of Hawaii are vain.
Great is the goodness of Jehovah in sending missionaries to turn us from these vanities to the living
God." They then united in a hymn of praise, and
bowed in prayer to Jehovah, the Creator and Governor of the world.

Her conduct in the vol-cano. (margin note)

There was rare moral heroism in this act of Kapiolani.   When, a few years since, the
writer stood by this grandest of volcanoes,
and saw the mass of molten lava upheaving and
surging over the breadth of half a mile, through the
agency of an unseen power, and beheld a group of
Christian native attendants seated thoughtfully by
themselves on the verge of the abyss, he would not
have deemed it strange if even they had some lin-
gerings of the old superstitious fears, though this
was almost forty years after the visit of Kapiolani.

Her Chris-tian heroism. (margin note)

Mr. Ely must have exercised an excessive caution
in receiving native converts into the church,
since Kapiolani was not admitted until
after this visit. The reception of Kamakau, the
old chief already mentioned, was still later. So late
as the close of 1826, Naihe was not an accepted can-
didate for admission, though believed to be not far
from the kingdom of heaven.

Admission to the church. (margin note)

Of Kapiolani, Mr. Ely speaks in strong terms of
commendation.   " She is, indeed," he says, "a
mother in Israel. No woman on the Islands, probably, appears better than she; and perhaps there is
no one who has so wholly given himself up to the
influence and obedience of the gospel. I am never
at a loss where to find her in any difficulty. She
has a steady, firm, decided attachment to the gospel, and a ready adherence to its precepts marks her
conduct. Her house is fitted up in a very decent
style, and is kept neat and comfortable. And her
hands are daily employed in some useful work."

The village of Kaawaloa, where this noble woman
so adorned her Christian profession, was Her domestic
situated on a bed of lava forming a plain of life.
from half a mile to a mile and a half in length, south-
east of which are the deep and quiet waters of Kealakekua Bay, and southwest the ocean. A precipice
of singular appearance rises hundreds of feet on
the northeast, and you perceive that it was once a
lofty cataract of molten lava, by which the plain was
formed. The arable lands are above and beyond the
precipice, and a road chiefly of modern construction
now descends along the face of the precipice to the
landing below. When Kapiolani built the stone
house still standing in the beautiful region two
miles above Kaawaloa, near where the house of the
Rev. Mr. Paris is now located, is not known to the
writer. He only knows that she removed to that
place to accommodate Mr. Ruggles, the successor of
Mr. Ely, whose health required a milder temperature
than could be found on the black lava of the shore.

It was in the village on the plain below, near the
sea-shore, that Naihe and Kapiolani resided when

they entertained Captain Finch, of the U. S. ship *Vincennes*, and the Rev. Charles S. Stewart, in the autumn of 1829; and there we shall see Kapiolani as she was at her own home. The writer imagines that, in the year 1863, he saw some of the forsaken remains of her dwelling. Her house was a spacious building, inclosed in a neat court by a palisade fence and painted gate, from whence she issued to meet them with the air of a dignified matron, her amiable and benignant face beaming with joy. I can do no less than quote the expressive language of Dr. Stewart.

"This chief," he says, "more than any other, perhaps, has won our respect and sincere friendship. She is so intelligent, so amiable, so lady-like in her whole character, that no one can become acquainted with her, without feelings of more than ordinary interest and respect; and from all we had known of her, we were not surprised to find the establish-
_{How she en-} ment she dwells in equal, if not superior,
_{tertained her}
_{guests.} to any we had before seen — handsomely arranged, well furnished, and neatly kept; with a sitting-room, or hall, in which a nobleman, in such a climate, might be happy to lounge; and bedrooms adjoining, where, in addition to couches which the most fastidious would unhesitatingly occupy, are found mirrors and toilet-tables fitted for the dressing-room of a modern belle.

"It was near tea-time, and in the centre of the hall a large table was laid in a handsome service of china; and, after a short stroll in the hamlet, and the rehearsal of the tragedy of Captain Cook's death on the rocks at the edge of the water into which he fell, we surrounded it with greater delight than I had before experienced, in observing the improvement that has taken place in the domestic and social habits of the chiefs. Kapiolani presided at the tea-tray, and poured to us as good a cup of that grateful beverage as would have been furnished in a parlor at home; while her husband, at the opposite end, served to those who chose to partake of them, in an equally easy and gentleman-like manner, a pork-steak and mutton-chop, with nicely fried wheaten cakes. A kind of jumble, composed principally of eggs, sugar, and wheat-flour, made up the entertainment. After the removal of these, a salver with a bottle of muscadine wine, glasses, and a pitcher of water was placed on the hospitable board. And every day we remained, similar generous entertainment was spread before various parties from our ship."

The *Vincennes* remained several days; and when, at the close, Captain Finch requested the Rev. Mr. Bingham, who had come with them from Honolulu, to express to Kapiolani the pleasure his visit had afforded him, and his thanks for her hospitality and kindness, her reply was, that the kindness of the visit had all been to herself, to the king and chiefs, and to the nation; "that he might have had some gratification in the visit, but he could have had no happiness like theirs; for our happiness," she exclaimed, clasping her hands and pressing them to her bosom, as she lifted her eyes, glistening with tears, to his, "our happiness is the joy of a captive just freed from prison!"

The closing of this domestic scene was beautifully characteristic. Messrs. Stewart and Bingham were to embark in the *Vincennes* at a

An interesting scene.

13

late hour in the evening, and Kapiolani had engaged
to send them on board in a canoe. Entering the
principal house to take leave, they found the family
at evening prayers. The parting scene, at midnight,
is thus graphically described by Dr. Stewart: —

"The paddlers of the canoe had been aroused from
their slumbers; other servants had lighted numerous
brilliant torches of the candlenut, tied together in
leaves, to accompany us to the water; and I was
about giving my parting salutation, when not only
Naihe, but Kapiolani also, said, 'No, not here, not
here, but at the shore;' and, throwing a mantle
around her, attended by her husband, she accompanied us to the surf, where, after many a warm grasp
of the hand and a tearful blessing, she remained
standing on a point of rock, in bold relief amid the
glare of torchlight around her, exclaiming again and
again, as we shoved off, 'Love to you, Mr. Stewart!
love to Mrs. Stewart! love to the captain, and to
the king!' while her handkerchief was waved in
repetition of the expression, long after her voice was
lost in the dashing of the water, and till her figure
was blended, in the distance, with the group by
which she was surrounded."

That the years which intervened between the death
of her husband and her own departure, were
filled with such acts of usefulness as com-
ported with her state of widowhood, with her advancing years, and (as is probable) with a diminished
income, is sufficiently evident in the notice of her
death by the Rev. Mr. Forbes, then, and for some
years, the missionary in that district. He wrote
thus: "Our beloved friend and mother in Christ,
Kapiolani, is gone to her rest. She died May 5, 1841.

Her death.

Her end was one of peace, and with decided evidence that your missionaries have not labored in vain. For twenty-four hours and more preceding her death, she was delirious, owing to the violence of _{Her charac-} the disease, which fell on the brain. This _{ter.} nation has lost one of its brightest ornaments; and speaking thus I disparage no one. Her life was a continual evidence of the elevating and purifying effects of the gospel. She was confessedly the most decided Christian, the most civilized in her manners, and the most thoroughly read in her Bible, of all the chiefs this nation ever had; and it is saying no more than truth to assert, that her equal, in those respects, is not left in the nation. There may be those who had more external polish of manner, but none who combined her excellences. She is gone to her rest, and we at this station will feel her loss the most. We cannot see how it can be repaired."

The hand of God is to be acknowledged in the consistent, Christian life, for twenty years, of this child of a degraded paganism. Hers was the religion of the Puritans, and the pious reader will desire that all those islanders, from the highest to the lowest, may be like her.

CHAPTER XXIV.

NATIONAL CALAMITIES OVERRULED.

1842-1846.

WE now come to a period in the history of the
Premature mission, in which the infantile government
diplomatic
relations. of the Islands was precipitated, by various
causes, into premature diplomatic relations with
some of the great powers of Christendom, and found
no small difficulty in preserving an independent
existence.

The Romish missionaries were fully tolerated, but
Opposition the sentiment of the nation was against
of Romish
priests. them, and against their religion. No prominent chief attached himself to them, though numbers of the lower order, disaffected with their rulers,
or hostile to the Protestant missionaries, became
enrolled as their neophytes. Among these were the
unruly spirits, who, in the days of Boki and Liliha,
were for restoring in some form the old idolatrous
rites. The Romish priests complained of the government, particularly in regard to the school laws,
and the laws concerning marriage. At first they
went so far as to remarry couples at their option,
and their partisans refused to pay taxes for the
public schools. They were encouraged in their seditious proceedings by the belief that France would
sustain them; and the French consul, under the

same belief, protested against restraint being put, even in the form of license, upon the traffic in ardent spirits.[1]

While affairs were in this state, on the 23d of August, 1842, the French corvette *Embus-* cade, Captain Mallet, arrived at Honolulu. The captain refused the customary salutes, and immediately forwarded a letter to the king, with demands more arrogant than those of Laplace. Their purport sufficiently appears in the response of the king, which has a historic value, and was as follows : —

Demands by a French naval officer.

"HONOLULU, *September* 4, 1842.

" To S. MALLET, Captain of the French sloop-of-war *Embuscade*.

" Greeting : We have received your letter dated the 1st instant, and, with our council as- sembled, have deliberated thereon ; and we are happy to receive your testimony that, if there are instances of difficulty and abuse in these Islands, they are not authorized by this government, and we assure you that we hold in high estimation the government of France, and all its estimable subjects. It is the firm determination of our government to observe the treaties with all nations. But the written laws are a new thing ; the people are ignorant, and good order can only be preserved on the part of the government by affording the protection of the laws to all who will appeal to them at the proper tribunals.

The king's response.

" On the introduction of the Roman Catholic religion, it was understood that toleration was to be fully allowed to all its priests and all its disciples, and this has been done as far as lay in our power,

---

[1] Jarves's *History*, p. 165.

and no one can prove to the contrary. But it is impossible to put a stop to disputes and contentions between rival religions, and the evils and complaints which result from them.

"The law favors literature, and as soon as the French priests are ready to found a high-school for the purpose of imparting it to their pupils, and teachers are ready, it shall find a location.

"The school laws were formed to promote education in these Islands, and not sectarianism; and no one should ask the government that they be altered to favor any particular sects. Any man qualified for teaching, being of a good moral character, is entitled to a teacher's diploma; this by reason of his acquirement, not of sect. No priest of either sect can give diplomas. Likewise marriage is regulated by law, and no priest of either sect can perform the ceremony, except the parties obtain a certificate from the governor, or his officer; and why should the laws be altered? Difficulties often arise on the subject, and we should regulate our own people.

"The laws require the people to labor on certain days; some for the government, and some for the landlords to whom the labor is due according to law; and the kind of labor is regulated by those to whom labor is due.

"The laws are not fully established in all parts of the Islands, and probably an ancient custom has been practiced, by which the owner of land would pull down the house of one who built thereon without his cheerful consent; but if the owner of the house complains to the judges, they should grant a trial; and if no satisfaction is obtained, then the governor will grant a trial; and if that decision is unjust, an

appeal must be made to the supreme judges, who
will sit twice a year.

" The ground occupied by the French priests in
Honolulu is held by the same tenure as that of the
priests of the Protestant religion, and some other
foreigners; and negotiations have been commenced,
which it is to be hoped will give equal justice to all.

" When John Ii arrives from Kauai, that case will
be adjusted, and if he denies the charge which you
have represented, a trial will be granted.

" Please do us the favor to assure the admiral, that
the present laws do not contravene the sixth article
of the treaty of the 17th of July. Brandy and wines
are freely admitted here, and if any one wishes a
license to retail spirits, he may procure one by ap-
plying to the proper officers. Those who retail spirits
without license are liable to punishment. Please
inform him, also, that we have sent ministers to the
king of France to beg of him a new treaty between
us and France.

" Accept for yourself the assurance of our respect
and our salutations.

KAMEHAMEHA III.
KEKAULUOHI."

Admiral Dupetit Thouars took possession, about
this time, on behalf of France, of Tahiti and the
Marquesas Islands. If his object, in sending the
Embuscade to the Hawaiian king with these imprac-
ticable demands, was to do the same with Demands not
the Sandwich Islands, the announcement enforced.
at the close of the king's letter, that he had sent
ministers to France with a request for a new treaty,
is probably the reason why the corvette left without
giving further trouble.

An evil now befell the nation greater in appearance than any which had preceded it, but providentially overruled, in the end, for good.

Mr. Charlton, the English consul, from the time of his arrival in 1825 had acted an unfriendly part, both towards the mission, and towards the government. He was by no means a fair representative of his own government, which appears to have been ever willing that the Sandwich Islands should rise and prosper under their native dynasty. Mr. Charlton's object was to make the islanders the subjects of Great Britain, which he in fact claimed them to be. His hostility to the American mission was in part the result of this policy, but more the overflow of a heart opposed to everything having the form of godliness. His motive in his active effort to secure a permanent footing for the French Roman Catholic mission, was to create an influence adverse to the American. And when at length, but too late, he perceived the direction of affairs from the impulse he had given them, and that they were urged onward by the naval power of France, he became desperate, and lent himself zealously to injuring the nation. An English party was created. Questions of jurisdiction were bitterly discussed; though when they afterwards came before the law adviser of the Crown in England, his opinion was given in favor of the Hawaiian king.[1]

Matters had come to a crisis in the spring of 1842; and just at this time Sir George Simpson and Dr. McLaughlin, high in the service of the Hudson Bay Company, arrived at the Islands. After a candid examination of the merits of the

Hostility of the English consul.

A friendly visit.

---

[1] Jarves's *History*, p. 107.

controversies between their own countrymen and the native government, they decided to use their influence in favor of the latter. As the king feared the effect of the false representations of the English consul and his partisans, Sir George advised the sending of commissioners to Europe and to the United States, with power to negotiate for an acknowledgment of the independence of the Islands, and for a guarantee against their usurpation by any one of the great powers.[1]

Sir George Simpson, Mr. Richards, and Timoteo Kahalilio, a native chief, were accordingly appointed commissioners. Sir George left immediately for England, and the other two directed their course for the United States. Dr. G. P. Judd, a physician connected with the mission, and long known to the government, was invited to take the place of Mr. Richards, and act as recorder and translator. This he did, resigning his connection with the mission. He was subsequently appointed President of the Treasury Board, and his services in this capacity were invaluable to the nation.

An embassy to foreign powers.

In September, two months after the departure of the commissioners, Mr. Charlton, apprehensive that the embassy might be prejudicial to him, left his consulate for London, assigning his official duties to Alexander Simpson. A characteristic letter to the king is given below.[2] No

Close of Mr. Charlton's career.

---

[1] Jarves's *History*, p. 173.

[2] "BRITISH CONSULATE, WOAHOO, *September* 26, 1842.

"SIR, — From the insults received from the local authorities of your Majesty's government, and from the insults offered to my sovereign, her Most Gracious Majesty, Victoria the First, Queen of the United Kingdom of Great Britain and Ireland, by Matthew Kekuanaoa, governor of this island: and for other weighty causes, affecting the interests of her Majesty's subjects in these Islands, I consider it my bounden duty to repair sooner was the attention of the British government called to this undiplomatic letter, than it led to the immediate dismissal of the official. The king declined to receive Mr. Simpson as vice-consul; but he insisted on retaining the office, and was able to do much mischief.

Mr. Charlton, on his way to England, fell in with Lord George Paulet, commanding H. B. M. frigate *Carysfort*, and found in him an instrument suited to his purpose. A despatch received by Rear Admiral Thomas from Mr. Simpson on the coast of Mexico, had induced him to order the *Carysfort* to Honolulu, for the purpose of inquiring into the matter. The frigate arrived on the 10th of February, 1843. The customary salutes were withheld, and an interview with the acting vice-consul seems to have prepared the commander for extreme measures, looking towards the transfer of the Islands to Great Britain. Usurpation by Lord Paulet. I do not deem it necessary to describe the measures, most humiliating and painful to the native government, which led, on the 25th of February, 1843, to a provisional cession; though under protest against the injustice of the demands, and with an appeal to the British government for redress.

immediately to Great Britain to lay statements before her Majesty's government, and have therefore appointed, by commission, as I am fully authorized to do, Alexander Simpson, Esq., to act as consul until her Majesty's pleasure be known.

"Your Majesty's government has more than once insulted the British flag, but you must not suppose that it will be passed over in silence. Justice, though tardy, will reach you; and it is you, not your advisers, that will be punished.

"I have the honor to be, your Majesty's most obedient, humble servant,

"RICHARD CHARLTON,
"*Consul.*"

"His Majesty, KAMEHAMEHA."

More than two months before this time, Messrs. Richards and Hahalilio had put themselves in communication with Daniel Webster, then Secretary of State at Washington, and had received his declaration, "as the sense of the government of the United States, that the government of the Sandwich Islands ought to be respected; that no power ought either to take possession of the Islands as a conquest, or for the purpose of colonization; and that no power ought to seek for any undue control over the existing government, or any exclusive privileges or preferences in matters of commerce." These declarations were virtually repeated by the President in a Message to Congress, on the 31st of December.

Successful embassy to Washington.

On the 11th of March, Mr. Simpson himself departed for England in a vessel belonging to the king, with despatches to the Foreign Office from Lord George Paulet. In the same vessel went Mr. J. F. B. Marshall, an American gentleman of excellent character residing at Honolulu, with a commission from the king to represent him in London; which, however, was not known to Mr. Simpson.

Embassy to London.

Meanwhile affairs at the Islands, and especially at Honolulu, assumed a distressing aspect. The law prohibiting violations of the seventh commandment was rescinded, and the barriers to intemperance were broken down; at a time when no less than four ships of war were in the port, two of them frigates, with twelve hundred men. The scene, for a month or two, reminded the older missionaries of the early period of their mission. The king finding himself divested of power, retired to

Deplorable condition of the government.

Maui; and Dr. Judd, fearing the seizure of the national records, withdrew them from the government house, and secretly placed them in
the royal tomb. There, among the deceased sovereigns of Hawaii, using the coffin of Kaahumanu for a
table, for many weeks he found an unsuspected asylum
for his own labors in behalf of the kingdom. "It
required no small degree of prudence on the part of
one so influential and beloved among the natives to
prevent an actual collision between the hostile parties.
With unshaken reliance on the justice of England,
the chiefs patiently awaited her decision. On the
6th of July, Commodore Kearney arrived, commanding the U. S. Ship *Constellation.* He immediately issued a public protest against the
seizure of the Islands. The presence of a ship of
war of a nation friendly to their sovereign rights was
encouraging to the chiefs. Commodore Kearney on
all occasions treated them as independent princes.
This courtesy exasperated still further Lord George,
who wrote the king that if he should suffer himself to
be saluted under the Hawaiian flag, he would forfeit
all consideration from her Majesty's government.
The king came from Maui on the 21st to hold communication with Commodore Kearney. So much ir-
rition was now manifested on both sides, that a violent
explosion must soon have occurred; when, unexpectedly to all, on the 26th of July, Rear Admiral
Thomas, in the *Dublin* frigate, arrived from Valpa-
raiso, having made all possible speed on receiving
the despatches of Lord George."[1]

Admiral Thomas, immediately on hearing of the
usurpation by his inferior officer, without
waiting for. instructions from his govern-

[1] Jarves' *History,* p. 183.

ment, hastened to the Islands, resolved to atone for
the indignity done to the king and his people as effectually and speedily as possible. The king was at
once, in the most formal and honorable manner, re-
instated in his authority. This was on the 31st of
July, 1843. The king and chiefs then re- The govern-
paired to the great Stone Church to offer stated.
thanks for the gracious interposition of Providence.
The deportment of Admiral Thomas toward all
parties, while at the Islands, was honorable to his
character, and he has ever since been gratefully
remembered.

Reference has already been made to a message
from the President of the United States to Congress
in December, 1842. The committee on foreign relations in the House of Representatives, through
its chairman, John Quincy Adams, made a report,
from which the following is extracted : —

" It is a subject of cheering contemplation to the
friends of human improvement and virtue, Report in the
that, by the mild and gentle influence of Congress.
Christian charity, dispensed by humble missionaries of the gospel, unarmed with secular power,
within the last quarter of a century, the people of
this group of Islands have been converted from the
lowest debasement of idolatry to the blessings of the
Christian gospel; united under one balanced government; rallied to the fold of civilization by a written
language and constitution, providing security for
the rights of persons, property, and mind; and invested with all the elements of right and power
which can entitle them to be acknowledged by their
brethren of the human race as a separate and independent community. To the consummation of their

acknowledgment, the people of the North American Union are urged by an interest of their own, deeper than that of any other portion of the inhabitants of the earth by a virtual right of conquest, not over the freedom of their brother man by the brutal arm of physical power, but over the mind and heart by the celestial panoply of the gospel of peace and love."

The independence of the Hawaiian nation was subsequently acknowledged by the United States and Great Britain, and by France and Belgium.

Independence of the Hawaiian nation.

The commissioners all returned to the Islands early in the year 1845, save Haalilio, who died of consumption at sea. He was a man of intelligence and judgment, of agreeable manners, and respectable business habits. While employed on his embassy, he read his Hawaiian Bible through twice. The proofs of his piety appeared in his love for the Scriptures, for secret and social prayer, for the Sabbath, and for the worship of the sanctuary. He was gratified by what he saw of the regard for the Lord's day in the United States and England, and was shocked in view of its desecration in France and Belgium. On Sabbath evening, just before his death, he said; "This is the happiest day of my life. My work is done. I am ready to go." Then he prayed; " O, my Father, thou hast not granted my desire to see once more the land of my birth, and my friends that dwell there; but I entreat Thee refuse not my petition to see thy kingdom, and my friends who are dwelling with Thee." His government and people were oppressed with grief when they heard of his early death.

Death of Haalilio.

The Rev. Messrs. Hunt, Whittlesey, Andrews, and Pogue, constituting the tenth reinforcement, arrived in 1844.

The Hawaiian government, from this time forward, had an acknowledged existence in the great family of nations. This was ten years be- *Practical recognition of the government.* fore the Prudential Committee ventured to make the formal declaration, that it was a Christian nation; and twenty years elapsed before it was fully and cordially recognized as such by the Christian Church. In 1843, the United States were represented at the Islands by a Commissioner; and Great Britain, in the year following, by a Consul General. The way was now opened for foreigners to become naturalized citizens; and all of foreign birth, who became members of the government, were required first to be thus naturalized. John Ricord, an American lawyer of considerable ability, was made Attorney General, after taking the oath of allegiance; Robert C. Wyllie, a Scotchman, was made Minister of Foreign Relations; and on the 20th of May, 1845, the king, for the first time in Hawaiian annals, opened the legislative chamber in person, by an appropriate speech, which was in due form responded to by the nobles and representatives. The several ministers afterwards read their official reports. On the 29th of March, 1846, a French ship of war returned the $20,000 exacted by Captain Laplace in 1839. The same vessel brought a special Commissioner from the King of France, entrusted with a treaty, concerted between England and France, by which all previous conventions were abrogated, and the objectionable clauses regarding ardent spirits and juries were modified so as to be more

acceptable to the king.   In October, 1846, Captain
Steen Bille, of H. D. M. S. *Galathea,* negotiated a
treaty in behalf of the King of Denmark ; which was
memorable as being the first convention entered into
by his Hawaiian Majesty with a foreign power, which
recognized, in all their amplitude, his rights as a
sovereign prince.[1]

The nation was composed of a mixed population,
Revision of   native and foreign, and the laws needed
the laws.   and received revision, with the competent
aid of the new Attorney General. The first two volumes of statute laws were issued in 1846.

[1] Jarves' *History,* pp. 197, 198.

CHAPTER XXV.

BARTIMEUS, THE BLIND PREACHER.

1843.

PUAAIKI[1] was born in East Maui, about the year 1785, a few years after the death of Captain His early Cook, and about as long before the visit of life. Vancouver. It is said he would have been buried alive by his mother, but for the intervention of a relative. The inhabitants were then wasting away under the influence of the most abominable vices, and he became as vicious and degraded as the rest of his countrymen. He early acquired a love for the intoxicating *awa*, and it is supposed that his blindness may have resulted from this, in connection with his filthy habits, and the burning tropical sun beating upon his bare head and unsheltered eyes. Before losing his sight, he had learned the *lua*, or art of murdering and robbing; the *kake*, a secret dialect valued for amusement and intrigue; and the *hula*, a combination of rude, lascivious songs and dances.

When the mission reached Kailua in 1820, he was there in the king's train, playing the buffoon for the amusement of the queen and chiefs, and thus he obtained the means of a scanty subsistence. It is not probable that he then knew anything of the missionaries. When the royal family removed to Honolulu,

[1] Pronounced Poo-ah-ee-kee.

14

in 1821, the blind dancer made part of their wild
and noisy train. There he suffered from illness and
neglect. In his distress, he was visited by John
Honolii, one of the Christian islanders brought by the
mission from America, who spoke to him of the Great
Physician. This interested him, and as soon as he
could walk, he went with his friend to hear the missionaries preach. The impression he made on them
was that of extreme degradation and wretchedness.
His diminutive frame bowed by sickness, his scanty
covering of bark-cloth, — only a narrow strip around
his waist and a piece thrown over his shoulders, —
his meagre face, his ruined eyes, his long black beard,
his feeble, swarthy limbs, and his dark soul, all made
him a most pitiable object.

Yet he was a chosen vessel, and the Lord Jesus was
such a Friend and Saviour as he needed.
Led by a heathen lad, he came often to the
place of Christian worship, gave up his intoxicating
drinks and the *hula*, and sought to conform to the
rules of the gospel as he understood them. His
heart was gradually opened, and the Spirit took of
the things of Christ and showed them unto him.
When now the chiefs again called for him to *hula* for
their amusement, his reply was: "*That* service of
Satan is ended; I intend to serve Jehovah, the King
of Heaven." He was now rising in the scale of being. Some derided him; but some of high rank,
and among them his patron the queen, had come so
far under the influence of the gospel, that they respected him for the stand he took. He even exhorted the queen, Kamamalu, to seek earnestly the
salvation of her soul, and his exhortations seemed
not to have been wholly in vain.

The progress of Puaaiki in divine knowledge can be accounted for only by the teaching of the His progress Spirit. His blindness did indeed favor his edge. in knowl- giving undivided attention as a hearer, and also the exercise of his powers of reflection and memory. His habit was to treasure up what he could of every sermon, and afterward to rehearse it to his acquaintances. It was thus he grew in knowledge, and at length became himself a preacher. In the fourth year of the mission, among the twenty-four chiefs and five hundred others then under instruction, though there were marked and happy cases of advancement, none seemed to have gone further in spiritual knowledge than Puaaiki.

In March, 1823, he accompanied Hoapili, the governor of Maui, and his wife Keopuolani, to Lahaina. Messrs. Richards and Stewart then became his religious guides. The insurrection on the island of Kauai was followed by a sort of insurrectionary effort, on the part of a heathen party on Maui, to revive some of the old idolatrous rites. Puaaiki and his His decision. associates, then known as "the praying ones," earnestly opposed this; and being called together by the missionaries, and instructed and encouraged, the blind convert was requested to lead in prayer. Mr. Stewart gives an account of his own emotions occasioned by that prayer : "His petitions were made with a pathos of feeling, a fervency of spirit, a fluency and propriety of diction, and above all, a humility of soul, that plainly told he was no stranger there. His bending posture, his clasped hands, his elevated but sightless countenance, the peculiar emphasis with which he uttered the exclamation, 'O Jehovah,' his tenderness, his importunity, made us feel that he was praying to a God not afar off, but one that was nigh, even in the midst of us. His was a prayer not to be forgotten. It touched our very souls, and we believe would have touched the soul of any one not a stranger to the meltings of a pious heart."

It was not until the spring of 1825, that Puaaiki was received into the church. The missionaries seem to have erred on the side of caution, in this case, as in that of Kapiolani.

Examination for admission to the church.

The darkness, pollution, and chaotic state of society was the reason, though perhaps that should have been a motive for receiving those little ones earlier into the fold. But Puaaiki's expression of desire to be united with the people of God, in the spring of 1825, could not be any longer resisted, and he was carefully examined by Mr. Richards, as to his Christian knowledge and belief, and the evidences of a work of grace in his heart. The following is a translation of a portion of his replies:—

" Why do you ask to be admitted to the church ?"

" Because I love Jesus Christ, and I love you the missionaries, and desire to dwell in the fold of Christ, and join with you in eating the holy bread, and drinking the holy wine."

" What is the holy bread ? "

" It is the body of Christ, which he gave to save sinners."

" Do we then eat the body of Christ ? "

" No; we eat the bread which represents his body; and as we eat bread that our bodies may not die, so our souls love Jesus Christ and receive him for their Saviour, that they may not die."

" What is the holy wine ? "

" It is the blood of Christ, which was poured out on Calvary, in the land of Judæa, to save us sinners."

" Do we then drink the blood of Christ ? "

" No ; but the wine represents his blood, just as the holy bread represents his body, and all those who go to Christ and trust in him, will have their sins washed away in his blood, and their souls saved forever in heaven."

" Why do you think it more suitable for you to join the church than others ? "

" Perhaps it is not. If it is not proper, you must tell me; but I do greatly desire to dwell in the fold of Christ."

" Who do you think are proper persons to be received into the church ? "

" Those who have repented of their sins and have new hearts."

" What is a new heart ? "

" One that loves God, and loves the word of God, and does not love sin and sinful ways."

" Why do you hope you have a new heart ? "

" The heart I now have is not like the one I formerly had. The one I have now is very bad. It is unbelieving and inclined to evil. But it is not like the one I formerly had. Yes, I think I have a new heart."

These answers are given as a sample. Mr. Richards declares the questions to have been all new to him, and that he answered them from his own knowledge, and not from having committed any catechism.

On the tenth of July, 1825, Puaaiki was admitted into the church at Lahaina, and received the name of *Batimea Lalana.* The name Lalana (London) was added at his own suggestion, in accordance with a Hawaiian custom of noting events. It was designed to commemorate the then recent visit of his former patrons, the king and queen, to London, and their deaths in that city. I shall use only the former of the two names, giving it the English form, *Bartimeus*.

It is needless to say, that this young convert had His temper- ceased from the use of all alcoholic drinks, ance. and of *awa*, long before his admission to the Christian church. But when a translation of Paul's Epistles came afterward into his hands, and he read, " Prove all things ; hold fast that which is good ; abstain from that which is of evil character," [1] he thought it his duty to relinquish the use of tobacco.

The Rev. Jonathan S. Green came to Lahaina three years after Bartimeus's public profession of his faith, and abode there a few months, and bore a most favorable testimony concerning him as a " consistent . Christian, adorning in all things the doctrine of God his Saviour."

In 1829, Bartimeus was persuaded to remove with Residence at his wife to Hilo, on the island of Hawaii. Hilo.   Here his field was wider and more necessitous than it had been at Lahaina. Several natives of talent and influence had there been hopefully converted, some of them through his influence. Among them was David Malo, a most active and promising youth. Moreover, Lahaina had been longer favored with the means of grace. Hilo — since so wonderfully blessed with outpourings of the Spirit — he was persuaded to make his home for several years. The resident missionary, at first, was Mr. Goodrich, the same who met Kapiolani at the volcano. In the following year, Kaahumanu, the ex-queen and regent of the Islands, visited Hilo, and this ex-

[1] As rendered in the Hawaiian version.

traordinary woman seconded the efforts of Bartimeus by her influence as a ruler, and still more by her example as a Christian. The cool climate of that windward district, its green fields, its clouded skies and frequent rains, exerted such a beneficial effect upon his eyes, that he made a painful and partially successful effort to learn to read ; but the effort aggravated the evil, and he reluctantly gave up the design. The light of the body did not increase in proportion to the light of the mind. Through the sense of hearing he was adding rapidly to his knowledge of the way of life. Every text and nearly every.sermon which he heard, was indelibly fixed in his mind. The portions of Scripture, which were then being printed in his native language, were made fast in the same way. By hearing them read a few times, they were fixed, word for word, chapter and verse.

Mr. Green removed to Hilo in 1831, and remained there a year and a half. He saw Barti- His activity. meus daily, became intimately acquainted with him as a man and a Christian, and bears the most favorable testimony as to the faithful coöperation of his native brother and fellow-laborer. Bartimeus never remitted his activity, attending little neighborhood meetings, accompanying the missionary, visiting alone, or accompanied by his wife, or some native Christian brother, and receiving the many who came to his own house, attracted by his social and affectionate disposition, and by his copious and spiritual conversation.

Some time in 1834, Bartimeus removed to Wailuku, on the island of Maui, where, and in At Wailuku the vicinity, he continued to reside, during the eight or nine years till his death. Here he was once more, during a part of the time, associated with Mr. Green, whose love for him, and confidence in him, and admiration for his character, appear to have increased to the last. In 1837, there were manifest indications of the great awakening, which so wonderfully pervaded the group of Islands in the following year. The infant church at Wailuku was revived. The members confessed their sins, and sought for pardon through the blood of atonement. No one seemed more deeply penitent than Bartimeus. No one was more importunate in seeking for pardon, on his own account, and for his brethren, and for the impenitent. When, during most of the year 1838, the Spirit of God moved upon the mass of the population, and caused multitudes to bow to the sceptre of the Son of God, the heart of the good old man seemed to overflow with joy, and he poured out the emotions of his soul in language not easily described. "None but those who saw him," says Mr. Green, "during some of those interesting scenes, can conceive the appearance of Bartimeus. No painter could do justice to the heaven-illuminated countenance of our friend. And yet no one that saw that glow, that index of unearthly joy, can cease to retain an affecting impression of it."

As a consequence of this outpouring of the Spirit, people resorted from all quarters to Wailuku for instruction, coming often a distance of fifteen or twenty miles. But this could not long be; the aged, the infirm, and the young could not come so far at all. The people, therefore, erected houses of worship in all the large districts of Maui, and it became a difficult question how to supply them with preach-

ers. Messrs. Green and Armstrong did the best
that seemed to them possible in the circumstances:
they selected a class of their most devoted and tal-
ented church members, and instructed them in the
Scriptures, in the elements of moral science, and in
church history. Bartimeus was a prominent member of this class. From our present point of view,
it seems as if he ought, long before this time, to
have been formally licensed to preach, if not ordained
as an evangelist, or even as the pastor of a church.
But the ideas of our missionary brethren at that
early period developed slowly in this direction.
Bartimeus was now set apart formally to the office of
deacon or elder. This appears to have been   Licensed as a
early in 1839. It was not until three   preacher.
years after this, that he received a formal license as
a preacher of the gospel. And it was not until February, 1843, the beginning of his last year   Ordained.
on earth, that he was ordained as an evangelist, — his services being then statedly required by
the people of Honuaula, twenty miles from Wailuku.

He entered upon his work in that place with his
accustomed ardor, proclaiming the glad tidings of a
Saviour's mercy in the house of God, by the way-
side, and from house to house. On the arrival of
Mr. Clark as pastor of the church at Wailuku, he went
over to welcome him to his new sphere of labor, and
spent a week or two. He then resumed his labors
at Honuaula. There he was arrested by sickness.
The attack being severe, he returned to Wailuku,
that he might procure medical aid, and   Sickness and
also be near his brethren with whom he had   death.
spent many years of delightful Christian intercourse.
He seemed to have a presentiment from the com-

mencement of his sickness, that he should not re-
cover. But the thought of death gave＊him no
alarm. He knew in whom he had believed. On
the Lord Jesus Christ he had, long before, cast himself for time and eternity. This surrender had been
succeeded by a sweet peace. He had the hope of the
Christian. Bartimeus did not leave as much of what
might be called a dying testimony, as many others
have done. There was less need that he should do
so. His daily conversation, his holy example, and
his unremitted labors in the cause of his blessed
Master, had borne ample testimony. For a day or
two before his decease, he sank under the force of
disease, so that he was unable to converse much.
He died September 17, 1843, and entered, as there
is the most cheering reason to believe, into the
joy of his Lord.

On the nineteenth, his funeral was attended by a
large congregation of sincere mourners.
Funeral.
The voice, which had so often been heard
in devout supplication, and in earnest entreaty calling the sinner to repentance, was silent in death.
A sermon was preached from 2 Cor. v. 1: "For we
know that if our earthly house of this tabernacle
were dissolved, we have a building of God, a house
not made with hands, eternal in the heavens."

The character of Bartimeus shines out so clearly
in the foregoing narrative, that little more need be
said. His calling to be a preacher was evidently of
God. He had original endowments for that service.

He was regarded as an ardent Christian, and as
the most eloquent speaker in the nation.
His elo-
quence.
His knowledge of the Scriptures, as well
as of general subjects, was remarkable, considering

his inability to read. No missionary could quote
Scripture more copiously and appositely in an off-
hand effort, than he. Even parts of Scripture that
had not been printed in the native language seemed
to be familiar to him, from merely hearing them
quoted in the pulpit and Bible class. His memory was
of the very first order. On moral subjects he often
evinced powers of discrimination that were aston-
ishing, as compared with most other natives. He was
a short man, rather corpulent, inferior in appearance
when sitting, but when he rose to speak he looked
well, stood erect, gesticulated with freedom, and as
he became animated, poured forth words in torrents.
Being familiar with the former as well as the present religion, customs, and modes of thinking, he
was often able to draw comparisons and make ap-
peals with a power which no foreigner could ever
command. " Often," says Dr. Armstrong, "while
listening with exquisite delight to the eloquent
strains of Bartimeus, have I thought of Wirt's
description of the celebrated blind preacher of
Virginia."

But perhaps he was even more distinguished for
the grace of humility. Although much
noticed by chiefs and missionaries, as well _{His humility.}
as by those of his own rank, and occasionally receiving tokens of respect even from a far distant
land, he was always the same. He sought the
lowest place, and always exhibited the same mod-
est demeanor, and appeared in the same humble
garb. His prayer was, " Lord, be merciful to me a
sinner." This was the more noticeable, as being
strongly in contrast with the natural character of
Hawaiians.

CHAPTER XXVI.

CHURCH AND HOUSE BUILDING.

CHURCH building, at native expense, made constant
Church building under difficulties. progress on the Islands, though generally under very great difficulties. At Kohala, on Hawaii, the people, in their effort to procure a new and more commodious house of worship, had to bring the timber six or eight miles from the mountains. The wood was hard and tough, axes were scarce, and there were few facilities for keeping them sharp. After the timber had been cut and hewn, from eighty to a hundred and fifty persons of both sexes laid hold of a long rope, made fast to one of the timbers, and a day was required to drag it up and down the precipitous ravines and through woods and brush, to the ground set apart for the building. Oxen could have done nothing were they obtainable, because of the ravines.

The fondness of the people of Kohala for the or-
Fondness for worship. dinances of the sanctuary, was very strikingly manifested. The district is subject at certain seasons to continued and violent winds and rains; and females, young and old, used frequently to come several miles in the rain, over precipices and ravines, to the place of worship, with a single scanty garment of brown cotton, and that garment, as well as their hair and entire persons, completely drenched. The author well re-

members his surprise at finding this same church filled with people one Sabbath morning in 1863, notwithstanding a furious rain-storm, in which they had travelled with great discomfort from their homes. Had they had umbrellas, they could hardly have carried them in so great a tempest.

The laborious efforts of the native churches to procure convenient houses for worship, At Keala-kekua. were further illustrated at Kealakekua, another name for the Kaawaloa station. The house was built of stone, and in the first place, every stone had to be carried by the church members on their shoulders an eighth of a mile. The lime had then to be obtained by diving for the coral in from ten to twenty feet of water. After a piece had been detached a rope was made fast to it, and the mass was drawn up, and put into a canoe. Thus the limestone was procured. To reduce it to lime, a large amount of wood was needed, and every stick had to be brought one or two miles. This was done by the men. The women carried the lime a fourth of a mile in calabashes, in all many scores of barrels, and afterwards as much sand, and about an equal quantity of water. The posts and beams were brought by the men from the mountains, each timber requiring the joint efforts of from forty to sixty men. Their labor was all gratuitous. To pay the masons and carpenters, each man subscribed according to his ability, varying from one to ten dollars, to be paid in such useful articles as they could command.

At Kaneohe, on the island of Oahu, when the old grass meeting-house was no longer in a condition to be occupied, the members of At Kaneohe the church, which contained not more than seventy-five able-bodied males, erected a stone edifice, ninety-five feet in length by forty-two in width.

The efforts of the church at Waimea, on Hawaii, to erect a new stone church, in the year 1842, were quite as extraordinary as those performed at Kealakekua.

At Waimea.

Among the means for building a stone meeting-house of considerable size on Molokai, was a subscription by the women of more than two hundred dollars, which they earned by making mats, though each earned no more than eight cents a week. The contributions from the men were chiefly the result of transporting firewood in canoes across the channel, twenty miles wide, to Lahaina, carrying seven sticks in a canoe, which sold for eight cents a stick. Timbers for the church had to be dragged ten miles by human strength.

On Molokai.

In 1844, places of worship were erected at four of the outstations in the Kailua district. Their walls were of mud, hardened in the sun, painted without and plastered within with lime mortar.

In the Kailua district.

The church at Waiohinu, in the district of Kau, on Hawaii, was completed in 1846; men, women, and children conveying the stones from several heathen temples; and coral, also, which was taken from the bottom of the sea, they carried seven miles to be converted into lime. The timbers had to be drawn from the mountain forests. It was a fine building, and the author had the pleasure of meeting and addressing a large Sabbath-school, and a still larger adult congregation, within its walls. The building was destroyed by the great earthquakes

In Kau.

of 1868; and has been since replaced by a neat
framed building, painted within and without, and
well seated, with a steeple and a bell. The cost was
two thousand two hundred dollars, and seven hundred dollars of this sum was contributed by sister
churches on the Islands.

What is known as the great Stone Church, at
Honolulu, was dedicated on the 21st of
July, 1842, in the presence of the king, his ^{At Honolulu.}
premier, the high chiefs, and an assembly of more
than three thousand.   Its cost was about thirty
thousand dollars.   The dimensions of the edifice are
one hundred and thirty-seven feet by seventy-two.
Galleries were afterwards introduced, and a tower
and steeple, with a bell and town clock. At the dedication, the king presented a deed of the building and
premises " to the church, and those of like faith who
should come hereafter."   It was five years from the
commencement to the completion of the building.

The present church edifice at Hilo has very much
the appearance of country churches in New
England.   It was completed and dedicated ^{At Hilo.}
in 1859; is a neat substantial building, fifty by seventy-five feet, finished on the outside with pilasters,
and roofed with zinc, with a tower rising thirty-six
feet above the ridge.   The inside is neatly finished,
and well seated, with galleries across one end, and
a pulpit.   The cost of the house and appurtenances
was about thirteen thousand dollars in money, besides a large amount of gratuitous labor by the people.   They very properly resolved not to consecrate
the house until it was paid for.   The requisite
amount was raised after several meetings, and there
remained a balance of more than three hundred dol-

lars in the treasury. The dedication was further
deferred two weeks for the arrival of a bell, weigh-
ing a thousand pounds, which had been ordered from
the United States. The people were jubilant when
it arrived. Multitudes rushed to the shore, and
lashing the bell to spars, bore it with shouting to
the church door. It was soon hoisted to its place
in the tower, where it sent out its 'inviting peals
over the hills and fields of Hilo.

At first, the people seated themselves in their
houses of worship upon mats, spread on the
ground; but they came gradually to feel
the need of seats. When a man had procured for
himself a pair of Sabbath pants, and a woman a cal-
ico or white dress, the next thing was to have a seat
in the meeting house, in order to keep their new
garments clean.

Introduction of seats.

The Hawaiian people now no longer worship in
thatched meeting-houses. With a very slight exception or two, all the churches are framed
or stone buildings. Most of them are
neatly finished, with seats or pews; a number of them have a gallery, or raised seats for the
choir, and almost all have steeples and bells. A considerable number of the churches are being furnished
with melodeons to assist in the singing, the instruments being played by some one of the people. The
number of the church buildings cannot be less than
one hundred and twenty; and the work of building,
repairing, and modifying, to suit the ever-improving
tastes of the people, is still in progress. In June,
1870, over ten thousand dollars, out of a total of
thirty-one thousand dollars contributed for religious

1870.
Extent of
church ac-
commoda-
tion.

purposes, was reported as expended for churches, and that is about the usual proportion. It is believed that two hundred and fifty thousand dollars would not replace the Protestant church buildings on the Hawaiian Islands, as they stand at the present time. It may be safely said, that very few communities in any portion of the Christian world have expended so much, in proportion to their wealth, on their places of worship. It is also true, that in but very few Christian lands are sittings provided for so large a proportion of the inhabitants.[1]

A number of the places of worship, erected during the period of rapid advance among the people, are significant monuments of the enterprise of chiefs and people. And it was natural, perhaps unavoidable, while the missionary himself minis- Where the tered to a large region, that church edifices too large. buildings are should be erected, which have proved too large for the permanent necessities of the people, and somewhat retarded the growth of smaller church organizations adapted to a native ministry. These large churches have also embarrassed the audiences now worshipping in them, which have been reduced, partly by the decline of population, but more by the multiplication of local churches, making them seem smaller than they would seem in rooms better adapted to the necessities, and involving also large expenses in their repairs. In a number of instances, however, these large structures, as in the case of the Stone Church at Honolulu, and the church built by Kuakini at Kailua, have been utilized by diminishing

---

[1] The Roman Catholics are said to have about one third as many churches as the Protestants, and to be multiplying them in many cases, much beyond the needs of their congregations.

15

the size of the audience room, and thus obtaining lecture-rooms, and places for Sabbath-school gatherings, that have proved very useful.

The large expenditure on churches that are constantly advancing in architectural taste, has had a very important effect on the style of private dwellings.

There has been a very marked improvement in Building of the dwellings of the Hawaiians within the dwelling- houses. last twenty years, and even the last ten years. The most striking evidence of this, is the number of small framed houses, or cottages, of one story, or of one story and a half; found most numerously of course near the larger villages, but also to be seen in the most distant and inaccessible regions of the group. Another grade of improvement is that of board floors, partitions, glass windows, and other conveniences, in modified Hawaiian houses thatched with grass or leaves from the ridge-pole to the ground, many of which make admirable residences.

Still another improvement in domestic life, even Furniture for where there is no special modification in houses. the houses themselves, is in the multiplication of conveniences, such as chests and trunks, for articles of clothing and other necessities.

It should be borne in mind, that the building of Cost of build- houses, even in the simplest Hawaiian ing. style, is more expensive than formerly, when timber, and grass, and labor were much more plentiful than they are now. The labor of procuring timber, stone, and lime for church building, already described, is comparatively as great for dwelling houses. Were not the necessary expenditures for food and dress comparatively light, it would be impossible for the Hawaiians to expend what they do in making their houses comfortable; and while it is proper to stimulate them to greater thrift in husbanding their limited incomes, it is often matter of surprise that they are able, with their small means, to accomplish as much as they do.

CHAPTER XXVII.

AMONG the missionaries who died in the period now under review, the reader will be glad of such notices as the materials at command will justify.

Mr. Edwin Locke died at Punahou, on Oahu, October 28, 1843. He was a native of Fitz- william, New Hampshire. The manual-labor school at Waialua, which he instituted, was an enterprise without precedent at the Sandwich Islands. But though it has been found hard to make such institutions successful elsewhere, this was an entire success. It was self-supporting. Mr. Locke possessed a generous nature, unbending principle, and great integrity of character. He was a kind, sympathizing, and excellent neighbor, and a true and faithful friend. His zeal was ardent. His qualifications for the department of labor he had chosen were preëminent, and his success was not only beyond the expectation of the friends of the school, but even beyond his own expectations.

Mr. Locke.

The Rev. Sheldon Dibble was a remarkable man. His talents were of a high order; and so was his devotion to the cause of the Redeemer; and so were some of the productions of his pen, though he did not live to give them that fullness and perfection of which he was capable.

Mr. Dibble.

Mr. Dibble was born at Skeneateles, New York, January 26, 1809, and became a member of the Church at the age of twelve years. He graduated at Hamilton College in 1827, pursued his theological studies at the Auburn Seminary, and arrived at Honolulu June 6, 1831. His health not being good at Hilo, where he was first stationed, he removed to Lahainaluna in 1834, and became connected with the Seminary. His wife dying in 1837, and his health failing, he came to the United States with his two motherless children. While here, he delivered historical lectures at the Auburn Seminary and elsewhere, and made an extended tour through the south and southwest, during which he often lectured to the edification of his hearers. These lectures, or an abstract of them, he published, before returning to the Islands.[1] Having again married, he was once more at Lahainaluna, his favorite post, before the close of 1840.

Mr. Dibble's "History of the Sandwich Islands," begun at the request of his brethren in 1841, was printed at Lahainaluna in 1843. As an authentic history — though far less comprehensive than the historical work of James Jackson Jarves, — it is of great value. His "Thoughts on Missions" were first printed at Lahaina, and were afterwards placed among the publications of the American Tract Society. They seem to have had their origin in the meetings of the mission in the years 1836 and 1837, where the "Great Awakening" had its commencement. Mr. Dibble is believed to have been the principal author of the "Appeal to the American

[1] This volume was entitled, *History and General Views of the Sandwich Islands Mission*, but I have not found a copy.

Churches," which emanated from the first of these meetings.

During the last six months of his life, he bled repeatedly at the lungs, and regarded himself as constantly descending towards the grave; but he appears never to have doubted the reality of his interest in the great salvation. Once, while bleeding profusely, he said, "How sweet to have a Saviour at such a time." Though greatly emaciated, his mental powers were clear and vigorous to the end. On the closing day of his life, having a presentiment that the time of his departure was at hand, he said to his wife, "I have nothing more to do, except to bless my wife and children, draw up my feet like good old Jacob, and go home." At ten o'clock that night he was evidently dying, and could speak with difficulty. He expressed a willingness to die, under the assurance that he was going home to his Father's house. There was no indication of pain, no mental anxiety, and on his countenance was a sweet, calm serenity. The night was occupied in prayer, in singing such hymns as "Jerusalem my happy home," and in repeating such passages of Scripture as are peculiarly adapted to support the soul in its passage out of the world. At three o'clock in the morning of January 22, 1845, he closed his eyes in death.

Mr. Horton O. Knapp died at Honolulu on the 28th of March, 1845. He was one of the large reinforcement of teachers, which reached the Islands in 1837. His native place was Greenwich, Connecticut, where he was born March 21, 1813. He joined the church in 1831, and commenced a course of study with a view to the Christian ministry, which he had in mind when he offered himself to go as a teacher to the Sandwich Islands. During the great awakening, his post of duty was at Waimea, on Hawaii, where that work of grace first appeared among the natives, and where the drain upon the vital powers must have been very great. It was too much for Mr. Knapp. He subsequently spent some time at Kailua, and at Lahainaluna, in the hope of recovering health, but without material benefit. Early in 1839 he removed to Honolulu, where he devoted his remaining strength to the schools.

Mr. Knapp was courteous, generous, and obliging in his intercourse with his brethren, just in his dealings, circumspect in conversation, and eminently active and consistent in his piety. His last days were full of pain and languishing ; but the gradual though sure advance of death gave him no alarm, for to him

"Dying was but going home."

The Rev. Samuel Whitney belonged to the first company of missionaries. He was born at Branford, Connecticut, April 28, 1793, and became hopefully pious in 1813. After spending two years in Yale College, he offered himself for the mission, and was accepted. On his outward voyage he had a narrow escape from drowning. Employed, for exercise and recreation, in painting the outside of the vessel, standing on a suspended plank, he was thrown from this position into the sea, while the vessel was under full sail. Retaining his self-possession, and being skillful as a swimmer, he gained a bench, which had been thrown over for him, and which is

Mr. Whitney.

still preserved by his family. A boat went to his assistance, and in less than half an hour he was safely on board.

Mr. Whitney received ordination in 1825, and his labors at Waimea, on Kauai, were greatly blessed. Near the close of his twenty-fifth year, his health began to fail, and he repaired to Lahainaluna, where, in the family of Mr. Alexander, he died, December 4, 1845. His mind was vigorous and active. Among his last words were these, which he uttered with great emphasis: "And is the victory won? Glory, glory, glory! Hail, glorious immortality! Can it be that this is death? That I, who all my life have been afraid of death, have come to this? Here all is peace, and light, and joy. The Saviour has me by the hand, leading me along. I soon shall be in heaven."

As the connection of the Rev. Hiram Bingham, one Mr. Bing- of the pioneer missionaries, with the Board, ham. was terminated at his own request in 1846, this would seem the most suitable place to pay a tribute to his memory; though he did not reach the close of life until November 11, 1869.

Mr. Bingham was born at Bennington, Vermont, October 30, 1789, graduated at Middlebury College in 1816, and at the Andover Theological Seminary in 1819. A visit to the Foreign Mission School at Cornwall awakened a desire to carry the gospel to the country of Obookiah. His appointment as a missionary of the American Board, and designation to the Sandwich Islands, were in 1819. His ordination, in connection with that of his Andover classmate, Asa Thurston, was by the North Consociation of Litchfield County, in Goshen, Connecticut, on the

29th of September, in the same year. It was then and there that Mr. Bingham found his wife, Miss Sybil Moseley, a native of Westfield, Mass., whose interest in the cause of missions had brought her to the ordination.

Mr. Bingham's history, until the mission became established, is substantially that of the mission itself, and has been given in the previous pages. His residence was at Honolulu, which soon became the permanent seat of government, and the chief resort of whaling and other ships of the North Pacific. It was also the stronghold of the Prince of Darkness in that island world, and the chief battle-ground for the overthrow of his kingdom. The missionary stationed there required a large amount of courage, and an inflexible will. . These, allied with good nature, cheerfulness, and calm persistency, Mr. Bingham possessed in a high degree. We may perhaps say, what is often said of eminent men, that he was made for the position. Two successive kings, and the chief ˙men and women who ruled in his time, deferred unconsciously to the moral power he was exerting upon them, and the strong-minded, strong-willed Kaahumanu was very much like him, after her conversion, in the best features of her mind and character. It is believed, that in matters of religion there was generally a mutual sympathy and coöperation between them. The traits of character, which sometimes embarrassed the deliberations when he was in council with his brother missionaries, and which perhaps prevented his acquiring a large personal influence among the churches of his native land, were among the things required in the peculiar circumstances of his position, in the first twenty years of the mission.

It may also be said, that as a missionary he was sincere and honest, without pretense, without selfish ends, an enemy to every form and species of wickedness, and fearless in rebuking it, of irreproachable character, loved by the good, dreaded and hated by the wicked. His relations beyond the circle of his own family, as he reflected upon them, and as they determined his daily thoughts and feelings, were chiefly with the native community. No wonder the natives loved him. It was affecting, in my tour through the Islands seven years ago, to hear aged women inquire, affectionately and in tears, after "Bináme," whom they seemed to regard as their spiritual father in Christ.

Mr. Bingham, six years after his return to the United States, published a history of the mission down to 1845, in an octavo volume of more than six hundred pages. Though somewhat diffuse and cumbrous, it possesses great value as a history, being generally accurate in its statements.

Mr. and Mrs. Bingham's return to this country was in the year 1841, and was in consequence of the failure of Mrs. Bingham's health. She never recovered sufficiently to encounter the fatigues and exposures of a voyage around Cape Horn, though both were ardently desirous of renewing their missionary labors; and she died at Easthampton, Mass., February 27, 1848, at the age of fifty-five. In the seven years which had passed since he left, the mission had been making rapid progress; great changes had occurred, and nowhere more than at Honolulu; and it was scarcely possible for Mr. Bingham, if returned to the Islands, to resume his old relations, and work with the ease and freedom of olden times. Missionaries were no longer insulated and independent forces. A Christian commonwealth had arisen, and a community of interests. It was understood to be the belief of Mr. Bingham himself, that, after so long an absence, he would not be able to accommodate himself to the new state of things. In this opinion he was probably correct, and hence, though retaining to the last an unimpaired interest in the mission, he did not resume his labors on the Islands.

In the year 1863, friends of missions in different parts of the country united in securing for him an annuity, by which he was enabled to pass a comfortable old age. He was expecting to revisit the Islands in 1870, and take a joyful part, with the Hawaiian churches, in the semi-centenary of the mission, which would come in that year; but such was not the will of the Lord. His death, at the age of eighty, was after a very brief illness; and it may be said of him, with the utmost confidence, " Blessed are the dead, which die in the Lord; they rest from their labors, and their works do follow them." It should be added, that three of his five children are now doing good missionary work in the islands of the Pacific.

The Rev. William Richards died at Honolulu, November 7, 1847, at the age of fifty-four. Mr. Richards. I have had frequent occasion to speak of his services, as a member of the mission, and in connection with the government. His native place was Plainfield, Massachusetts, and he was born August 22, 1793. His education was at Williams College and the Andover Theological Seminary.

He was dearly beloved by the good people of

Lahaina, who loaded him with their simple presents when departing for the United States in 1836; presenting them with tears, and often clasping his feet with loud lamentations, lest they should see his face no more. Perhaps no man has ever shared more largely in the affections of the Hawaiian people, than did Mr. Richards. He was ever looked up to by them as a friend and father, in whom they could safely confide; and when the king and chiefs felt compelled to seek a teacher and adviser from the mission, they chose him, as on the whole the most suitable person for that respectable post.

His connection with the king and chiefs as their teacher and adviser, has been sufficiently noted. It was chiefly through his aid, that they were enabled to frame the constitution of 1840, with a bill of rights founded on the Word of God, and containing all the outlines of a constitutional and responsible government. It was a bold and successful attempt to curb the arbitrary power of the king and chiefs, to define and secure the rights of property, to encourage industry, and introduce a government of law and order.

His subsequent diplomatic services, in connection with others, resulting in the acknowledged independence of the island-government, are already known to the reader.

These and other invaluable services Mr. Richards performed without the opportunity of making provision for the future support of his family; and it was honorable to the government, that it settled a generous stipend on his widow, which was promptly paid until her decease.

The mission suffered a great loss in the year 1849,

by the death of Mr. Levi Chamberlain, for twenty-
six years the senior superintendent of its   Mr. Cham-
secular affairs. Probably no man has lived   berlain.
at the Islands who was more generally respected and
beloved.   Called, in the year 1822, to labor some
months with him at the Missionary Rooms of the
American Board, in the absence of Jeremiah Evarts,
then Corresponding Secretary and Treasurer, and
closely connected with him in correspondence ever
after till his decease, I knew and greatly admired his
disinterested spirit, his enlarged benevolence, his
undeviating integrity, and his unreserved consecra-
tion of time, talents, and property to the cause of
Christ.   But for the failure of his health, he would
perhaps have been Mr. Evarts's successor as Treasurer of the Board.   The post assigned him at the
Islands was responsible and honorable, but difficult
to fill.   He accepted it cheerfully, and in the discharge of its duties probably did as much as any
other man to insure success to the mission.

Mr. Chamberlain was born in Dover, Vermont,
August 28, 1792, and consequently lived almost to the
age of fifty-seven.   His early years were spent with
an uncle in Boston, by whom he was trained to
the mercantile profession.   He became a member of
Park Street Church in 1818.   When of age, he commenced the mercantile business for himself in Boston, and in a few years made such progress, as to
have the almost certain prospect of accumulating
wealth.   But his heart was drawn towards the gospel ministry; and after consulting with judicious
friends, he closed his business, and commenced a
course of study in the Academy at Andover.   Indications of the disease which ultimately proved

fatal, along with the exigency at the Missionary
Rooms, led to a change in his life-plans. Placing
his little property where its avails would help forward the cause of missions, he accepted an invitation to join the first reinforcement of the mission to
the Islands, and arrived at Honolulu, April 27, 1823.

He entered upon his new labors with a self-devo-
tion which never wavered. He brought to his work
a vigorous mind, a sagacious judgment, a body,
though slender, exceedingly active and efficient, and
a spirit supremely devoted to his Redeemer, and the
good of his fellow-men. His toils were incessant
and perplexing. But he shrank from no sacrifice,
no self-denial. He was ready to take the lowest
place, the poorest fare, and the hardest toil; ready
to be a " hewer of wood and drawer of water," in
building the temple of the Lord on those Islands.

But the range of his fine mind was by no means
restricted to the secular concerns of the mission.
His correspondence with his brethren of the mission,
and his patrons at home, touched upon almost every
vital interest, and was truly wonderful in its quantity,
its matter, and the neatness and accuracy of its execution. Long and wearisome days he devoted to
the examination of native schools; and being himself a proficient in penmanship, he early took pleasure in imparting the art to the more advanced of
the native pupils. Among his first pupils was Haalilio, who afterwards became the king's secretary,
and his ambassador to the United States, England,
and France.

Mr. Chamberlain's experience, judgment, and
piety gave him influence with his brethren as a
counselor. He leaned to the side of self-denial,

prudence, and caution, and his opinions were frankly and kindly expressed.

About the year 1845, Mr. Chamberlain was induced to try the effect on his health of a voyage to China. This voyage he extended to the United States, where he was permitted to meet, once more, his two eldest sons. After eighteen months from the time of his departure from the Islands, and a voyage around the world, he was again at his beloved home, but with health very little improved. Physical strength was declining, but his mind and spirit were as vigorous as ever. Early in 1849, he suffered from a profuse hemorrhage, and it seemed as if he must soon die; but he revived, and lingered six months longer, yet on the verge of the grave. He waited patiently, joyfully looking forward, and on Sabbath morning, July 29th, he had a peaceful departure to the " rest which remaineth to the people of God," leaving a widow and seven children.

Mr. Chamberlain may be said to have adorned every relation he sustained. As a husband, as a father, as an agent entrusted with great responsibilities, as a member of the mission and of the foreign community, he was the same conscientious, devoted Christian, seeking not his own, but the things which are Jesus Christ's.

The Rev. John S. Emerson and the Rev. Asa Thurston were members of the mission until their deaths, which occurred in 1867 and 1868, and memorials of them will naturally come further on in the volume.

CHAPTER XXVIII.

1848–1851.

THE year 1848 was signalized by measures professedly intended to bring the mission to a close.

There were then about one hundred and thirty children of missionaries at the Islands, of whom more than a third were ten years old and upwards. An application was received from five families for permission to come home, with twenty-five children, to The problem provide for the support and education of for solution. the older ones; and there were sixteen other families in the mission, that would soon be similarly situated. This resulted from the method of prosecuting missions by married missionaries, in connection with the extraordinary healthfulness of the Islands, favoring the increase of families. The bearing of this new development upon the welfare, and even the existence of the mission, was at once perceived, and thus the case came up for consideration. Should an unqualified assent be given to those asking permission, the next year might be expected to bring home twelve other members of the mission, and more than thirty children. With such precedents, should they be followed, it would require but a few years to withdraw almost every family; nor did it seem probable, in view of past experience, that many of the returned families would ever resume their residence on the Islands.

In the conduct of missions to the heathen, choice was of course to be made between employing married missionaries, and men unmarried. Experience was decidedly against the latter course for the general system. The result of celibacy in the Papal ministry had not been such as to encourage a Protestant trial of the system. Missions prosecuted by married missionaries, had thus far worked well. The family had proved a better agency, and more truly economical, than the celibate. But it had not been fully demonstrated, that the natural feelings of parents would continue so under the control of religious principles, on which the self-sacrificing work of missions depends for success, as to prevent the modern system from being overloaded by partially occupied and dependent families, withdrawn from the missionary work, and residing amid the churches from which the funds were derived. The history of missions had not then given the needed aid for the solution of this problem.

What the Prudential Committee had to do, was to devise a method for retaining those families in the field, without incurring expenses that could not be borne; and, at the same time, in view of the vast success of the mission, prepare the way for its early close.

The healthful oceanic climate of the Sandwich Islands, along with the Christianized state of the people, and the progress of civilization, *Manner of its solution.* suggested a solution of the novel problem, which I will now briefly state.

1. No objection was made to the brethren becoming Hawaiian citizens, should any of them choose

to do so; taking, at the same time, a qualified release from their connection with the Board.

2. Brethren, with the approval of the mission, might purchase from the Board the houses in which they lived, with all their appurtenances; and be subject to no other restrictions in the investment of their private property, than popular sentiment imposes on pastors at home.

3. Brethren, after declaring their intention to remain on the Islands in the continued prosecution of Christian labors, and taking a release from their connection with the Board, might receive their proportional part of property held by the Board at their respective stations.

4. When it had been satisfactorily shown, that brethren, thus released, could not obtain a full and proper support from their churches, from their glebe lands, from the avails of private property and other sources, the Prudential Committee would make grants, for a time, to aid in their support, after the manner of the Home Missionary Society.

5. The government of the Islands also engaged, on these conditions, to confirm to the brethren, individually, the possession of the lands thus made over to them.

This was no doubt a somewhat venturesome step on the part of the Prudential Committee, involving the risk of not a few evils; but it was the only apparent method of escape from greater evils.

It appeared, from letters not received until after these propositions were actually on their way to the Islands, that the mission had become in some meas-
The mission in sympathy. ure prepared for such an arrangement, by considering the very facts that had opera-

ted so forcibly on the minds of the Prudential Committee.

The letter of the Committee was dated July 19, 1848. The mission assembled in the following April, and assented substantially to the proposal.

Mr. Wyllie, Foreign Secretary of the Government, was then on rather confidential terms with the mission. Shortly after the adoption of the proposals made by the Prudential Committee, the mission received a letter from him, earnestly requesting that Mr. Armstrong might take the place of Minister of Public Instruction, vacated by the decease New Minister of Public Instruction. of Mr. Richards. The state of things at the Islands was no longer purely missionary, but approached the mixed condition of our new settlements ; and it was necessary, in bringing the mission to a successful close, that special attention should be given to the education of the people, and that the expense of it should be assumed as soon as possible by the native community. A self-sustaining religious community required a system of common schools ; and much would of course depend on the faithfulness and skill of the person in charge of that system. There could, therefore, be no reasonable doubt that it was Mr. Armstrong's duty to accept the proposed office, and a transfer of his relations was made in 1849.

Consequently upon this, and soon after, was a proposal from the mission to transfer the Lahai- Lahainaluna Seminary naluna Seminary, hitherto owned and sup- transferred to the government. ported by the Board, with everything belonging to it, to the Hawaiian government; but with the provision, that the institution should be continued; at the expense of the government, for the cultivation of sound literature and solid science, and that no religious tenet or doctrine should be taught there contrary to those heretofore inculcated by the mission. In case of non-fulfillment or violation of the conditions upon which the transfer was made, the institution was to revert to the mission, to be held in behalf of the American Board; or else the government should pay the sum of fifteen thousand dollars. This agreement was subsequently ratified by the Legislature of the Islands, and also by the Prudential Committee.[1]

Working of the new construction. The new construction worked far better than the Committee had ventured to expect. There had been no experience to throw light upon the path, but an obvious Providence led the way, and strengthened their confidence that they were proceeding in the right direction.

A collegiate institution. The next step in the process, was converting the school at Punahou for missionaries' children into a Collegiate Institution, which afterwards grew into the Oahu College. It greatly diminished the anxiety of parents to send their children to the United States for education, since it removed all necessity for so doing; and being a school of high order, it ever after relieved the Board from the necessity of paying anything for the education of the children elsewhere.

Beginning of the native pastorate. Another highly important step was the commencement of the native pastorate. On the 21st of December, 1849, almost thirty years after the commencement of the mission, James Kekela, a graduate at Lahainaluna, was ordained pastor of the church of Kahuku, which is still existing with a pastor, on the island of Oahu. The native churches of

---

[1] See Annual Report of the Board for 1849, pp. 198, 239-243.

the Island all took part in the ordination. Several Hawaiians had been licensed to preach, but Kekela was the first to receive ordination, and become the pastor of a church. He still lives, and we shall hear of him again as a successful leader in the native mission to the Marquesas. In the following year, a second native was installed pastor of a church at Waianae, still existing on the western side of the same island; and a third was installed pastor of a church at Kanapali, on the island of Maui, since divided into two churches.

The manner in which the missionaries extended their care over their large charges, is favor- Missionary supervision. ably illustrated in Mr. Coan's account of his tour through Hilo and Puna, at the close of 1850: " In company with four school superintendents, all the schools were visited and examined, all our juvenile cold water army, a thousand strong, was called out, marshaled, marched, etc.; and our anniversary dinners were prepared and eaten by hundreds at a sitting. Our meeting-houses were crowded, on these occasions, with parents and children. Hymns and temperance odes were sung; addresses were delivered; prayer was offered; sermons were preached; contributions were taken up; candidates were received into the church; the roll of communicants was called; discipline was attended to; reports were heard; instructions were given; children were baptized; and the Lord's Supper was administered. These anniversary celebrations were held at eleven stations, several days having been spent at each."

After these celebrations, there was a convention of all the teachers and trustees of the schools in those districts, in connection with the officers of the church.

Nearly two hundred were present. The sessions were continued two days, and questions were discussed of the first importance to religion and education. There was much unity of spirit, order, and quiet. The essential rules of deliberative bodies were observed, though with less formality.

Another interesting step towards the construction *Foreign resi-* of a well-ordered Christian community on *dents' church.* the Islands, was the institution of an evangelical church among the foreign residents of Honolulu. It was at once self-supporting, and it did much towards bringing the foreign community into harmonious and active coöperation with the mission and the government.

A radical change was effected, though not without a somewhat protracted correspondence, *Salaries in place of common stock.* in the method of supporting the missionaries. It was a change from the common-stock system to salaries. This system was originally derived from the well-known Baptist missionaries at·Serampore, in India, through the Bombay mission. It involved the keeping of a depository at Honolulu, stocked with all the articles supposed to.be needed by families, and these the families obtained at cost. This was deemed a necessity during the first decade or two, while the Islands were in a barbarous state; but in many respects it did not work well. The salaries, once established, were on the whole more economical, and prepared the way for progress in the direction of independent native churches.

Among the efforts of a tentative nature, but having only partial success, was an attempt to *Missionary support from native churches.* induce the large native churches to assume the whole or a part of the support of their

missionary pastors. It was probably some help to
the missionary in overcoming a natural reluctance
to break loose from dependence on the Board; and
it must have made it seem easier, in the course of
events, for the native churches to assume the much
smaller salaries needed by their native pastors.

Pressed by pecuniary exigencies, the Prudential
Committee took what now seems a step A practical
in the wrong direction. The boarding- error.
school at Wailuku for native females, was converted into two self-supporting boarding-schools, for
boys and girls whose mothers only were native.
The school-building and apparatus were condition-
ally made over, for this purpose, to Mr. Bailey and
Miss Ogden; and these teachers were to gain their
support from the schools. The common schools,
which were then supported by the government, numbered three hundred and eighty-eight, with eleven
thousand seven hundred and ninety-two pupils.

This year was signalized by the development of a
practical conviction, that the Islands could What led to
not rise to an independent existence as a a foreign
mission from
Christian nation, without developing the the islands.
spirit of foreign missions. Both the native churches
and the missionaries, in the present advanced stage
of the work, needed that invigorating influence. So
obviously was the foreign missionary spirit a necessity
to the Hawaiian churches, that members of the mission proposed the forming of a new mission in one
or more of the groups of coral islands westward,
called Micronesia, though two thousand miles distant; to be in part sustained by laborers and contributions from the native churches. The collections of these churches at their monthly concerts of

prayer, even then amounted to fifteen hundred dollars a year. It was believed that the Hawaiian churches would support the missionaries sent from their own number, and that they would be all the more ready to multiply the gospel institutions among themselves. The Prudential Committee came fully into these views, and immediately entered upon the incipient measures.

On the 10th of November, 1851, Messrs. Snow, Sturges, and Gulick, and their wives, embarked at Boston for Micronesia, going by way of the Sandwich Islands. Arriving at Honolulu, a schooner was chartered, and it was decided that Mr. Clark, secretary of the Hawaiian Missionary Society, and Mr. Kekela should accompany the mission, to aid in its establishment, and to bring back a report to the Hawaiian churches. Two Hawaiian missionaries were added, and the new mission sailed July 15, 1852, followed by the prayers of thousands of native Christians, recently emerged from the same heathen darkness from which they would rescue the Micronesians. Mr. Kekela, after his return, visited all the churches on Oahu, Maui, Molokai, and Hawaii, informing them of the moral desolation he saw on those Islands, and of their need of the gospel. His statements were illustrated by specimens of the wickedness and barbarism of the people, which he had brought with him, and were exceedingly interesting to the native churches. He was thus preparing, doubtless, though unconsciously, for his own mission to a still more barbarous people in another direction.

The Rev. Messrs. Dwight and Kinney were added to the mission in 1848, and Dr. Wetmore in the following year. It was about this

Mission to Micronesia.

New missionaries.

time the discovery of gold in California awakened an almost universal interest. The influence was felt in the Sandwich Islands. Among the native islanders drawn to that region, were cer- *Native Christians in the gold mines.* tain members of Dr. Baldwin's church at Lahaina, fifteen of whom went to California to dig for gold. Their conduct was marvelous. Not one of them was known to have dishonored his Christian profession. Among a people of dissolute habits, they stood aloof from gambling, drinking, Sabbath-breaking, and other evil practices. Most of them gave a share of what they obtained to promote the cause of piety; and one, finding that he had cleared four hundred dollars, gave fifty to make his missionary an Honorary Member of the American Board.

Another outrage was committed by Roman Catholic France, for which it is hard to account, *Another French aggression.* except on the supposition of a design, should circumstances render it possible, to take possession of the Hawaiian group, as they had done of Tahiti. Rear Admiral Tromelin arrived at Honolulu, August 15, 1849, in the frigate *La Poursuivante*, and, some days after, misled perhaps by Mr. Dillon, the French Consul, took military possession of the fort at that place, of the government offices, the custom-house, the king's yacht, and other vessels sailing under the Hawaiian flag; all avowedly to punish the Hawaiian nation for not complying with demands which every unprejudiced person would regard as unreasonable and unjust. The fort was dismantled, the arms, powder, etc., destroyed, and the yacht sent off to Tahiti. The government offered no resistance, but the representatives of the United States and Great Britian made formal protest. The king and his government were firm, and the admiral did not deem it prudent to press the case farther. [1]

In the following year similar demands were re-newed by Mr. Perrin, who came in the cor-vette *Serieuse*, as commissioner of the French Republic. He was prepared to enforce his demands as before; but Providence so ordered, that the United States ship *Vandalia*, Captain Gardner, came into port at the critical point of the negotia-tion. The presence of this vessel, and the impres-sion that she would resist any acts of violence, in case the United States flag were raised by the gov-ernment, had the effect to lead the French com-missioner to waive his most offensive demands. Thus the Lord again interposed, and the French government did not repeat these dishonorable pro-ceedings.

Still another, and the last.

The two princes, who have of late occupied the Hawaiian throne, sons of Kekuanaoa, and grandsons of Kamehameha I., visited Eng-land and the United States in 1849, and made everywhere a favorable impression by their in-telligence, their graceful manners, and the propriety of their deportment. These representatives of the Hawaiian nation, had a formal interview with the Prudential Committee at the Missionary House, when the Chairman addressed them, and presented to each of them an elegant pocket Bible. A reply was made by Dr. Judd, the ambassador whom they had accompanied to Europe and America, and written acknowledgments were afterwards received from the interesting strangers.

Visit of the two princes to the United States.

[1] For a more full account, see *Missionary Herald*, 1850, pp. 61-66.

CHAPTER XXIX.

A CENSUS. — MARQUESAN MISSION. — OAHU COLLEGE.

1850-1853.

A CENSUS of the Islands, taken in January, 1850, gave the population at eighty-four thousand one hundred and sixty-five. The deaths in that year were four thousand three hundred and twenty, and the births one thousand four hundred and twenty-two; being an excess of the deaths over the births of two thousand eight hundred and ninety-eight. The males under eighteen years of age, were twelve thousand nine hundred and twenty-three, and the females ten thousand three hundred and eighty-three; from eighteen to fifty-three they were about equally divided. The blind were five hundred and five, and the deaf two hundred and forty-nine.

There had been extraordinary causes of mortality during the year preceding that census. The decrease in the population had been constant, though greatly checked by the prevalence of Christianity. Of unmarried foreigners, there were five hundred and sixty-five; of foreigners having white wives, there were one hundred and sixty-eight, and their children numbered three hundred and fifty-nine. Foreigners with native wives were three hundred and twelve, and they had five hundred and fifty-eight children. The number of pupils in five Eng-

Population of the islands.

lish schools was four hundred and thirty-eight, and the high schools contained two hundred and two. The primary and common schools were five hundred and forty, containing fifteen thousand six hundred and twenty pupils. Four hundred and thirty-seven of the common schools were Protestant, and one hundred and three were Catholic. The Protestant schools had thirteen thousand two hundred and sixty-one pupils, and the Catholic schools two thousand three hundred and fifty-nine. The total outlay for these schools during the year by the government, was $21,989.84, of which $17,-051.84 were paid as teachers' wages, and $3,160.51 were expended for school-houses. There were also two select schools supported by government, the expense of which, for the year 1849, had been $6,545; and eight other select schools were reported, which were sustained in different ways, some by subscription, some by parents of the pupils, and two by the American Board. These ten select schools embraced in all four hundred and fifty-seven pupils, of which two hundred and sixty-seven were Hawaiian, one hundred and five half-caste, and eighty-five pure white. Three other English schools were said to be in operation, embracing about seventy scholars, most of whom were native children.

A remarkable relapse into intemperance at Waimea, on Hawaii, about this time, and a no less remarkable recovery, are described by Mr. Lyons. Both illustrate the singular impressibility of the people. The agents of evil came, and found those who were willing to coöperate with them. "From the hills and vales," says the missionary, "the smoke of the *ki* root ovens ascended,

[marginal note: National education.]

[marginal note: Remarkable relapse and recovery.]

and the deluded people were busily engaged day and night in manufacturing the intoxicating beverage, or in drunken festivals, with the old songs and dances. There were magistrates, but they had been drawn over."

Thus matters stood for a time. Mr. Lyons shall describe the recovery from this relapse in his own way. "A waking up of a part of the magistracy, and a change in another part, with the prayers of the saints that remained firm, and help from on high, restored order and tranquillity. For some time the heavens seemed to be brass above us. The fires of the *ki* root ovens had gone out; drunkenness and revelry had ceased; yet the Spirit of the Lord, except in a small degree, was not among the people. Few repented of their abominations. But prayer was unceasingly offered, and efforts were constantly made to reclaim the wanderers. In November a series of meetings was held, and the Holy Spirit was with us. There was a movement among those who had disgraced their profession, and also among those who had never come out on the Lord's side. Confessions were made; the desolations of Zion were repaired; the Sabbath congregations increased; the church arose, and put on her beautiful garments. Additions were made from the ranks of the impenitent.

"Meanwhile the reviving influence spread to the out-stations. In November and December I made a long tour through my field. It was a very precious season. Meetings were everywhere well attended. The churches, for the most part, presented an encouraging appearance. The cause of temperance flourished again, and temperance celebrations passed off well. In some places revivals were in progress.

The spirit of benevolence was cheering. Schools had their usual appearance, though some of them were not so promising as formerly. Ninety-nine individuals have been received into the church on examination, and some sixty or seventy stand propounded for admission. A great number of wanderers have been reclaimed, and among them are some Romanists."

Mr. Bishop, writing at this period, and speaking of Hawaiian converts from the low vices of heathenism, compares them to the reformed drunkard. There is a constant struggle with the old passions and habits, and perhaps in some unguarded moment a fall; but he rises again, and, with much to lament in his course, holds on to the end, and dies in the hope of immortality. So with many a Hawaiian Christian. His pastor and his more established brethren stand in fear of him, and exhort him, and pray for him, because his light does not shine as it ought, and because his faith is feeble, and Satan's temptations are strong. But the Lord is gracious to him while he lingers like Lot on the plain, and he is finally carried through in safety, a ransomed heathen, a sinner saved by grace.

The mission to the Marquesas Islands had a singular origin. Some time in March, 1853, a chief from one of these Islands, named Matunui, with a son-in-law of his who was a native of Maui, arrived at Lahaina on board the whaleship *Tamerlane*. He was from the island of Fatuhiva, which he left in February, and his object in visiting the Sandwich Islands was to induce missionaries to go and live with his people, and teach them the word of God. He very much de-

(marginal notes: Hawaiian piety characterised. — Rise of the native Marquesan mission.)

sired at least one white Protestant missionary; but
rather than return alone, he would take two or three
native missionaries. The Hawaiian churches were
greatly moved by this appeal, and felt, as did the missionaries, that it ought to be responded to as a call
from God. This could be done only by sending a
native mission. The Rev. James Kekela, the first
of the ordained native pastors, the Rev. Samuel
Kauwealoha, Mr. Lot Kuaihelani, a deacon and
teacher in the church at Ewa, and Mr. Isaia Kaiwi,
a graduate of Lahainaluna and several years a
teacher and deacon in the second church at Honolulu, offered themselves for the service. They were
all married men. Mr. James Bicknell, a pious lay-
man, born in England, also offered himself, and was
a useful member of the mission for several years,
but is now residing at the Sandwich Islands. The
expense of the mission was to be borne by the native
churches. The Rev. Mr. Parker, of the mission,
one of the company which had visited these islands
several years before, was to go with them, to advise
and assist at the outset; and an English schooner
was chartered to take the company to Fatuhiva.

This mission was not allowed to go without impressive valedictory services. A great mis- Farewell
sionary meeting was held in the Stone missionary
meeting.
Church at Honolulu. The house was crowded above
and below. The eight Hawaiians there to be consecrated to the foreign missionary work, and to
receive their instructions, presented a thrilling
scene. It was so to the missionaries. Not many
years before that time, they had worshipped in a
house near the one in which they were assembled,
made of poles, strings, and grass, resembling any-

thing else rather than a church, and with a congregation clothed mostly in kapa. They now sat in a house built by the same congregation, which, for magnitude and durability, might vie with almost any house of worship in an American city; and the people were assembled to send forth missionaries from among their own race to other and distant heathen lands.

The mission was successfully commenced, and Mr.
The mission commenced. Parker left them hopeful as to the future. He reported the Fatuhivans as a superior class of Polynesians in their physical appearance. The men were athletic, healthy, and free from cutaneous disease; but were exceedingly savage in their appearance, by reason of their tattooed faces, arms, and limbs. The females were generally small, with regular features and light complexions, and were better looking than the females of the Sandwich Islands.

A year later, the mission, though quietly pursuing its work, had met with some discouragements. The people of the different valleys were often at war. There was very little government. The papists had come in to oppose them, and spent the Sabbath, after mass, in teaching the people amusements. Matunui, the chief who had asked for the mission, had not proved to be all the brethren hoped to find him. The attendance on worship and schools was irregular. But a comfortable house had been built, and a garden inclosed, and the mission wrote in good spirits.

Seventeen years have elapsed since this mission
Persistence of native missionaries. was commenced; and Kekela, Kanwealoha and Kaiwi, of the first company of

missionaries, are still there. The results of their self-denying and patient labors are far from being limited to the narrow bounds of their own missionary field. They have demonstrated what a native ministry may do, through the grace of God, among savage heathen people of a kindred race. And the reacting influence of their mission was found to be such in their native islands, after ten years, as to prepare the way for a cheerful concession of independence to the native ministry and churches over all those islands.

The Hawaiian Missionary Society, though to some extent a disbursing agent of the American Board, was now beginning to act as an independent body. The Marquesan mission being com- Hawaiian Missionary posed of Hawaiian missionaries, its rela- Society. tions were wholly with that Society; and so were the relations of the Hawaiian missionaries in Micronesia. The Society began, about this time, to direct a portion of its efforts to the feeble churches and destitute places on the several islands of its own group.

The papists seem not to have been making much progress in the way of converts, but the Inroad by Mormons became troublesome for a time. Mormons. Five or six Mormon priests labored in Honolulu and vicinity for a few months. Their doctrines, instructions, and practices were such, that the most abandoned and licentious characters were among their first converts. They licensed several of this class, who were graduates of Lahainaluna, to expound their texts. Baptism by immersion was with them a saving ordinance. Moreover, they taught their converts, that they would have nothing to pay for

17

the support of their ministers, or for the building of churches, or for foreign missions.

The Punahou institution received a charter in Oahu College chartered. 1853, with the name of Oahu College. The charter describes the object of the College to be "the training of youth in the various branches of a Christian education." It further states, that "as it is reasonable that the Christian education should be in conformity to the general views of the founders and patrons of the institution, no course of instruction shall be deemed lawful in said institution, which is not accordant with the principles of Protestant Evangelical Christianity, as held by that body of Protestant Christians in the United States of America, which originated the Christian mission to the Islands, and to whose labors and benevolent contributions the people of these Islands are so greatly indebted."

There was also an additional security for the institution in the following article, namely: "Whenever a vacancy shall occur in said corporation, it shall be the duty of the Trustees to fill the same with all reasonable and convenient dispatch. And every new election shall be immediately made known to the Prudential Committee of the American Board of Commissioners for Foreign Missions, and be subject to their approval or rejection; and this power of revision shall be continued to the American Board for twenty years from date of this charter."

This institution was in some important sense the Its object. *palladium* of the nation. That part of the community, which, though born on the Islands, was of foreign descent, more especially the children of the missionaries, was fast becoming an

influential and important element; and all that then
seemed needful to make them a blessing to the Islands, was an adequate and proper education. This
the College was designed to afford. To- Its endow-
wards its endowment the government gen- ment.
erously gave three hundred acres of excellent land,
valued at ten thousand dollars. Twelve thousand
dollars, resulting from the sale of these lands and
individual donations at the Islands, are invested at
the Islands; and about nineteen thousand are invested in the United States, the result of donations
in this country. Of this latter sum the American
Board contributed five thousand dollars. Among
the larger individual donors was the late James
Hunnewell, Esq. The College, though founded by
the Board, is governed by an independent body of
Trustees residing on the Islands.[1] It is open to
youth of all races. The number of pupils
from 1841 to 1866, was two hundred and Its pupils.
ninety, of whom one hundred and seventy-three
were males, and one hundred and seventeen females.
Only twenty had died. A score of these pupils have
since graduated at colleges in the United States,
where a majority took high honors. It is matter
of regret that so many, after receiving the very valuable instruction at Punahou, should not have returned to the Islands on completing their education
in the United States.

[1] When Kamehameha the Great conquered Oahu in 1794, he gave Pu-
nahou to one of his principal warrior chieftains, who was the father of
Hoapili. Upon the death of the father in 1802, the land became Hoapili's.
Hoapili gave Punahou to his daughter Liliha, upon her marriage with
Boki. In 1829, just before starting on his fatal expedition in search of
sandal-wood, Boki gave the land to the Rev. Hiram Bingham; and Mr.
Bingham, before leaving the Islands in 1840, generously gave it to the
mission school, which afterwards became the Oahu College. He is there-

It should be stated in justice to the College, that
Its value to the Islands. a number of the most useful and prominent
members of the island community, male
and female, in the ministerial, legal, and educational
ranks, received their entire education at this institution, and that this number is sure to increase.
Though established with primary reference to the
children of missionaries, it now (as was anticipated
from the beginning) derives the larger proportion of
its pupils from other classes in the community. The
condition of the Islands would have been far less prosperous and satisfactory, at the present day, had there
been no such institution during the last quarter of
a century; and without it the national prospects
would be far less cheering than they are.

The small-pox invaded the Islands early in 1853,
A pestilence. and was dreadfully fatal in certain districts.
Mr. Bishop, who encountered every risk to
save his people, reports the deaths in Ewa of twelve
hundred out of a population of twenty-eight hundred. Nearly one half of the eight hundred church
members were victims of the pestilence. From
morn to night the missionary visited the sick and
dying, lying helpless on the ground, where, in most
cases, they were destitute of every comfort, except
such as he carried to them, and administered with
his own hands. For a while it was difficult to find
persons to bury the dead. But some were found
willing to undertake the task for a large reward;
and when they could not be found, friends performed
the duty, of course at the risk of their lives. Many
in this way contracted the disease. The indications

fore to be numbered among its founders. These facts I gather from a
Historical Essay on the College, published at Honolulu in the year 1866.

of decay were so rapid, that immediate interment was necessary. A hasty grave was dug near the place; the body was rolled in its clothes and mats, and without ceremony was hurried to its last resting-place. For three months there were no funerals, no mourners. A short prayer was sometimes made over the grave, but very seldom, as no one dared to approach the place, except the grave-digger. The number of sick in the district, at one time and for more than three months, was not less than three hundred, and the deaths averaged from twenty to thirty a day.

CHAPTER XXX.

1854.

KAMEHAMEHA III. died on the 15th of December,
Death of the king. 1854. Though not free from faults, especially in the early part of his reign, he
possessed many excellences as a sovereign prince.
He largely inherited the amiable disposition of his
mother, and was generally beloved while a youth. It
His charac- ter. was his misfortune to come young to the
throne, and to be subject for a time to the
influence of unprincipled and crafty foreigners, when
the national mind was feeling the reaction consequent on the great awakening. It is not supposed
that he cordially embraced the gospel, though he
seems ever to have been impressed with its truth and
importance. The Protestant missionaries enjoyed
his confidence to the last, and he thankfully availed
himself of such aid in promoting the welfare of his
subjects, as they could properly render. He was
the friend and benefactor of his people; and few are
the sovereigns, who have been as ready to relinquish
their prerogative and their sources of private wealth,
to improve the condition of their subjects. His noble
stand in the cause of temperance, of which this history has made repeated mention, was continued for

years, and he manifested an unfailing interest in the civil and social institutions of his nation.

The reign of law may be said indeed to have commenced before his time; but there was no constitution, and the people had no well-defined rights. Even the right of parents to their children was not clear. Those who occupied houses knew not how soon they might be ejected, and those who cultivated fields were in constant fear of being deprived of the products. The people were mere vassals, with no participation in affairs of government. The constitution given by this sovereign put both chiefs and people in the same relation to the laws. He gave Hawaii her Magna Charta, and it was with him a voluntary gift. Her existence as a constitutional state, dates from the year 1840, and she will cherish his memory while blest with a national existence.

The younger of the two surviving grandsons of the first Kamehameha, a son of Kinau, suc- Kamehaceeded to the throne. Born March 17, meha IV. 1814, he received his education in the Chief's School, under the care of Mr. and Mrs. Cooke, members of the mission, as did his brother, the present sovereign. In 1849, both of them, fine looking young men, enjoyed the advantages, and experienced the disadvantages, of foreign travel.

The address of the young king, on the occasion of his inauguration, which was delivered in Testimony of the young both Hawaiian and English, strikingly ex- king. emplified the progress of the nation. I make a single extract: "With the accession of Kamehameha II. to the throne, the *tabus* were broken, the wild orgies of heathenism abolished, the idols

thrown down; and in their place was set up the
worship of the one only living and true God. His
was the era of the introduction of Christianity, and
all its peaceful influences. He was born to commence the great moral revolution which began with
his reign. The age of Kamehameha III. was one of
progress and of liberty, of schools and of civilization. He gave us a constitution, and fixed laws;
he secured the people in the title to their lands, and
removed the last chain of oppression. He gave them
a voice in his councils, and in the making of the laws
by which they are governed. He was a great national benefactor, and has left the impress of his
mild and amiable disposition on the age for which
he was born."

CHAPTER XXXI.

1857–1862.

THE mission, assembled at Honolulu in the year 1857, bore the following testimony, in its annual letter, to the general progress at that time:

" When we contrast the present with the not very remote past, we are filled with admiration and gratitude in view of the wonders God has wrought for this people. Everywhere and in all things we see marks of progress, unmistakable to every intelligent and candid observer. Instead of troops of idle, naked, noisy savages gazing upon us, we are now surrounded by well-clad, quiet, intelligent and self-possessed multitudes, who feel the dignity of men. Instead of squalid poverty, we see competence, abundance, and sometimes luxury. Instead of brutal howlings and dark orgies, we hear the songs of Zion, and the supplications of saints. The little dirty kennel, dingy with smoke, from which the light of the sun was nearly excluded, has given place, in numerous cases, to the neat cottage, or the commodious dwelling of wood or stone, well provided with the furniture of the civilized. All this is true in instances too numerous for specification. Yet we would not be understood to affirm, that it is true of the masses.

While a general progress is most evident, and
marked by many prominent and striking indices,
there are still many, as in all lands, who are too in-
dolent, too ignorant, or too vicious, to put forth the
efforts necessary for the improvement of their condition.

" Yet our towns are rising, our roads are improving.
Signs of   Agriculture and industry are assuming in-
prosperity. creasing importance.   Our government, in
its legislative, executive, and judiciary departments,
has acquired organic form, and is moving on in the
discharge of its functions.   Our schools are sustained.   Our islands are being dotted over with improved church edifices.   Law is supreme; order
prevails; protection of all human rights is nearly
complete; there is little complaining or suffering in
the land; shocking crimes are rare; and it may be
doubted whether the sun shines on a more peaceful
people.   All this and more, through the grace of
God, has been accomplished during the last thirty-
seven years; and for all this we do and will praise
the Lord.

" The social state of the people improves from
Social condi- year to year; and it is a remarkable fact,
tion.   that life, liberty, and the avails of industry
and enterprise, are nowhere more safe, than in the
Sandwich Islands.   Foreigners of all nations are
kindly received, and their rights, personal, social,
civil, and religious, are respected.   No resident and
no subject, who conducts himself uprightly and dis-
creetly, has just cause to complain that his rights
are invaded."

The testimony at the close of the foregoing extract is well sustained by a remarkable passage in

the report to the government of Chief Justice Lee,
as early as the year 1853: "In no part of the world,"
he says, "are life and property more safe than in the
Sandwich Islands. Murders, robberies, and Security of life and property.
the higher class of felonies, are quite un-
known here; and in city and country we retire to
our sleep, conscious of the most entire security. The
stranger may travel from one end of the group to
the other, over mountains and through woods, sleep-
ing in grass huts, unarmed, alone, and unprotected,
with any amount of treasure on his person, and with
a tithe of the vigilance required in older and more
civilized countries, go unrobbed of a penny."

Mr. Shipman, who joined the mission in 1854,
was stationed at Waiohinu, in the district of Kau.
Excepting three or four sons of missionaries, he was
the last to receive an appointment as a missionary
to the Islands, and he died at his post after seven
years. Mr. Shipman was a man of strong intelligence, and much among the people; and after four
years he bore this emphatic testimony concerning
the reality of their piety: "Nothing but Testimony as to native piety.
the Holy Spirit could have wrought in them
what we now see. Many of them live among us
monuments of his power in converting the soul.
.Whether it was by a mighty outpouring of the Spirit,
in what is termed a revival, or by a gradual work
of grace in the community, I know not; but that
the Lord has been here, with regenerating power,
there can be no doubt. Neither education, nor legislation could have produced what we now see. All
the improvements of this kingdom will fail to do for
the younger portion of the population, what has
been done by your missionaries. through the blessing
of God, for the older portion."

The Hawaiian Evangelical Association decided, in
Revision of 1859, that it was inexpedient to attempt a
the Scripture
version. new translation of the Scriptures; but that
the existing version should be suitably revised, with
the addition of clearly relevant proof-texts, or references.

According to the report of Dr. Armstrong, Presi-
The national dent of the Board of Education, in that year,
schools. the statistics of free schools, supported by
the government, then stood as follows: —

Raised by the school-tax in 1858 . . . . . $34,994.00
Raised by the school-tax in 1859 . . . . . 31,491.49
   Number of free schools in 1859 . . . 285
   Number of scholars 8,628
   Schools where English is taught . . . 16
   Native youths in them 804
   White children in schools 190
   Mixed children in schools 166
                                                   ———
   Total in the schools 9,788

The excess of boys over the girls in the free
schools, was one thousand five hundred and seventy.
One hundred and forty of the schoolmasters were
from the seminary at Lahainaluna. Conventions of
teachers, of from five to ten days' continuance, were
held on the islands of Kauai, Oahu, Maui, and at
three places on the island of Hawaii. Essays were
read, and exercises performed in reading, writing,.
arithmetic, and geography; and a variety of subjects
were discussed, all pertaining to the office and work
of the schoolmaster. About four-fifths of the free
schools were composed of the children of Protestant
parents. The chief reading-book in the schools was
the New Testament, both on account of its cheap-
ness, and the desire of the parents that their children should be instructed therein; and portions of

the Hawaiian version were often seen in the hands of Roman Catholic children.

In addition to free schools, the government supported the Lahainaluna Seminary, with one hundred and twelve students; the royal school at Honolulu, with fifty-five; and the free school at Honolulu with seventy-eight. This last was made up of a mixed class of Hawaiians, Americans, English, Welsh, Irish, Scotch, Germans, Chinese, Tahitians, Peruvians, Hindus, and Africans. There were also Hawaiian-English schools containing eight hundred pupils.

The select schools, not under the government, were the Oahu College, with seventy-three Select students; the boarding-school at Hilo, with schools. sixty-three; and a manual labor school at Waioli, on Kauai, with sixty-two. The school at Hilo had been in operation twenty-four years, and had cost the Board seven thousand five hundred dollars, in addition to the support of Mr. Lyman, the teacher. Of its five hundred and forty-three pupils, nearly four hundred were in many different kinds of business, at the time now under consideration, scattered through the Sandwich Islands, Oregon, California, the Marquesas Islands, and Micronesia.[1] In this school, as well as in Mr. Wilcox's, at Waioli, the pupils cultivated the soil during a portion of each day. These three schools derived their support chiefly from the American Board.

In 1860, the government system of school education experienced an irreparable loss, as it Death of Dr. proved, in the death of Dr. Armstrong, as Armstrong. a consequence of injuries received by a fall from his

---

[1] The school at Hilo, in 1868, received from the government a new and perpetual charter, under the old Board of Trustees, composed of the American missionaries on Hawaii, with power to fill vacancies when they occur

horse. He had labored during fifteen years effectively in the distinctive character of a missionary, and thirteen years in connection with the government of the Islands, as President of the Board of Education, with other responsible offices attached. The king was greatly moved by his death, and ad-
Tribute to dressed the following touching note of sym-
his memory. pathy to the afflicted widow : —

" My dear Madam : — I hope I shall not appear intrusive upon your first grief, if I hasten to tender you and your family my sincerest condolence for the great bereavement you have sustained under a heavy dispensation of Providence.

" Your husband, so suddenly removed, at the very time when all who knew him, or appreciated his usefulness, were hoping to see him return to his important avocations, was a valued friend of mine, and an efficient officer of the government, and I am, to a very large extent, a sharer in your loss.

" Believe me, Madam, when I assure you, that so suddenly did this blow reach me, that it is only by degrees that I appreciate the magnitude of the loss* which you and I, and the country, have sustained.

" Yours, very truly,

" LIHQLIHO."

" PALACE, *September* 24, 1860."

He also prepared an obituary notice of Dr. Armstrong in Hawaiian, for the native newspaper. The closing sentence reads thus : " It is suitable that the whole nation should mingle their weeping with the tears of the widow and children of the deceased, for, in our prosperity, he rejoiced in our joy, and when trouble came upon us, he was afflicted in our affliction."

About this time there was a great diminution in the calling of whale-ships at the Islands. Whale-ships call less frequently. They could obtain their supplies more advantageously elsewhere. While this relieved the islanders from one of their most demoralizing influences, it deprived them of their principal means of obtaining money and the productions of other lands. But measures were soon in progress to promote the cultivation of sugar, rice, wheat, and other products for exportation, and the industrial interests of the Islands were thus promoted.

Mr. Lyons, of Waimea, appears to have regarded his district as embracing the equivalent of Church-building on Hawaii. fourteen parishes, to each of which he furnished a native sub-pastor, acting in subordination to the missionary, with deacons and elders; and he labored hard, in the years 1859 to 1861, to have each of these parishes supplied with a neat and comfortable house of worship. One or two of them, which I saw on the uplands while sailing along the northern shore, had the unmistakable church appearance.

Concerning the Papists, at this time, it will be sufficient to avail myself of information received Papists at Hilo. from Mr. Coan, writing under date of August 21, 1861. The papists made a strenuous effort to gain numbers and influence in Hilo. Their temple had been completed, and it was consecrated with much pomp and ceremony. "The French Bishop was there, with a number of his clergy; and papists were called in from every part of Hawaii, and from all the islands in the group. Music, paintings, harangues, feasting, horse-riding, bell-chiming, and many other diversions were in full play, to attract the multitude. No efforts were made to prevent the Protestant peo-

ple from witnessing the show, and of course many
were there from idle curiosity, and many others from
an honest desire to see, compare, and judge for
themselves.   Numbers joined the Romanists, but
they were mostly strangers from other parts, ignorant laborers on the plantations of Chinamen, and a
few decidedly wicked and base characters from the
neighborhood, — notorious liars, dishonest debtors,
adulterers, and men who had been convicted and
punished by the laws of the land; and there were
enough of this class left.   It is believed that no
man joined them who gave evidence of piety."

CHAPTER XXXII.

1860–1861.

WHILE the year 1860 had its trials, it was specially distinguished for revivals of religion over a large part of the Islands. In no one of the previous twenty years, had there been such evidence of the Holy Spirit's presence in the churches. The voice ^{Extent of the} of rejoicing for spiritual mercies came up ^{revival.} from nearly all the stations. Churches were revived, backsliders reclaimed, the fallen raised, the weak strengthened, the timid made brave for the truth, and hardened sinners converted to God.

At the annual meeting of the mission in May, the missionaries came together mourning over the desolations of Zion. These were painfully evident in Honolulu, and many other places. But even there the Lord had begun to revive his work. The ^{Where it} first distinct signs of spiritual interest were ^{commenced.} at Kaneohe, on the island of Oahu, under the ministry of Mr. Parker. This was as early as October, 1859, and among a very irreligious class of persons. There was a decided increase of pious feeling and activity in the church. Fifty-nine suspended or excommunicated members were restored to fellowship, and about the same number of hopeful converts were added by profession. There was also a manifest growth in grace in the older members of the church.

18

Early in the year 1860, the revival extended along
Extends over Oahu. the northern side of the island to the district of Hauula, where the native pastor
Kuaea was laboring. The number of hopeful converts
there, within the space of a few weeks, was scarcely
less than a hundred. At the close of the general
meeting, Messrs. Coan and Parker made a tour of
the island, and brought back a favorable report,
not only from the two places just named, but from
Waialua. The churches in Honolulu came now
within the reviving influence. A sermon preached
in June, by Mr. Kuaea in the Second Church, under
the pastoral care of Rev. Lowell Smith, was evidently blessed to the people. He then made a
preaching tour through Oahu, accompanied by a
number of deacons from his own and other churches.
The people came out freely to his meetings, and
urged that the labors might be prolonged. The
lay helpers were with special reference to visiting
from house to house.

Their united labors on returning to Honolulu were
very useful; and from that time, there was a precious work of grace at all the stations on Oahu. In
September, Mr. Smith also made a preaching tour
through the island, accompanied by twelve deacons.
Their visit to Waialua appears to have been specially
successful, and they had great reason for rejoicing
through the whole tour. Many who had been infatuated by the wild *hulas*, and not a few Roman Catholics and Mormons, became regular attendants on the
Protestant meetings.

Mr. Emerson, of Waialua, has left a pleasing record
An interesting case. of his visit to Waianae. He was there the
guest of Kapuiki, formerly judge of the

district. After bathing and refreshment, the family assembled for evening devotion in the well-finished house, floored, papered, ceiled, glazed, shingled, clapboarded, matted, and surrounded by a deep verandah. At night, the guests retired to separate apartments, furnished with beds filled with dried grass, and surrounded by mosquito bars. Twenty-five years before, the owner of this house was an obstinate heathen, often intoxicated, and having no fellowship with the church, of which he was now the main pillar.

A series of meetings was held at that place, for prayer, instruction, and inquiry, preparatory to the celebration of the Lord's Supper on the following Sabbath, in all of which much interest was manifested. The good people afterwards spoke of the communion season which followed, as being more joyful than any one ever before.

At night the room in which the missionary lodged was separated from one occupied by natives only by a thin partition, and two or three times each night while he remained there, the natives rose for prayer, each offering a short but fervent petition for the outpouring of the Holy Spirit upon the people and themselves. One night he listened to not less than nine of these prayers after he had retired to rest.

The admissions to the churches on the Island of Oahu, as the result of this revival, were nearly nine hundred. *Number of converts.*

As a consequence of the special religious interest on the Island of Kauai, the church at Koloa received one hundred and two members *On Kauai.* by profession, and the church at Waioli twenty-one.

Mr. Alexander returned to his field at Wailuku,

on Maui, in June 1860, after an absence in the United States of eighteen months, and was "deeply impressed with the low state of piety among the people." But brighter days were near. In October, there was cheering evidence of an unseen power moving on the hearts of the people. The morning prayer-meetings, which had been greatly neglected, were attended by increased numbers, and there was an evident increase of solemnity in those who attended public worship on the Sabbath. Backsliders spontaneously confessed their wanderings, and asked an interest in the prayers of God's people. Some of the most careless and profligate evinced great concern for their soul's salvation, and Christians prayed as they had not before been heard to do. Fair professors of religion, who had been living in secret sin, were constrained to come forward and confess their wickedness, and beg the prayers of their brethren. The members of the church and the awakened were drawn together, and together they sought the Lord. For successive weeks, they met for prayer and exhortation three times a day, and sometimes they protracted the afternoon meetings till eight or nine o'clock in the evening; and a few times they continued all night in prayer and mutual exhortations. Fearing evil would result from such protracted meetings, the missionary advised their discontinuance. Young converts sought out former companions in wickedness, and endeavored to bring them to Christ. Brethren of the church went in companies of two, three, four, or five, and visited every house, whether of professed Christians, Papists, or Mormons. Multitudes were thus brought

On Maui.

Characteristics of the work.

under the influence of the gospel, who, living far up the valleys and ravines, were almost inaccessible to their pastor. A wonderful change indeed came over the whole community.

For six months and more, prayer-meetings were held as early as the dawn of day, in as many as eight different places, and the people seemed to take delight in meeting each other at that early hour. Scripture knowledge was valued and sought as it had never been before. Many entered upon the practice of reading the whole Bible through in a year. Pious women also were very active in their efforts to promote the revival.

In the districts of Hilo and Puna, on Hawaii, the awakening influence was nowhere so strong as in 1837–40; but in many places back- slidden church members came with confessions and tears, to renew their covenant vows. Numbers of the most hopeless of them returned more humble, penitent, and sincere than ever before. In many places daily meetings were kept up morning and evening, and fully sustained. A great and good work was thus wrought in the church itself. Many of the youth, who had seemed to have only a name to live, became active and zealous members, and the churches stood upon a higher level.

If the work was less marked and decisive at other stations, outside of the churches, there was nevertheless an excellent quickening influ- ence among the better portion of the members, and a reclaiming of many wanderers. The piety that pervaded the nation was, on the whole, purified and strengthened.

There soon followed indeed a reaction. The prog-

ress of the gospel, in 1860 and 1861, was like a
swollen river; in the next year, it was like
the same river in a season of drought.

A reaction.

But the lines were being more distinctly drawn
between the Church and the world. There
were antagonist and conflicting forces.
Whereas once scarcely a native could be found who
would refuse to admit the claims of the gospel,
many were now ready to advocate the doctrines of
infidelity, and boldly rejected the truth. In the
legislative councils, they sought to overthrow the
laws in favor of temperance and correct morals, and
scoffed in private at all religion. This naturally had
the effect to arouse the godly, and the contest between light and darkness became more active and
decided. Notwithstanding the apparent decline of
fervor, there was a growth of principle, and an
increase of feeling in the churches, that they were
bound to support the gospel at home, and to send it
abroad.

General re-
sults.

As the result of this revival of religion, nearly
fifteen hundred were received into the
churches on the Islands in 1860, and
more than eight hundred in the following year.

Admissions to
the church.

In the year 1860, the pastors, foreign and native,
and the churches on the island of Maui,
organized themselves into a Presbytery.
Not long after, the missionaries on the island of
Hawaii, uniting with an equal number of delegates
from the native churches, formed an Evangelical
Association; and about a hundred were admitted as
honorary delegates, to assist in the deliberations of
the body, but not to vote. The proceedings were to
be in the Hawaiian language. The first meeting of

Ecclesias-
tical organ-
izations.

the Association was at Hilo, and continued through
an entire week, with the most satisfactory results.
Similar associations were formed on Oahu and
Kauai.

These ecclesiastical bodies, whether called pres-
byteries or associations, were formed on much the
same basis, and had the same great object in view,
— to become what might be termed nurseries of the
infant Hawaiian churches. It was also hoped, that
they might be repositories of knowledge and experience, when the experience and counsels of the missionary pastors should be no longer available. Although some took the name of presbytery, and
others that of association, none of them were
strictly either Presbyterian or Congregational, the
circumstances of the native churches requiring
modifications. Another fact to be noticed is, that
these bodies were in no way connected with similar
ecclesiastical bodies in the United States. They
grew out of the exigencies of the work there; and
it was not seen to be desirable or feasible to connect
them with similar bodies in other lands.

CHAPTER XXXIII.

RECONSTRUCTION OF THE CHRISTIAN COMMUNITY.

1863.

IN so novel a process as bringing a mission to a close, some practical errors were unavoidable. As we now judge, in the light of experience, it was an error in this mission for the missionaries to retain the undivided pastoral charge of their large churches for some years after 1848; and another, that they drew from those churches a part of their support. At any rate, these arrangements were found at length to stand in the way of extending the native pastorate, since they inclined the brethren, when the ordaining of such pastors was urged as a present duty, to attach what proved to be an undue importance to the difficulties in the way. Never was the apparent want of adaptation to the pastoral office among the Hawaiian people so earnestly set forth by a portion of the missionaries in their correspondence, as in 1861 and 1862, more than forty years after the commencement of the mission. The few that were ordained pastors had indeed lived without reproach, and the larger number sent as ordained missionaries to Micronesia and the Marquesas Islands, had all a good report. The pastors on the Hawaiian Islands, however, had been held in subordination to the missiona-

Practical errors.

Backwardness to put forward a native ministry.

ries of their respective districts, and not having enjoyed a full personal responsibility, were unable fully
to demonstrate their capabilities. So great was this
lack of confidence on the part of some of the older
missionaries, that they even regarded many more
years of trial as needful, before they would deem it
safe to confer a full pastorate on many of the native
ministers.[1]

Nor was this difficulty peculiar to the Sandwich
Islands. At that time only thirty-eight of the one hundred and seventy churches connected with the missions of the American Board, had
native pastors. There were nine in the African, Syr-
ian, and China missions. The Ceylon and Mahratta
missions had only four each; which was also the
number at the Sandwich Islands. The Madura Mission had only six; and there were but eleven in the
three missions to the Armenians of Turkey. This
was after the lapse of thirty, forty, and fifty years.
Yet it was not for the want of pious, educated natives in the employ of the missions; there were then
as many as four hundred of these, most of them virtually preachers, and many actually licensed as such.
Neither had the Secretaries of the Board failed to
press upon their brethren the great importance of
the pastorate, as a means of securing an efficient native ministry. Nor were the missionaries less im-
·pressed with the desirableness of so organizing the
native churches, as to secure self-government and

[1] One of the Reports at the General Meeting of the Mission in 1863, has
the following declaration : " Your Committee are of the opinion, that all
or nearly all the stations now occupied by foreign pastors, should be so occupied for many years to come." The foreign pastors were then seventeen
in number, and there were twenty-one churches. — *Proceedings of the
Hawaiian Evangelical Association*, 1863, p. 71.

self-support at the earliest practicable time. The obstacles had been unavoidable, and were such that it
Causes of this back-wardness.
would require some time to surmount them. They existed in the want of experience; in the lack of precedents; in ideas and habits carried by the missionaries from their native land; in early impressions as to the native character; in the fact that the education of the native ministry was begun prior to any proper development of native churches, and of course before it was known exactly what was needed; in certain errors that had been unavoidable in the higher education, by reason of which many of the young men became disinclined to such pastorates; in the absence of a well-defined and settled purpose among the missionaries, to assign churches to the pastoral care of a native ministry; and to the consequent fact, that the native preachers, with few exceptions, were not avowedly educated for the pastoral office, and therefore were not in the expectation of it; and so the idea had not that place in their thoughts, nor that hold upon their consciences and hearts, which it has with a very large number of the pious young men in the colleges and higher schools of our own country.

It was not easy to overcome these difficulties, espe-
Why hard to be overcome.
cially as two thirds of the churches in the missions of the Board were what is called *station* churches, whose acting pastors were missionaries. Moreover, there had been such a lack of development in those native preachers, who had been long licensed to preach, especially in the matter of judgment and decision, — owing in part, doubtless, to their not having had more responsibility thrown upon them, — as rendered it difficult for missionaries,

who had known them long, to believe it safe to commit to them the pastoral care, even though exercised for a time under missionary supervision.

The difficulty was not alone with the missionary. The native preacher, having his eye upon a better and surer maintenance, often preferred remaining in the service of the mission, where his pay was certain, to incurring the risk of a smaller and ill-paid salary as the pastor of a native church. It was, moreover, a somewhat frequent experience that the licensed preacher yielded to the allurements of office, or trade. The laws governing the human mind are everywhere the same. The fixed relation between "demand and supply," can no more be disregarded with the graduates of mission colleges, than with those of American. The pastoral office is of divine appointment, and sustains a peculiar relation to the sanctified nature of man. Hundreds of the best pastors in the United States spend their lives cheerfully as such on salaries that would by no means content them in mere worldly pursuits. The pastorate, once clearly apprehended in its relations to the person and work of the Redeemer, is far more desirable and influential than that of "reader," "catechist," or mere "licentiate." It has a great attractive power in the church at home, and may be made to have the same in foreign fields. But there must be a well-defined prospect of such a pastorate. The inward call of the Holy Spirit to this work, needs the coöperating influence of providential openings. There must be the expectation of a waiting people. Thus we obtain our gospel ministers. Were no pastorates in prospect, or were the most important pas-

The difficulty not alone with the mission-ary.

Universal interest of the pastoral office.

There must be the prospect of pastorates.

torates to be filled by foreign preachers, our educated young men would do as too many of our highly educated native converts abroad have done.

There was the additional difficulty at the Sandwich Islands, that a numerous body of lunas — deacons and elders — had long been accustomed to act as lay preachers in the smaller divisions of each parochial district; and these were naturally averse to surrendering their public functions to pastors of their own race.

Additional difficulty at the Islands.

But the time had come at the Islands when the difficulties should be met and overcome. The reverence for missionary authority, inherited in some sense from the chiefs, could not be expected long to survive the race of chiefs; nor was official subordination in the native ministry to individual missionaries favorable to creating self-reliant, self-governing churches. It was time to give compactness and efficiency to the native Protestant community, and to devolve upon it the responsibilities of self-government in ecclesiastical matters; thus preparing the way for committing to its direction the working of all its religious charities. It was time to concede to the native clergy and people as much agency in the management of their religious affairs, as they then possessed in the affairs of the state.[1]

The time for an independent ministry arrived.

The very delicate relations of the foreign and native pastors were to be so adjusted that there would be no conflicting interests. A method of self-government was to be devised, which should be efficient, and at the same time acceptable

What was to be done.

---

[1] The time here mentioned was under the Constitution of Kamehameha III.

to pastors and people. The Protestant churches on the different islands, though separated by rough ocean channels, were to be made to feel as one body in Christ, and one in interest, by means of appropriate bonds of union. It had become needful, moreover, that a more weighty responsibility should rest on that community in its larger sense; that it should assume the whole direction of the work of building up Christ's kingdom on the Sandwich Islands, and on the islands farther'west; while it should be relieved of the support of the old missionaries, and assured of such pecuniary aid, for a time, as would enable and embolden it to assume the new responsibilities.

The reason for sending the author to the Islands in 1863, was chiefly the depressed tone of feeling at the time, in the letters of so many of the missionaries. The reaction following the general revival of 1860, was no doubt severe, and it seems to have affected both the pastors and people. There was reason to believe it would be transient, as in fact it was.[1] But with so great tendency to discouragement, it seemed scarcely possible to bring about the desired changes at the Islands, by the slow process of correspondence. Accordingly, at the close of 1862, the Prudential Committee resolved, that it was expedient for the Foreign Secretary to repair to the Islands, and aid the brethren, by per-

Why the author was sent to the Islands.

---

[1] The Hawaiian Evangelical Association, at its meeting in June of the next year, used the following language: "We believe our churches are growing in knowledge and in grace. There never was a time when we had more decisive evidence of genuine piety, or a larger number who would suffer persecution, and death if need be, for the name of the Lord Jesus."

sonal conference, in the reconstruction of the Christian community, which had grown up through the divine blessing on their labors. Though shrinking from the responsibilities of such a mission, at his somewhat advanced period of life, his duty seemed clear. Going by way of the Isthmus of Panama and San Francisco, he landed at Honolulu on the 27th of February, 1863.

After spending three months in the most gratify-

Personal intercourse. ing personal intercourse with the missionaries at their several homes, he attended a meeting of the Hawaiian Evangelical Association, which was prolonged a full month. The results were embodied in nine reports, drawn up by committees after the subjects had been discussed, which reports were afterwards adopted with great unanimity.

As the results of these deliberations, the large

The reconstruction. churches were to be divided, with convenient territorial limits ; the missionaries retaining the pastoral care of the central churches, where circumstances favored it, while native pastors were to be placed, as fast as possible, over the others.

Native pastors and laymen were to be associated with those of foreign birth or origin, in all the working religious bodies on the Islands.

While the old missionaries, from their age, experience, and superior attainments, would naturally continue to exert a salutary influence upon the churches and pastors near them, the ecclesiastical control would be exclusively with the local ecclesiastical bodies. They were to organize the churches, define their territorial limits, ordain and install the pastors, and remove them when it was desirable so to do; and their supervision extended to doctrine, discipline, and practice. The details of this supervision were left, in a considerable degree, to the ecclesiastical bodies of the several islands, and from their decision there was ordinarily to be no appeal; though the local bodies would be at liberty to refer cases of peculiar difficulty, for advice and counsel, to the general body in its annual meeting at Honolulu. The missionaries thus divested themselves of a responsibility, which they had exercised from the beginning, and which, at the outset of those infant churches, was as needful as it is in a young family.

The Hawaiian Evangelical Association had before consisted of the missionaries of the American Board residing on the Sandwich Islands, together with other resident evangelical ministers of foreign birth who were in sympathy with them; but it was thenceforward to consist of all native and foreign Congregational and Presbyterian clergymen on the Sandwich, Micronesian, and Marquesas Islands; of lay delegates, appointed annually by the local ecclesiastical bodies; and of such laymen as should be elected, from time to time, by a two-thirds vote.

A Board was formed, called " The Board of the Hawaiian Evangelical Association," to consist of not less than eighteen members, one third of whom were to be natives; and the hope was entertained, that the American Board would see fit to transfer to this Board its responsibilities for directing the work at the Sandwich Islands and in Micronesia.

The deliberations and records of the Association, which until that time had been in the English language, were thenceforward to be in the Hawaiian language, as also were those of the Hawaiian Board.

That there might be no unnecessary hindrances to the dividing of the great churches, and to the multiplying of native pastors, and obtaining their support from the native community, it was proposed, that the American Board resume the support of the old missionaries, as far as should be needful.

It was expected, that the native churches would assume the entire support of their native pastors, and of their foreign missionaries; but it would be needful for a time that the American Board should make grants in aid to the Hawaiian Board for certain other purposes.

The children of missionaries at the Oahu College were to give a prescribed attention to the Hawaiian language, as a condition of receiving aid at the College from the funds of the American Board. A theological class of native students was to be formed, under Mr. Alexander at Wailuku,[1] and a boarding-school for native females was to be commenced, to raise up suitable persons to become teachers in female schools, and the wives of native pastors.

On the return home of the Secretary, these proceedings received the cordial sanction of the Prudential Committee, and also of the American Board.

Confirmation of the proceedings.

The reader is already aware, that the missionaries at these Islands, some years before, were released from their special connection with the Board. The relations of the Hawaiian Christian community as such, to the American Board, and to the churches for which the Board

Changed relations of the American Board.

---

1 Mr. Coan also taught a class of Theological Students at Hilo.

acted, were now radically changed. The Board ceased to act any longer as principal, and became an auxiliary. Its responsibilities were transferred to the Hawaiian Board; with no other obligations remaining upon it, than to make grants in aid of certain departments, so long as they should be needful to enable the community to get fairly under way. Of course the Board was to have assurance that these grants were properly expended.

Much remained, however, to be done by the Hawaiian community — composed as it was of the native Christians, the missionaries and their children, and pious foreign residents on the Islands — before the newly created religious community would become fully self-governed and self-reliant. There was to be a reconstruction of the native churches, increasing their number, and defining the territorial limits of each. Natives were to be sought out who might probably be fitted for the gospel ministry, and the pastoral office, and suitably educated. The churches on some of the Islands were to be more perfectly associated ecclesiastically, for mutual aid and the better discharge of their ecclesiastical duties. The risk was to be incurred of admitting native pastors and delegates into the Evangelical Association of the Islands, with equal rights to deliberate and vote, with the native language as the medium of business. In view of all this, the missionary brethren at that time gave expression to their sentiments in the following language: —

"We stand to-day, with our Christian community on these Islands, as far removed from the abominations of heathenism, which existed when our fathers landed on these shores, as light is

19

from darkness. ' Old things have passed away.' The whole structure of society is new. We have civil and religious liberty, schools, seminaries of learning, churches and ecclesiastical associations, and the needful appliances for carrying forward the work of the Lord among this people.

" We say, then, that we believe the mission, re- garded as one of the missions of the American Board of Commissioners for Foreign Missions, has accom- plished its work. And it has been a glorious work, and we believe it will ever be regarded as a monu- ment of·the grace of God.

" We believe the time has come, when it is expe- dient to change the base of our operations. The Christian community on these Islands, composed of all evangelical foreigners and natives, is well able to assume the responsibility, and take the lead in build- ing up and maintaining our religious institutions.

" To the officers and patrons of the American Board of Commissioners for Foreign Missions, who have so long sympathized with us in our trials, joys, and sorrows, aided us by their prayers and wise counsels, and provided so abundantly for our wants, we tender our sincere and most hearty thanks. We do not doubt that the American Board will continue to make such grants-in-aid as we may need; and though our relations change, they will feel a deep and tender interest in the prosperity of all our in- stitutions; and we are assured of their sympathies and prayers.

" We anticipate the happiest results, because the change is urged upon us by the providence of God, and because we have earnestly sought the divine aid and guidance in making it. There has been so

much unanimity in our counsels, notwithstanding
the existence of so many diverse interests, that we
perceive the hand of a higher power, guiding us to
wise conclusions. And we have reasons for the
hope, that the change will prove salutary, not only
to the churches and pastors on these Islands, but to
the American Board itself, and to its patrons, and to
the missions beyond us that may be transferred
to our care.

"The change," they add, "must be salutary, inasmuch as it will permit the Church of Christ in
these Islands to avail itself of a feeling of religious
patriotism and nationality, by placing the religious
community here in a position of independence, as
one among the many Christian communities of the
world. Analogous to our position politically, as an
independent people, our church, being manifestly
an outgrowth of the spiritual life of our own people,
must be dearer to them when it no more appears
like a colonial dependency sustained by the spiritual
life of a foreign people."

The Evangelical Association on the large island
of Hawaii was divided into two associa- Reorganiza-
tions, called the Eastern and Western; churches.
and the two recognized nineteen new churches, and
installed native pastors over eight of them.

The working of the new system has proved to be
all that could be expected or desired. A Working of
member of the Association, writing after system.
four or five years' experience, speaks thus of the
Hawaiian members of the Evangelical Association.

" Our attention was drawn mainly to the fifty or
sixty Hawaiian members, ministers and delegates of
the churches, who constitute the bulk of the assem-

bly. They are an earnest and wide awake body of
men. Not generally eager to speak, but paying
careful and respectful attention to the counsels of
the fathers, and responsive to the propositions of the
young leaders; generally rather cautious, and in-
disposed to advance new and radical measures, but
ever ready to fall in with the progressive ideas of
the few who, in such a body, are fitted to lead.

" The Hawaiian ministers are constant and intelligent readers of the weekly and monthly
newspapers published in their language.
They are leaders in every educational movement;
having been the main agents — owing to the decay
of the government school system — in the establishment of perhaps twenty independent schools in
their various parishes. They are the conservative
element, the guides of the people."

The Ha-
waiian min-
isters.

Next year another missionary, one of the oldest,
who was perhaps among the least hopeful in 1863
as to the success of a native ministry, bears the following testimony: " Our meetings of the Association have been full and earnest. For the first time,
we elected a Hawaiian for moderator. He
is a good man, and he did well. We wish
to induct our native pastors into all the duties, to
which they may be hereafter called."

A Hawaiian
moderator.

And here I will quote the testimony of the late
Rev. Franklin Rising, an Episcopal clergyman, and one of the Secretaries of the
American Church Missionary Society, as to the success of the mission. Mr. Rising visited the Islands
for the benefit of his health; and he thus states the
results of his observations during the four months
of his residence, writing in 1867.

Testimony of
an Episcopal
clergyman.

" As the controversy growing out of the Reformed
Catholic mission — which is not an undertaking of
my own Church, but simply of individual members
thereof — had filled the very air with conflicting
stories, I resolved to find out for myself, so far as I
could, just what had been done, and what had been
left undone, by your missionaries, as well as by
those of the Roman Catholics and the Reformed
Catholics. This resolution I sought to carry out in
the fear of God, and for my own satisfaction, as a
Christian man, and as an Episcopalian minister.
To this end I visited thoroughly the chief islands,
nearly every mission station on the whole group, and
so far as facilities were given me, all the religious,
educational, and social institutions. I attended
Sunday and week-day services; made the personal
acquaintance of the major part of the missionaries
of all creeds; conversed with persons of many professions and social grades. The deeper I pushed my
investigations the stronger became my conviction,
that what had been on your part necessarily an experimental work in modern missions, had, under
God, proved an eminent success. Every sun-rising
brought me new reasons for admiring the power of
divine grace, which can lift the poor out of the dust,
and set him among princes. Every sun-setting gave
me fresh cause to bless the Lord for that infinite
love, which enables us to bring to our fellow-men
such rich blessings as your missionaries have bestowed upon the Hawaiian race. Here I feel bound
to say, that I use the phrase 'eminent success' in a
relative, not an absolute, sense. All has not been
accomplished that could have been desired; but
more has been done than could have been expected.

Less than half a century is too short a time, as missionary annals teach us, *to complete* the process of Christianizing a heathen people. It has been long enough in this case, to transfer the whole race from the despotic sway of heathenism to the plastic influences of the gospel and to mould that race, up to a certain point, after the pattern of Christ. To me it seems marvelous, that in comparatively so few years, the social, political, and religious life of the nation should have undergone so radical and blessed a change as it has. And I would not have made this limitation, were it not that so many fail to appreciate how far removed heathenism is from Christianity, and how potent must be the power which induces the abandonment of the one and the embracing of the other.

"Looking then at the kingdom of Hawaii-nei, as it to-day has its recognized place among the world's national sovereignties, I cannot but see in it one of the brightest trophies of the power of the Cross; one of the most gratifying seals set by God upon the labors of his servants; and one of the strongest encouragements to press our missionary enterprises into all lands, and to sound the gospel unto every people. In using these words of warm commendation, I feel that I am exalting what the Lord has done for a people redeemed with his precious blood, rather than what man has done for a once degraded race." [1]

[1] For the whole statement of Mr. Rising, see *Missionary Herald* for 1867, pp. 225-231.

CHAPTER XXXIV.

1862–1870.

THE principal building connected with the Seminary at Lahainaluna was burned to the ground in July, 1862; involving the destruction of the chapel, the recitation and dining rooms, the cabinet of minerals, and most of the philosophical apparatus; together with the rooms of fifty students, some of whom were injured by leaping from the windows, but no lives were lost. The government promptly furnished the means, with some aid from private donations, for rebuilding on an improved plan. *Destructive fire at Lahainaluna.*

This popular institution had ninety pupils at the time of the fire, of whom thirty-eight had a good standing in the church. Of the seven hundred and seventy-one pupils in the twenty-five classes since 1831, four hundred and thirty-eight belonged to the nineteen years, while the seminary was supported by the American Board, and three hundred and thirty-three to the thirteen years of its subsequent support by the government. *Usefulness of the institution.*

A very large majority of the whole, after leaving the seminary, had engaged in teaching for a longer or shorter period. They were to be found in this work at every nook and corner of the land, from

Hawaii to Niihau. The institution still holds an intimate relation to the Protestant mission and churches upon the Hawaiian Islands, although under the care of the Government Board of Education, and receiving its support from the national treasury.[1] It numbers among its graduates the best qualified teachers of the common schools, and a large proportion of the natives in employments implying a good degree of education, such as surveyors, lawyers, and judges. A majority of the pastors of the Hawaiian churches received their literary education there, as did most of the more prominent Hawaiian missionaries in Micronesia and the Marquesas Islands. The medium of instruction is the Hawaiian language, though the English is taught to some extent.

Kamehameha IV. died suddenly on the 30th of November, 1863. The hopes inspired by his capacity, and the first years of his reign, were not fully realized. This was owing, in part at least, to a certain lack of self-control, but more to his unfortunate devotion, in his last years, to the eccentric mission of Bishop Staley. Yet he could hardly have regarded with satisfaction, had he lived, the demoralized condition of the common-school system, not long after the time of his decease, chiefly as the consequence of measures originated by him, or with his supposed sanction.

Death of the king.

His successor does not appear to have inherited the ecclesiastical proclivities of his brother, but seems for a time to have misapprehended the opinions and spirit of the mission. The arbitrary changes made by him in the Constitution of the

Kamehameha V.

[1] See Chapter xxviii. p. 243.

Third Kamehameha, were certainly lamented by the missionaries, as they were by a large body of the people, and the evil was aggravated by the modifications already referred to in the national schools, begun under the former administration, and continued under this. The public mind was disquieted. Political party spirit was awakened; and a tendency to spiritual lethargy, indifference, and skepticism appeared in the churches. Houses of worship were not well filled; prayer-meetings were not fully attended; the Sabbath was desecrated; benevolent contributions declined; and there were few manifestations of the power of the Holy Spirit. Religious decline.

Yet the testimony is decisive, that there were even then many thousands of Christians walking in the steps of those who, through faith and patience, inherit the promises. It is cheering to read, about this time, of the native preacher who had been called to the pastorate of the church at Waialua, on Oahu, where the health of the resident missionary had failed. His sermons were described as full of thought, and many of them as replete with illustrations, beautiful and perfect in their adaptation to the purpose of conveying religious instruction to Hawaiian minds; such sermons as no foreign-born missionary in the land could preach for Hawaiians. Hopeful indications.

Mr. Bond makes a statement concerning the state of his church at Kohala, in 1864, and the effect of a faithful exercise of discipline, which is too suggestive and interesting to be passed in silence. For fifteen years there had been no scenes of drunkenness in that district. But occasion was taken, during his absence, and the prevalence of a Successful church discipline.

report that he was not to return, by certain Hawaiians in the vicinity of the papal house of worship,
to introduce an intoxicating liquor made from the
ki plant, which all were persistently tempted to drink.
A new justice had come into the place, who was in
sympathy with the offenders, and at first seemed to
throw every obstacle in the way of executing the
laws; but ere long, finding that he might derive pecuniary advantage from a more stringent course, he
convicted near seventy individuals of drunkenness,
much to the relief of the community. Thus sustained, inquiry was made how many of the church
members had brought dishonor on their Master's
cause. After the most thorough examination, only
eleven were found to have thus subjected themselves
to the discipline of the church. These were suspended promptly ; and it speaks well for the individuals, that, instead of taking offense, and turning
their backs upon the people of God, as it was feared
a part of them might do, they all, with one exception, gave such evidence of repentance that they
were restored to their former standing in the church.
There had been a long season of coldness and de-
clension, but now there was an increasing regard for
religion and morality. The Sabbath-school, numbering two hundred pupils, became more interesting.
The church, also, after much discussion, resolved to
divide, and set off a new church, with a Hawaiian
pastor, deriving his support from his people, and one
of the deacons was invited to become the pastor of
the new organization, to which he assented.

The annual meeting of the Hawaiian Evangelical
Association, at Honolulu, in 1865, was full
of promise. A majority of the members
present were Hawaiians, and the business

The native element in the Evangelical Association.

of the Association was conducted in the native language. The impression left on the missionaries was, that there was no natural barrier to the free, equal, and harmonious working together of the two races, in civil, political, and ecclesiastical relations.

The annual sermons on foreign and home missions were delivered before large audiences; and the one on foreign missions was by a native pastor from Maui, and is described as a noble effort. Near the close of the session a union meeting was held in the Stone Church, at which three foreign and two native ministers spoke with power and effect; and in the afternoon, twelve hundred communicants united in celebrating the Lord's Supper.

The Rev. Lorrin Andrews, the first Principal of the Lahainaluna Seminary, published his Hawaiian Dictionary of the Hawaiian Language, on dictionary. which he had been long employed, in 1865. He had collected and defined fifteen thousand and five hundred words; as many as were in the first edition of Dr. Johnson's English Dictionary. The pages were five hundred and fifty-nine. President Alexander, of the Oahu College, contributed a valuable Introduction; and an English and Hawaiian vocabulary and a chronological table of remarkable events were appended. The Hawaiian government aided in its publication; yet the work must be numbered among the results of the mission to those Islands. Its publication was really due to the characteristic enterprise of Mr. H. M. Whitney, son of one of the first missionaries.

In January, 1866, the United States steam frigate *Lancaster*, Rear Admiral Pearson, made Visit of Admiral Pearson. a visit of a week at Hilo. During this visit the people assembled in the church, and an hour was devoted to music, in which the native choir was assisted by the band from the frigate. The Admiral then made an address, expressing his satisfaction with what he had seen at the Islands. He admired the prevalence of peace, order, and kindness. He was happily surprised at the amount of intelligence, and the extent of its diffusion among the people; pronounced a hearty encomium on their teachers, and exhorted all to abide by the instructions they had received, and to be steadfast in pursuing the right.

In the same year, there occurred a celebration at Celebration of the National Independence. Hilo, on the 31st of July, which affords a pleasing illustration of the native character in its Christianized form. It was on the anniversary of the restoration of the National Independence by Admiral Thomas. That day is to the Sandwich Islands, somewhat as the 4th of July is to the United States. There was no burning of powder, no booming of guns; there were no rockets, yet there was music and excitement. Arrangements had been made for a great meeting in the church. Several speakers had been engaged, and pieces of music had been prepared. The programme included the lowering of the Hawaiian flag, under the command of Lord George Paulet, with a mournful dirge or lament, and its restoration, with joyful music, at the command of Admiral Thomas. At nine o'clock in the morning, the people came in by companies from different districts, some with banners, some in uniform, all neatly dressed for the occasion. The church was soon crowded, and all could not gain admission. The services opened with music and prayer. Next came schools and companies from different sections of Hilo, with their free-will offerings for re-roofing and otherwise repairing the church. The collections amounted to one thousand and twenty dollars, and the assembly was jubilant on the announcement. The women vied with the men, many of them giving five and ten dollars each.

In the festive arrangements following the exercises, Mr. Coan was invited to dine with about thirty native females, at a table loaded with a variety of viands, foreign and native, followed by tea and coffee. The guests were all well dressed, and their deportment was most exemplary. Among the after dinner speeches was one from Dr. Judd, who was also an invited guest, and whom the reader will remember during the usurpation of Lord Paulet, as pursuing his labors for the government in the mausoleum of the Hawaiian kings. He gave an interesting history of the stirring events in those dark times.

And so the day passed, with music, addresses, feasting, and thanksgiving, leaving none but pleasant memories.

Six months later, on occasion of the annual conference of the churches of Hilo and Puna A Sabbath-school celebration.
at the same place, there was a Sabbath-school celebration, and a procession of four hundred children, with banners and flags. Several young men from Mr. Lyman's school were present with their flutes, and the Hawaiian children, having an ear for simple airs, sang in remarkable harmony as they marched along. At ten o'clock, the procession entered the church, and took seats previously assigned. The house was full. The exercises lasted an hour. These were prayer, singing, and instru-

mental music, interspersed with short, animated speeches.

The "week of prayer" was observed at the open-ing of 1867, by all the Protestant churches on the Islands, native and foreign. The two foreign churches at Honolulu, had experienced a reviving influence before the new year came in, and that week greatly deepened the interest. Several men of business in the town, and several youths in the Oahu College, were among the hopeful converts. There were many indications of an improved religious condition in several of the native churches, especially on the island of Molokai, in connection with the ministry of Rev. A. O. Forbes. A powerful revival had been in progress there for several months. There was also an interesting state of feeling in the female seminary at Waialua, on Oahu, under the care of Rev. O. H. Gulick and wife, which was commenced in Kau, on Hawaii, in 1863, and was transferred to Waialua, in 1865. Most of the fifty-seven girls in the seminary were over twelve years of age, and fifteen of them were previously professing Christians; but now seriousness came over the whole body, and a number gave very satisfactory evidence of conversion. The female seminary under Miss Mary Green, at Makawao, on Maui, was similarly blessed. In Mr. Alexander's Theological School at Wailuku, eight young men, graduates of Lahainaluna, and who had been two years in the school, were ready to enter the ministry of the gospel.

It was distressing, however, to witness the decline in the government day-schools. Many of them had been discontinued, and others were not properly conducted. As a consequence, the pupils were irregular in their attendance, and parents became disaffected, and longed for schools in which there would be religious instruction. Some churches went so far as to provide schools for themselves, independent of the government.

The contributions by the native churches for a year, as reported in June, 1867, are worthy of mention. They were as follows: —

Annual contributions.

For support of pastors, ...	$6,246.72
For church building, ...	12,550.41
For boarding-schools, ...	639.14
To Hawaiian Board, ...	4,004.09
Miscellaneous, ...	3,668.58
Total, ...	$27,108.94

The value of these contributions will be appreciated, when it is considered that they were in gold.

As in some parts of the United States, so in the Sandwich Islands, the Chinese are an increasing element of the population. A Chinese, named Aheong, became a Christian and a Christian preacher. The first notice I find of him is in an account of the annual meeting of the Evangelical Association in 1867. He was spoken of as one of the lay delegates from Maui, and was described as having a literary turn, good sense, and as being one with the brethren in the bonds of the gospel. He was brought to the Islands about sixteen years before in the capacity of a coolie, but had been educated above his condition, and came at length to be numbered among the merchants of Lahaina. His Christianity had not changed the expression of his face, or shortened the length of his

A Chinese evangelist.

cue, or led him to drop the comfortable loose dress
of his oriental home. Aheong joined freely in the
discussions of the Association, being fluent in the
Hawaiian language, and was always listened to with
respect and attention.

He was employed by the Hawaiian Board as an
evangelist among his countrymen, and had learned
the English and Hawaiian languages, using the latter with much power. Dr. Gulick describes him in
1869, as a very attractive speaker in any of the languages he uses.

The mission of Bishop Staley to the Sandwich Isl-
The Reformed ands,[1] commenced in 1862, to which he gave
Catholic Mission. the name of the "Reformed Catholic Mission," was from the ritualistic portion of the Church
of England; yet had the sanction of the Society for
the Propagation of the Gospel, and apparently of the
British Queen. It was not what the Episcopal foreign residents had requested, nor what the king had
originally desired. Yet, coming with such prestige,
the king was persuaded by his prime minister (who
had been the leader in calling for an Episcopal bishop)
to throw the weight of his influence into it. As a
consequence, the king became unnaturally estranged
from the American missionaries, to whom, under God,
he and his people were mainly indebted for their religion, their intelligence, and their independent position among the Christian nations. But neither
king, nor bishop, nor foreign minister seriously
retarded the reconstruction of the Protestant community, as already described. In the absence of a

[1] The rise and early proceedings of Bishop Staley's mission are sufficiently described in my work on the *Hawaiian Islands,* published in 1864,
pp. 331–359.

personal hold on the people, the results of this un-
courteous interference were seen chiefly in the national school system, the bishop being placed by the
king on the committee in charge of that system.
The changes there effected seemed to have for a
leading object to root out the evangelical element
from the instruction.

The representations made by Bishop Staley concerning the Sandwich Islands, and the influence of
the American mission upon their inhabitants, in his
published statements, and during his visits to this
country and England, were, to say the least, very extraordinary, and seem hardly consistent with a sound
state of mind. His career was not one that could
possibly succeed. His hostility to the Protestant
mission and churches on the Islands was more in-
discreet and reckless, than was that of the Roman
Catholics; and so extreme was the ritualistic development, that the Hawaiian people looked upon the
" Reformed Catholic " religion as so much like the
Roman, that they thought they might as well follow
the latter religion, if they should relinquish the one
they had already embraced. The bishop and his
clergy obtained very few followers. In the spring
of 1869, Dean Harris was officiating at Honolulu,
and had a small congregation, and a boarding-
school for girls, and a day-school for boys, neither
of them largely attended. Deacon Mason was then
preaching at Lahaina, and kept up a day and boarding-school for boys, and a boarding-school for girls.
The pupils of the schools constituted the Sabbath audience, almost no one else attending. At Wailuku,
also, on Maui, the Rev. Mr. Whipple had a day-school
for boys and girls, and his Sabbath services wer? at-

tended by from ten to twenty foreign residents. The Rev. Mr. Williams had a small school in Central Koua, on Hawaii, which, with a few adults, foreign and native, composed his Sabbath congregation.

The bishop was absent, at this time, on a visit to England. Meanwhile, there is good authority for stating, that a letter was addressed to the Society for the Propagation of the Gospel, signed by almost the entire membership of the " Reformed Catholic Church " in Honolulu, declaring their dissent from the doctrines and practices of the clergy sent to the Islands under the auspices of that Society, and suggesting or requesting their withdrawal. What they desired was a " low-church " pastor for Honolulu, without a bishop; and they pledged themselves to support him without assistance from abroad. It is also affirmed that a letter was written, by one of the cabinet ministers, stating that the king had withdrawn his patronage, and did not wish a cathedral to be erected on the land given by his brother, the late king, on which a chapel had already been built.[1]

The bishop returned to the Islands in the autumn of 1869, but received no cordial greeting. He took possession of the church on the following Sabbath, but almost no one came to hear him. Becoming at length convinced that his mission was a failure, he resigned his bishopric, and in May, 1870, he took steamer on his return to England. The archbishop has accepted his resignation.[2]

---

[1] *Missionary Herald*, 1869, p. 208.

[2] The authority for this last statement is the *London Observer*, as quoted by the *New York Observer*. The author received a letter from the Rev. Artemas Bishop, of Honolulu, while writing this chapter, dated February 8, 1870, confirming his previous impression, that Mr. Wyllie was the

The year 1868 was remarkable for earthquakes and volcanic eruptions on the island of Hawaii. Destructive earthquakes. These almost ruined the missionary station in Kau, and would have been very destructive of life in that and other parts of the island, had there been a numerous population. The three stone churches in Kau were shaken to the ground, but happily no one was in them at the time. The mission house occupied by Mr. Pogue and family, though a framed wooden building, was very much racked; and for hours they were harassed by erroneous reports of lava flowing down upon them from Mauna Loa.

Mr. Coan has always taken a special interest in the volcanic phenomena of Hawaii, and has given a description of these earthquakes. The shocks became frequent and vigorous in March, and were felt in all parts of the island. The mighty convulsion, which overthrew the churches in Kau, and many dwelling houses, and by its immense tidal waves swept whole villages from the shore, was on the 2d of April. Nothing like it is known in the traditions of the Islands. The earth rose and sank, and its surface rolled like the ocean in a storm. Hills swayed to and fro; stone walls fell flat; framed houses trembled and reeled; articles of furniture started from their places, and many were thrown down with vio-

originator of the "Reformed Catholic Mission." Mr. Bishop had just been assured of the fact by Bishop Staley, in a personal interview. "Mr. Wyllie," said the Bishop, "was the original author of that idea, and he put up the king to send for a mission from England." Mr. Wyllie's own ecclesiastical plan for the Islands, in connection with Bishop Staley's mission, as he stated it to me while we were on our voyage together from Oahu to Kauai, was to have a national Episcopal Church, with the Island-kingdom divided into ecclesiastical provinces. He intimated that our instituting independent local churches so extensively on the Islands was a serious obstacle (as it doubtless was) to the realizing of his plans.

lence; chimneys fell; timbers, ceilings, partitions
and plasterings cracked; and there was great destruction of glass and earthen ware. The earth
opened in seams and fissures, and avalanches of rocks
and earth fell from the precipices along the coast.
The terrific shock is said to have lasted three minutes, and there was of course great consternation.

In one part of Kau, near the abode of Mr. and
Mrs. Lyman, — both children of missionaries, — in
the night and without warning, a terrible landslide
occurred, an eruption of mud, earth, and rocks,
three miles long, half a mile wide, and from six to
thirty feet deep; burying a village in its way, and
thirty people, with flocks of goats, and five or six
hundred cattle and horses. It was so sudden and
rapid, that there was no escape for those within its
range. The noise was terrific, and the atmos-
phere was filled with dust. All rushed from their
dwellings; but the ground rocked and heaved with
such violence, that no one could keep his feet. Even
horses were thrown down. Mr. Lyman and family,
the native pastor and his family, and many others,
fled to a hill near by, and spent the night in exercises of devotion under the open sky, with no certain knowledge as to the extent of their danger.

The fires of Kilauea raged, at the same time, with
intense fury, surging against the walls of the great
cauldron; and the mountain itself was pouring
a stream of lava down to the sea, westward of the
mission station.

The Sandwich Islands are believed to be all of volcanic origin; but the volcanic agencies of all, except
Hawaii, have been slumbering from times anterior
to the historic period. Hawaii may be regarded as

still in the forming process; and, in the amazing extent and power of its internal fires, it is perhaps the most wonderful among this class of wonders.

Kilauea is on the side of Mauna Loa, four thousand feet above the level of the sea, and is the largest known volcano in constant action; but its eruptions pass off to the sea in directions which make them comparatively harmless. Mauna Loa rises ten thousand feet above Kilauea, and it is from its higher regions, and sometimes from its very summit, or near it, that the destructive eruptions come. To go back no farther than the year 1855; an immense river of fire then flowed down the north side for the space of sixty miles, to within a few miles of Hilo. It spread over nearly three hundred square miles, and continued thirteen months. Four years later, Mr. Lyons, on the western side, had a distinct view, from his house at Waimea, of a broad stream of lava descending from near the summit forty miles to the sea. The eruptions of 1868 were on the side opposite to Waimea, and descended north and south of the station of Waiohinu, at some distance from it.

CHAPTER XXXV.

1867–1868.

His Excellency M. Kekuanaoa, father of the fourth
and fifth Kamehamehas, and President of
the Board of Education; died in the year
1868. His death occurred on the 26th day of November, twenty-nine years after the death of his
wife, the excellent Kinau, and five years after that
of Kamehameha IV. His character was in keeping, on the whole, with his fine physical form.
Bishop Staley represented him as forming part of
his ecclesiastical establishment, and no doubt the
king did all in his power to make it so, but the
brave old chieftain remained to the last a
member of the First Church in Honolulu,
and firmly attached to its interests. Nor was his
friendship for the missionaries, and his grateful
recognition of his own and his nation's obligation to
them, ever shaken. His daughter, Victoria, who was
heir presumptive to the throne, died two years
before him. Her character was not like his;
though, like him, she retained her connection with
the Protestant community. My recollections of the
old governor are of a very pleasing character.

The Rev. John S. Emerson, whose death occurred

March 28, 1867, was a member of the mission nearly thirty-five years, having arrived at Hono- Mr. Emer-lulu on the 17th of May, 1832. He was son. born at Chester, New Hampshire, December 28, 1800, and was consequently in his sixty-seventh year at the time of his decease; which was the result of a sudden attack of apoplexy.

Mr. Emerson was educated at Dartmouth College and the Andover Theological Seminary. His missionary life was spent at Waialua, with the exception of four years passed as an instructor in the seminary at Lahainaluna, — from 1842 to 1846. An apoplectic stroke in 1859, and another in 1863, made it necessary for him to resign the pastoral care of his station in 1864; in which he was succeeded by Mr. Kuaea, a native pastor. His funeral brought together a large assembly, which manifested an affectionate interest in the occasion. In no part of the Islands had the people been more in the habit of reading the Scriptures. Mr. Emerson had so arranged their reading, that they were accustomed to read the entire Bible through once in three years. An old Hawaiian, belonging to the Waialua church, on being asked, said he had read the Bible through nine times.

Mr. Emerson had an efficient coadjutor in his wife. For years, she conducted the singing in the church, and was unwearied in administering to the wants of the people in sickness and health; as she continues still to do.

The Rev. Asa Thurston, one of the first missionaries, finished his course on the 11th of Mr. Thurs-March, 1868, after a residence at the ton. Islands of forty-eight years. During all this time,

he never visited his· native land. His labors at
Kailua have been frequently mentioned in this history, and were unremitted until the expiration of
forty years, when his mind failed under the pressure
of long and arduous service. Then, after visiting a
married daughter in California, he took up his abode
in Honolulu.

Mr. Thurston was a native of Fitchburg, Massachusetts, and was born October 12, 1787 ; consequently he (as well as his associate Mr. Bingham)
reached the good old age of fourscore. He was a
graduate of Yale College, and of the Andover Seminary. His wife who survives him, and is a resident
at Honolulu, was Miss Lucy Goodale, of Marlborough, Massachusetts.   Mr. Thurston is entitled to
a high rank among missionaries.   With physical
powers perhaps unsurpassed in his· day by those of
any other resident upon the Islands, whether native
or foreign, he was indefatigable in his labors.   His
letters to the Corresponding Secretary of the Board
were excelled in fullness and accuracy by none from
his associates, and show a noble work . performed
by him for Christ, in what was once the favorite
abode of the Hawaiian kings.   His knowledge of
the native language and character was thorough.
As a preacher, he was much esteemed by the people.
In the labor of preparing the Hawaiian version of
the Scriptures, it fell to him to translate parts of
Genesis, Numbers, and Deuteronomy, and the whole
of Samuel, and Second Kings.   Only when repeated
strokes of paralysis had rendered him incapable of
further service, did he consent to retire from his beloved charge.

I saw him in California, on my return from the

Islands. His step was still elastic, and his flowing white beard gave him a venerable appearance, but his mental powers were clouded. There was a constant serenity of manner, which showed that with him the conflicts of life were over.

Though so many of the missionary fathers have passed away, and the few that remain must The Hawaiian foreign in the ordinary course of nature soon fol- missions. low, their works will testify concerning them. Among these are the missions to Micronesia and the Marquesas Islands.

The mission to Micronesia, commenced, in the year 1852, by Messrs. Snow, Sturges, L. H. Mission to Gulick, and their wives, with two married Micronesia. Hawaiian assistants, has proved a success.[1] The groups nearest the Sandwich Islands, though two thousand miles distant, are called the Gilbert (also Kingsmill) and Marshall Islands. They are coral formations, low, and covered with cocoa-nut groves. Passing beyond these, westward, the first missionary station was established on Kusaie, or Strong's Island, between four and five hundred miles from the Gilbert group. The second station was on Ponape, or Ascension Island, three hundred miles still farther west. These islands belong to the Caroline group, and are both mountainous, with a rich soil, and healthful climate. Mr. Snow occupied the former, and Mr. Sturges and Dr. Gulick the Begun in the Caroline latter, and each station had one of the Ha- group. waiian missionaries. Mr. Snow's Hawaiian associate .

---

[1] For a somewhat extended account of the groups of islands in Micronesia first occupied, and the incipient events in this mission, see *Missionary Herald* for 1853, pp. 81-90.

died the next year. Mr. and Mrs. Doane reached Ascension in 1855, accompanied by a married Hawaiian assistant; and in October of the same year, Mr. Snow's seclusion was relieved by the arrival of Dr. and Mrs. Pierson, with Kanoa and his wife, natives of Hawaii. Dr. Pierson had opportunity, on his way, to visit seven of the sixteen islands in the Gilbert group, and five of the thirty Marshall Islands. The last named group is composed of two chains, perhaps a hundred miles apart. Dr. Pierson strongly recommended Apaiang, on the Gilbert, and Ebon, on the Marshall Islands, for new stations.

In 1856, a brigantine of one hundred and fifty-six tons, at the expense of Sabbath-school children, The Morning was built for the especial use of the Micro-Star   nesia mission, and named the Morning Star. She arrived at Honolulu in April, 1857, with Mr. and Mrs. Bingham as passengers. In her first voyage to Micronesia, she took them and a married Hawai-The Gilbert ian helper to Apaiang, and removed Messrs. and Marshall Islands. Doane and Pierson and their wives from their former station to Ebon.

It was a remarkable preparation for the safe oc-A remark- cupation of this latter station, that, while able prepara-tion. Dr. Pierson was residing on Kusaie, five canoes, with ninety people from the western chain of the Marshall Islands, being driven off their course, were providentially guided, after fifteen days, to that island. It was well known to these natives, that their lives, and also their means of returning to their native islands, were owing to the friendly influence of the missionaries. They reached their home safely in their canoes, in the favoring monsoon; and as some of them had seen Dr. Pierson on his visit to Ebon, two years before, this must be regarded as a very noticeable providence, preparing the way for the missionaries.

Captain Moore, of the *Morning Star*, was warned by a shipmaster, who had been at Ebon, to put up his boarding nettings, and not permit a single native to enter his vessel. On nearing the island matters looked somewhat threatening, for seventeen canoes were seen approaching the vessel, with an average of six persons in each. The boarding nettings were up; but one man in the foremost canoe, upon being addressed in his own language by Dr. Pierson, immediately recognized him, and exclaimed, "Doketur! Doketur!" (Doctor.) He was one of the party drifted to Strong's Island, in April, 1856, and who started for their homes in canoes, a part of which they had built at Strong's Island. The news soon spread through the fleet of canoes, and when they learned that Dr. Pierson was expecting to return to Ebon in the course of one or two moons, they were greatly delighted. The object of the delay was that Dr. Pierson might introduce Mr. Bingham to his old acquaintances at Apaiang.

Apaiang and its kindred islands did not furnish very eligible abodes for missionaries. The soil is extremely poor. The natives raise only a coarse kalo, not to be compared with the ordinary article of the same name at the Sandwich Islands, and subsist chiefly on the pandanus, and cocoa-nuts, which grow spontaneously. The sea yields a good supply of fish, but there is no wood suitable for fuel. The Gilbert language has a prevalence of voweled syllables, and is therefore better adapted to Hawaiian missionaries, than those of the Marshall and Caroline Islands.

The failure of Dr. and Mrs. Pierson's health obliged them to remove to California, and Dr. and Mrs. Gulick took their place at Ebon for a year.

The Hawaiian associate of Mr. Sturges died in
Death of a faithful native missionary. January, 1859. He had been an earnest and faithful missionary, an example of everything lovely and of good report. It is cheering to record of these humble missionaries, as of Kaaikaula, that he died as only a Christian can die, and that his wife bore her loss as one who knows how to cast all her burdens on the Lord Jesus. His widow returned to Hawaii with her orphan children; but being attached to the missionary work, she some time after resumed her mission on Micronesia, as the wife of Aea, a native missionary who was well reported of by his brethren, and who proved himself a valuable laborer at Ebon.

In 1861, Mahoe, one of Mr. Bingham's Hawaiian native assistants, was ordained during a meeting of the mission at Ponape. A printing-press had early been established in the Gilbert branch of the mission, and the amount of printing for the three branches of the mission, up to 1861, was thirty-two thousand one hundred pages for Ponape, nine thousand for Ebon, and twenty thousand for the Gilbert Islands.

Printing in native languages.

Dr. Gulick, Mrs. Sturges, and Mrs. Doane visited the Sandwich Islands in 1861, in the hope of recovering health. Mrs. Doane, however, died on the 16th of February. She had endured great trials, but was cheerful and happy under them, and many of the dark-minded inhabitants of these beautiful islands will hold her in grateful remembrance. During her protracted illness, she

Death of Mrs. Doane.

received the constant attentions of a faithful Ebon-
ite female, whom she had been the means of raising
from the depths of heathenism.

Mr. Snow removed to Ebon in August, 1862,
leaving a church at Kusaie of twenty-seven Church at
members, whose main dependence was to Kusaie.
be upon occasional visits from Mr. Snow. He saw
them the next year; and admitted eleven out of
twenty-seven candidates, among whom were two
chiefs, and the wife of one, "the most beautiful
young woman on the island." Mr. Snow now left
at Kusaie his translation of the Gospel of John,
which had been printed at Honolulu, and which
many of the people had become able to read. In
1869, he visited the island again, in the *Morning
Star*, in company with Mr. Pogue, a delegate from
the Hawaiian Board, who gives the following interesting account : —

"The 'gem of the Pacific,' as this island is called"
by some, is so in more senses than one. The population is six hundred, with no white man. There is
one church of one hundred and fifty-nine members,
with a native of the island for pastor. There are
three stone church-buildings, and one built in the
style of the island. As we landed at the wharf, near
Mr. Snow's house, we were greeted by the 'Good
morning' of many, who had come together to welcome their missionary, on his return to visit them
for a short time before his departure for the father-
land. It was delightful to see old and young, men
and women, boys and girls, coming around, taking
him by the hand, and greeting him with kind salutations. As I have seen loving children flock around
a father returning to his home after a long absence,

so this people gathered around our brother, whom
they regard as their spiritual father. They seemed
more like Hawaiians, than any other people with
whom I came in contact in Micronesia. They were
for the most part dressed in foreign clothes, and I
was struck with the mild, quiet, loving counte-
nances of many. They looked as if they were full of
happiness. And what were these people eighteen
years ago? Naked, degraded, sensual, smokers of
tobacco, drinkers of awa, superstitious, ignorant of
books, and of the true God. They are now clothed,
and in their right minds, read the Bible, sing the
songs of Zion, have a Sabbath, worship the true
God, and show by their lives the truth of the religion which they profess with their lips."

In 1863, in compliance with the recommendation
of the Hawaiian Evangelical Association, the Micronesian mission came under the direction of the Hawaiian Board of Missions. Kanoa and his wife were

Kanoa and his wife. then on a visit to Hawaii, his native isle,
for the benefit of his health; and he visited
all the churches on the island, the people coming
together everywhere to hear what he had to say concerning the mission in Micronesia. He had a horse
for his wife and infant child, but travelled on foot
himself. The author met him at Kilauea, the great
volcano, while on this missionary tour, and there
baptized his child. Kanoa received ordination before
returning to Micronesia.

At Ponape the number of church members, in 1865,
was one hundred and seventy-nine. Mr. Sturges

Church at Ponape. had been joined by Mr. Doane, and believed
that at least half of the people of Ponape
were in sympathy with them. The report of next

year was very cheering. "High chiefs, with their entire people, are taking their places with the missionary party, which now seems to be the party of the island. Our Christians are no longer trembling and crouching, and the heathen party no longer bully and swagger."

Mr. and Mrs. Sturges and Mrs. Doane were obliged by illness, in 1869, to retire from the island for a season, leaving Mr. Doane alone, with not a white person to whom he could look for companionship and counsel. Though much tried by the drinking propensities and other bad habits of the king, yet early in the following year, he was rejoicing over several chief men and their wives, in one of the districts, asking admission to the church.

Kanoa, on his return to Micronesia, was first stationed at Apaiang. In 1866, we find him once more at Kusaie, his first field, where he was cordially welcomed. In 1867, being no longer needed there, he returned to the Gilbert group, and was stationed on the island of Butaritari. In March, 1869, Mr. Mahoe, who had been left in charge of Apaiang in Mr. Bingham's absence, was severely wounded _{Calamity at} by one of a rebel party of natives, who _{Apaiang.} sought his life. The rebellion seems to have arisen, in part at least, from an attempt of the king (of whose Christian character the missionaries had good hope) to enforce a code of laws against murder, theft, adultery, and other crimes. The mission houses were destroyed, and the cocoa-nut trees around them cut down. Yet the mission seems to have gained a hold on the islands of Tarawa, Butaritari, Makin, Tapitauea, and the adverse occurrences at Apaiang may yet turn out for the furtherance of the gospel.

The whole number of hopeful converts received
Number of converts, 1870. into the churches of the Micronesia mission,
is 667; namely, 250 on Ponape, 226 on
Kusaie, 140 on the Marshall Islands, and 51 on the
Gilbert Islands. The printing amounted to
Printing. 2,408,218 pages; namely, for Ponape, 381,-
600 pages; for Kusaie, 223,200; for the Marshall
Isles, 381,726; and for the Gilbert Isles, 1,050,192.

The singular origin of the mission to the Marque-
Mission to the Mar-quesas Isl-ands. sas Islands, and its establishment in 1853,
have been described.[1] It was deemed essen-
tial to the success of the enterprise, that
the Hawaiian Board, along with their annual supplies, should for a time send also a delegation. The
delegates have generally been an American missionary and a lay member of some one of the Hawaiian
churches.

The mission, in 1857, had four stations and five
State of the mission. schools, and Isaia Kaiwi received ordination during the visitation of that year.
Owing to a necessary and unexpected delay in the
visit, there had been some suffering, and clothes,
plates, knives, and forks had gone to pay for food.
Yet the brethren were all resolved on continuing
their mission; and, not fearing the natives, and
being needed in many places, they resolved each one
to occupy a separate station. In 1863, the six missionaries were all Hawaiians. Five years later, forty-
seven persons were admitted to the church in the
space of twelve months. Three of the original missionaries sent out in 1852, are there still, and have
shown great energy and perseverance, as well as

[1] See Chapter XXIX.

good judgment, in their labors among the fiercest tribes of Polynesia.

The reacting influence of the Marquesan and Micronesian missions upon the Hawaiian churches has been highly salutary. The announcement of letters received, or of the return of a missionary brother from either field, is sure to make a sensation in a native audience; and rarely is a prayer offered by an Hawaiian, without at least one petition for his brethren, who have gone to carry the gospel to other islands.

Reacting influence from these missions.

21

CHAPTER XXXVI.

1870.

THERE can be no reasonable doubt, that the American Board was right in beginning as early as 1848 to bring its mission at the Sandwich Islands to a close; though the untried process, in every stage for the next fifteen years, was full of perplexity. Never did the Prudential Committee find it possible to see far ahead. Only from step to step did it please God to make the way plain. Nevertheless the belief was ever confidently entertained, that the leadings of his good providence were followed.

This belief was confirmed in the year 1863, when the missions no longer saw cause for delaying to place the native churches on an independent footing, with a native pastor as soon as possible for each church, whom the people would be expected to support. Nor can we too much admire the courage which then freely opened the doors of the annual business meetings of the mission to native pastors and delegates; substituting the native language for the English, and giving an equal vote to all, whether natives or foreigners, though with the certainty of being numerically outvoted by the native-born members at an early day. There are

The closing process commenced at the right time.

The satisfactory result.

now fifty-eight churches on the Islands, with a membership of fourteen thousand eight hundred and fifty. There are thirty-nine native ordained ministers,[1] all but three of whom sustain the pastoral relation, and five native licentiates with the care of churches. Besides these, nine ordained native ministers and seven licentiates are employed in the foreign missions on Micronesia and the Marquesas Islands. The whole number of ordained native ministers, therefore, in the home and foreign service, is forty-eight, and of licentiates twelve; making a total of sixty. The cost of this native ministry, wherever laboring, is defrayed wholly by the Hawaiian people. This native ministry, as a whole, is gaining in the estimation of their flocks, and of the missionaries. Discipline is faithfully administered in most of the churches; the interests of education are cared for, and there is an increasing sense of responsibility for the advancement of Christ's cause. The amount contributed by the native churches for Christian objects, in the year ending May, 1870, was thirty-one thousand and seventy dollars in gold, which would average a little more

[1] DISTRIBUTED AS FOLLOWS.

	Pastors of Foreign Origin.	Native Ordained Pastors.	Native Licentiates.	Vacant Churches.	Total.
Hawaii	5	17	1	–	23
Maui and Dependencies	1	10	3	3	17
Oahu	2	8	–	3	13
Kauai	–	4	1	–	5
Total	8	39	5	6	58

than two dollars for each church member on the Islands.[1]

The entire pastorate on the island of Oahu is now *The pastorate chiefly na-tive.* in the hands of native-born inhabitants, two of them being sons of missionaries. One of these missionary sons has a partial support from abroad, but the other, and all the Hawaiian pastors, are sustained by their respective churches. The pastorate on the island of Kauai is wholly in native hands; also on Maui, Kauai, and Molokai, with the exception of the college church at Lahaina luna. Three American missionaries remain pastors of churches on Hawaii; but their work is passing more and more into the hands of natives, of whom there are seventeen already ordained on that island. From the time of Mr. Thurston's retirement, North Kona, as well as South, were under the supervision of Mr. Paris, and the seven church organizations — all of them with ordained native pastors, with almost twice that number of neat substantial churches built by native enterprise wisely stimulated and directed, — happily exemplify the missionary's true policy of devolving all possible responsibility and labor upon the people and the native ministry.

The supply of native ministers promises at present to meet the demand. Mr. Coan has been educating them for the churches in his district. The Theological School at Wailuku, under Mr. Alexander, is a successful enterprise. Sixty-two have been

---

[1] Some readers will be interested in knowing, that the average contributions of each member in nine of the churches under native pastors, for the year under consideration, was four dollars and ten cents. Of twenty-five of the churches under native pastors, it was two dollars and forty-seven cents; and the average contribution of each member, in six churches under pastors of foreign origin, was two dollars and eighty-three cents.

members of the school since its commencement in 1863, and half of these have entered the ministry, and twelve are yet prosecuting their studies. The students have derived their support chiefly from the hospitality of the people around the institution, and from their own industry.

The success of the native ministry on the Islands is a point of inestimable importance. Dr. Success of the native ministry. Wetmore, an intelligent medical missionary residing at Hilo, after attending the annual meeting of the Evangelical Association at Honolulu, wrote as follows in 1867 : —

" Our native ministers and delegates are, as a body, a very respectable class of men. We are not ashamed of them, and we ought not to be. They stand up nobly on every question of importance, and discuss and vote as intelligently (I was about to say) as the majority of the missionary fathers; and I think such an assertion would not be untruthful. Four years ago, there was considerable trepidation in regard to allowing them to have an equal part and lot in the ministerial work, but now such fears have vanished, and the hand of fellowship is extended heartily. We rejoice greatly over it; as Paul said, we ' thank God and take courage.' "

" Sabbath-schools," he adds, " both here and throughout the group, or at least in the Prevalence of Sabbath-schools. most important localities, are receiving increased and increasing attention ; the children are being gathered into them in greater and more constant numbers. Instead of a missionary here and there engaged in teaching a large school, with almost proverbial inattention, we find a score or more of apparently devoted teachers engaged in impart-

ing instruction, and thus staying up the hands of
the pastor and greatly encouraging him in his work.
The Sabbath-school celebration here (in Honolulu)
on Saturday of last week, was a soul-cheering scene.
How I wish you could have witnessed the long procession of seven hundred children, marching with
their banners, and flags, and music. Their beaming
faces told how much they enjoyed the various exercises of the day; the speeches were very interesting, and were listened to with close attention; and
when the last address had been pronounced, the last
hymn or song sung, and the benediction received,
the hungry, thirsty ones dispersed quietly, to occupy their designated places for partaking of a
bountiful repast provided for the occasion."

The Sabbath-school Association, whose anniversary meeting is described above, had its
origin in the necessities of the times.
When the government, under "Reformed Catholic"
influence, became for a time antagonistic to evangelical interests, and this appeared in the national
schools, there was a call for increased exertions in the
religious instruction of the youth. Under the lead-
ership of children of the missionaries, scattered
through the land, with the active coöperation of
the native ministry and a large lay element in the
churches, a Sabbath-school Association was organized in 1866, which has had a very important agency
in staying the tide of infidelity and irreligion. This
Association meets annually at Honolulu, at the same
time with the Hawaiian Evangelical Association, and
consists of Protestant ministers, superintendents of
Sabbath-schools, and lay delegates from the schools.
Sixty-five schools were represented in 1869, in which

was an average attendance of five hundred and
twenty-two teachers, one thousand seven hundred
and forty-seven boys, one thousand four hundred
and eighty-four girls, and two thousand five hundred and ninety adults, making an average attendance of six thousand three hundred and forty-three.

The preceding chapters contain only a partial
statement of the supply of books for the Supply of books.
religious and moral instruction of the peo-
ple. The Hawaiian language was reduced to writing
about the year 1822. Since then not less than one
hundred and fifty different works have been prepared and printed, and the printing exceeds two
hundred and twenty millions of pages. To a very
large extent, these works have been sold to the
people. They include, besides the Old and New
Testaments, a variety of publications, — doctrinal,
practical, educational, scientific, historical; together
with a dictionary of the language, and at different
times, as many as thirteen periodicals, secular and
religious.

Twenty thousand Hawaiian Bibles and thirty thousand Hawaiian Testaments were printed in the space
of thirty years; and recently the American Bible
Society has published a beautiful electrotype edition
of the Hawaiian Scriptures, for family use; and also
an edition of the New Testament for the use of
schools. More than a hundred thousand hymn-
books have been printed in successive editions, with
constant improvements, and latterly with tunes annexed. The children have also a hymn and tune
book.

The press not being exclusively in the hands of
the evangelical community, the existing Character of the secular literature.
secular literature is gradually assimilating

to that of other Christian lands. Many of the religious works already printed by the mission are now out
of print, and deserve- republication, and there is
urgent demand for many new ones. The assistance
needed in publishing, either in the Hawaiian language, or in any of the other five languages, in which
the Islands churches are carrying on foreign missions, is chiefly indirect. The Hawaiian churches are
comparatively poor, and cannot pay the large sums
in advance, which are needful for the publication of
works, but are able to purchase the books when
published and offered to them. Hence their applications to Bible and Tract Societies. The American Tract Society has lately been requested to
publish a Bible Dictionary, a Bible Text Book, a
Commentary on the three first Gospels, and a Hymn-
book with six hundred hymns, — one edition without tunes, and another with them. The Hymn-
book is represented to be the most popular book
with the people, next to the Pocket Testament.

The education of the Islands is now sustained
The national wholly by the island community, native and
education. foreign. The government expenditure for
common schools, in the year 1869, under direction
of the Board of Education, was $38,865. Add to
this $3,929 for common school-houses, and $2,625 for
school-books, and the sum is $45,419. The addi-
tional expenditure, in the same year, for what are
called Hawaiian-English schools, in which the English language is more or less supplemented by the
Hawaiian, was $29,128; raising the grand total of
the expenditure of the government for education,
in the year 1869, to $74,547. The pupils of the
latter class were about fifteen hundred. In the

common schools, the attendance was five thousand nine hundred and thirty-eight, of whom three thousand four hundred and twenty-seven were boys, and two thousand five hundred and eleven were girls.[1]

Several schools not apparently embraced in the government report, are deserving of special notice. Miss Green's Makawao female seminary, on Maui, has twenty pupils. Instruction is given in English, and the school is nearly self-supporting, but is aided by the government, and by the Hawaiian Board. The Kawaiahao female seminary, at Honolulu, taught by the Misses Lydia and Elizabeth Bingham, was begun in April, 1867, in buildings belonging in part to the American Board. The Hawaiian Board appropriated $1,096 to fitting up the school rooms, and the Honolulu community generously gave $1,950 to purchase an additional building. The school receives its support from the community at Honolulu, and has twenty-four boarding scholars. The Makiki female seminary at Honolulu, was begun by Miss Ogden in 1859. Her pupils, ten years later, were twenty-five. Her labors on the Islands began as long ago as 1828, and her influence has been felt in hundreds of Hawaiian homes. The Koloa female seminary, on Kauai, was begun in 1862 by Miss Knapp and Mrs. J. W. Smith and her two daughters, and thirty girls have been in attendance. Mrs. Shipman, of Hilo, Mrs. Lyons, of Waimea, Mrs. L. H. Gulick, of Honolulu, and Miss Mary Paris, of Molokai, have each had small family schools; and Mrs. Coan a larger one at Hilo.

Somewhat over one hundred adult children of missionaries are now resident on the Islands; and it is due to them and to the mission fam-

Schools under private patronage.

Children of missionaries how employed.

[1] Biennial Report of the Board of Education.

ilies to state the following facts. They are all Hawaiian citizens. One of them is President of the Oahu College; one is Principal of the Lahainaluna Seminary; one is editor of two influential newspapers at Honolulu, one in English, the other in the native language; and fifteen have received ordination as ministers of the gospel, — four to labor on the Hawaiian Islands, two in Micronesia, two in China (one of them deceased), one in Japan, and six in the United States; twenty females and five males are now employed as teachers on the Islands, and more than half as many more have been thus employed in past times.

The island community, as a whole, is prosperous The national in its material interests, though such prosperity. prosperity is less with the native population than could be desired. Foreigners too largely engross the business. The annual exports have risen, in the last ten years, from $807,459 to $2,366,358; and the annual imports, from $1,223,740 to $2,040,-068. The former exceeds the latter by $326,290. The receipts of the government, during the *two* years ending March 31, 1870, were $834,112; and its expenditures $934,100. It has a funded debt of $112,900.[1]

In the opinion of Dr. L. H. Gulick, recently Corresponding Secretary of the Hawaiian Board of Mis-

---

[1] Speaking of the district of Hilo, in 1866, Mr. Coan writes thus: "Nothing is more clearly demonstrated by fact, than that Hilo has made strides in the path of temporal advancement, — in intelligence, agriculture, and commerce. Our roads, bridges, yards, gardens, fields, and dwellings, are being improved. Our market furnishes, besides sugar and molasses, coffee, arrow-root, fungus, wood, beef, hides, goat-skins, and other exports; and the amount of money in circulation, is annually increasing. Probably from five hundred to a thousand framed buildings are sprinkled over the district, many of them presenting a neat and inviting aspect. As nearly as I can ascertain, the district of Hilo has used half a million feet of lumber during the past year." — *Missionary Herald*, 1866 p. 274.

sions, who has had great opportunity of knowing
the moral condition of the Islands, the Moral condition of the
Islands.
number of virtuous men and women has
been steadily increasing from the beginning of the
missionary work. He regards the churches, taken
as a whole, as never so free from immoralities, as
they are now. He says: "The breakwater against
the terrible ocean of license which surged around
our Hawaiian Zion, has been laid deep and permanent. It has in many places so nearly reached
the surface, that female virtue is a known fact on
these sunny Isles, where, a few years ago, the name
was unknown, and the fact unheard of. Virtue that
stands these trials is virtue. Our preachers, whether
foreign or native, give no uncertain sound on questions of morality. A public sentiment is being
gradually created, by the influence of the gospel,
assisted by the teachings and example of a number
from foreign lands, in spite of terrible counter influences. There are many parents willing to make
effort, and to practice self-denial, to have their children kept from vice, and to raise them above the
vicious community around. We do not open a
school for boys or girls, but it is filled to its utmost
capacity, and many apply for admission who cannot
be received."

"But for the conserving effects of the Gospel,"
continues Dr. Gulick, "during the last half The race
preserved by
the gospel.
century, there would have been now scarce
an Hawaiian left to tell the story of the extinction
of the race, through foreign vices grafted upon
native depravity. That the race still continues to
decrease is no wonder; but that it is in existence to-
day, with many manifestations of true Christianity,
is one of the modern miracles of grace. That there

is so much vice and immorality should astonish no-
one; but that there is any virtue, any piety, any
civilization, should cause us to shout over the
triumphs of redeeming mercy." [1]

"We are laboring," Dr. Gulick adds, "not alone
The future for the Hawaiians of the present, but with
of the Isl-
ands. an eye also to the Anglo-Hawaiians of the
future; and the higher we lift the Hawaiian race,
the more influence do we exert for good on the
people who are to succeed them. The history of
this people has been a marvelous one, shedding
great glory on the missionary enterprise. The
frailties of the people, no less than their virtues,
come from their being one of the most impressible
of races, easily influenced to good, and too easily
drawn to evil. With so much amiability, and now
with so many Christian advantages, we may hope
for much from the Hawaiian nation, and the Hawaiian church."

[1] In a table compiled from the records of births and deaths, kept at the
office of the Board of Education, and derived from the quarterly reports of
the School Agents in the several districts throughout the country, it is
stated, that the births, in the years 1867, 1868, and 1869, were six thousand
and twenty-four, and the deaths nine thousand four hundred and eighty-
nine. The excess of deaths over births for three years, was three thousand
four hundred and sixty-five; showing an annual decrease of one thousand
one hundred and fifty-five. The National Board of Health, in their Report to the Legislature of 1870, published the following testimony of Dr.
Beratz, — a gentleman who had travelled for four months on the island of
Hawaii, and an independent observer, — as having a most favorable bearing
on this subject. He says: —

"The impression received from various books, before I visited the Hawaiian Islands, in regard to syphilitic diseases among the natives was
much changed when, during my stay on the island of Hawaii, I had an
opportunity to observe and form an idea of the state of things. I really
think there is not more fresh syphilis to be found among the natives of
these Islands, than among any other population of the same number in any
European or American country. During my stopping several weeks at
the principal places, where sick people of all sorts made their appearance
asking for advice and medicine, I am glad to state that the number of
patients afflicted with constitutional syphilis was only a small one,"

CHAPTER XXXVII.

THE SANDWICH ISLANDS EVANGELIZED.

1870.

A FOREIGN Missionary Society may be said to have completed its appropriate work among a *When a mis-sion is com-pleted.* heathen people, when a Christian commu- nity has resulted from its labors, that is self-govern-ing, self-sustaining, and imbued so with spiritual life as to give promise, not only of living after the Society has withdrawn from the field, but of being a leaven that may be expected ultimately to leaven the whole lump. In this view, it will not always be needful that the people of the entire national terri-tory shall have been first Christianized. Indeed, experience has shown, that native churches' must be aggressive, as well as self-sustaining, in order to their full development. They must have the benefit of what to them will be a foreign mission. The effort to carry mission churches through a long series of years, and to create a self-reliant and efficient Christian community, without the help of such an agency, must generally prove unsuccessful. Home missions will be the stronger for the foreign missions, but alone will not suffice. If there be no accessible heathen outside the national territory, then the mission should be withdrawn, if that be practicable, before that territory has all come under the power of the gospel; while there is land yet to be possessed, while something like a stern necessity exists for acting on the defensive, and pressing the war of conquest.

Some may think that, in missions like the one at the Sandwich Islands, the presence of Romish missionaries ought to keep the Protestant missionaries in the field. There is of course discretion to be used in respect to this matter, especially when Rome can command the armed support of some one of the great Catholic powers. But experience at the Islands has shown the wonderful vitality of spiritual forces even under such assaults, as well as the animating reason we have to look for providential interpositions. Besides, such is the inherent weakness of Romish missions, that they are obliged always to keep missionaries in fields they would retain for their Church. In all their great missions of past ages, these have been just as indispensable after the lapse of a century, as they were at any previous time, and the missions perished on the failure of the foreign supply. We need not wait for them to retire, as indeed we cannot, nor should we greatly dread their presence. All things considered, the mission churches at the Sandwich Islands are perhaps the better for the proximity and the assaults of their uncompromising foes. The wrath of man has been made to praise God, and the remainder he has restrained. Indeed the presence of an opposing if not a persecuting power, is almost a necessity in the early stages of missionary success. Witness Madagascar.

A more mischievous form of interference, is a rival mission from some Protestant Church, acting under the same banner, but with different doctrines, different forms of worship, and conflicting interests, — such as the late mission of Bishop Staley at the Sandwich Islands.

We cannot help believing, that missions have not been prosecuted with enough positive reference to an early termination. The mission to the Sandwich Islands has had a duration *Importance of aiming at an early close.* of half a century; and would have been protracted much longer, but for the counsels of the directing body. The error was in underestimating the spiritual vitality of the native church and pastorate, and in overestimating the importance of a prolonged discipline and training for the native ministry, in a newly formed Christian community. There was, also, too little thought of the enlightening and elevating influence that must attend the all-pervading agency of the Holy Spirit; warranting the belief, that at least in every hundred converts a man might be found with sufficient natural endowments, under Biblical instruction, to take the charge of one of the early churches gathered among a heathen people. Had the American missionaries at the Islands and their directors been prepared, from the outset, to act decidedly on this assumption, the work of the Missionary Board might have been shortened, possibly a score of years.

The relations at present sustained by the Sandwich Islands missionaries to the Board, and to the native Christian community, *Peculiar relations between the Board and the missionaries.* are somewhat peculiar. Their official connection with the Board, as missionaries, terminated in the manner and for reasons elsewhere stated, in the years immediately following 1848; but was so far renewed in 1863, that a reasonable support was guaranteed to them, while remaining on the Islands with the purpose of doing what they could for the advancement of Christ's kingdom. Their present relation to the island churches is that of missionary fathers. They are members of the Hawaiian Evangelical Association, with the right of voting, and with all the influence in that Association, and in the native community, which their characters and the remembrance of their services will command. They are Hawaiian citizens, as are their children, and have a deep personal interest in all that concerns the welfare of the nation.

The matter of support for the missionary families subsequent to the year 1863, was virtually decided by the missionaries themselves, at their general meeting in that year, in free conferences with the Foreign Secretary of the Board; and this is their account of the settlement.

Support of the missionaries.

"It is plain that the salary cannot be based on the principle of paying for services rendered. Missionary salaries have never been based on this principle. The missionary is not strictly the employé of the Board, or of the churches, but a servant of Christ engaged in doing the work of his Master. The Board only enables him to do this work to the best advantage. For this purpose a salary is granted, regulated according to the various wants and circumstances of the individual. It is obvious that, in returning to this missionary salary, the houses, lands, etc., placed at the disposal of the missionary in 1848, must be taken into account. And as one design of that arrangement was to place missionaries in a position to secure a support for

Their own account of the matter.

themselves and families at the Islands, it is reasonable that some regard should now be had to the means and advantages which this change may have placed in their possession. It is also understood, that these means and advantages, whatever they may be, may now be employed toward the support of the families in such way as will not interfere with missionary usefulness, so that we are not in fact placed on the same basis as before the change in 1848, with the same claims to a full support from the Board. These principles will aid us in coming to a just estimate of the various salaries.

"The salary now to be fixed upon, is to be regarded as a permanent arrangement, not to be revised from year to year, and not to be altered, unless some obvious reason shall make it necessary: the individual to be at liberty to receive the whole, or a part, or nothing, as his own sense of duty shall dictate. No grants are to be made for repairs of houses, or for ordinary medical aid. Applications for extraordinary medical aid should be considered as they shall occur. Aid will be granted to widows and superannuated missionaries as heretofore, according to the actual necessities of the case."

The Micronesian and Marquesan missions are the foreign missions of the Hawaiian churches. The native missionaries supported by natives. The eight Hawaiian missionaries and four assistant missionaries, with their wives, all derive their support from the Hawaiian churches, through the Hawaiian Board, and have no direct connection with the American Board. But it has been necessary that the support of the American laborers in Micronesia, and the expenses of the *Morning Star*, should be borne by the Board.

The number of ordained missionaries employed on
Whole num-
ber of the
missionaries.
the Sandwich Islands from the beginning,
is fifty-two; of lay teachers and helpers,
twenty-one; of female missionaries, chiefly married,
eighty-three; making a total of one hundred and
fifty-six. Ten of the ordained missionaries died in
the field, six of them past the age of fifty. Fourteen of the clerical missionaries returned for various
reasons to their native land, where six of them have
since died. The average duration of service per-
Average
length of
service.
formed by the ordained missionaries who
died at the Islands, was twenty-seven years.
The sixteen who are now living at the Islands have
been there from twenty-six to forty-seven years, and
their average service is thirty-seven years. These
remarkable facts speak well for the Hawaiian climate.

That so large a number of clerical missionaries is
Why so
many mis-
sionaries are
now on the
Islands.
still resident at the Islands, at what may
be regarded as the close of the mission, is
owing in part to the salubrity of the climate already noticed, and in part to the peculiar
constitution of the Hawaiian nation. Incorporating
the mission families into the civil community which
the mission had been mainly instrumental in forming, was part of the process, for reasons almost peculiar to those Islands, in closing the work of the
mission; and the lay members are now all in the
discharge of duties as citizens, as also are many
children of the mission. Most of the missionaries
Their claim
for support.
being far advanced in years, some of them
beyond the period for active service, they
generally feel, that they have a claim for such grants
in aid from the Board, as in addition to their private
means will make them comfortable; and this aid

can be rendered far more economically at the Islands, than it could be in the United States. Their residence, too, among the churches they have planted, now that those churches form an independent religious community, may perhaps be necessary to the ultimate success of those churches, and cannot fail to be useful. It seems at least to be obviously a part of the Divine plan, and the future historian will doubtless have pleasure in tracing its results. The Sandwich Islands lie on one of the great pathways of the world's commerce, and modern civilization is flowing in upon them quite fast enough for the religious interests of the nation, and for the temporal welfare of the native population. The presence of the religious fathers of the nation, for a few more years, as counselors and aids, will be among the best safeguards of the national welfare.

The missionaries and their directors have always favored the independence of the Islands. The present king, misled at one time by the representations of unfriendly persons, publicly expressed an opinion, that the missionaries were in favor of annexing the Islands to the United States. But this was wholly a misapprehension. If the Islands were thus annexed, an emigration would flow there from the United States, which, while it might enrich a few large native landholders high in rank, would at once impoverish the mass of the native people, and lead to their speedy extinction. The existence of the Hawaiian nation is inseparably connected with the religion to which it owes all its prosperity. Nor are the Protestant religious institutions now existing there for the native inhabitants alone; and these institutions will doubtless remain, and give character to the long future, whatever form the civil government shall assume. But the native element must rapidly disappear with the loss of independence; and the prospect of such an event is exceedingly painful to an observer from the missionary stand-point.

The cost of the Sandwich Islands mission, up to the year 1869, was one million two hundred and twenty thousand dollars; and that of the Micronesian mission, one hundred and fifty thousand dollars. Should we compare this cost of an enterprise extending through half a century, with that of railroads, steamships, iron-clad vessels, naval expeditions, or a single active week in our late civil war, the sum total would not appear large. The actual value of the results of this expenditure indeed is inestimable. It is vain for an objector to state the good this money might have done, if expended in some other quarters, or for other purposes. It could not have been obtained for other purposes. Its contribution was the result of the interest awakened by this very mission. And the mission, by its reacting influence on the sympathies and faith of the Christian community, has far more than supported itself. The Isles of the Pacific have been a productive working capital, both in this country and Great Britain, by reason of the early and great success of missions among them at the outset of the mighty enterprise for the world's conversion. They were missions to the more accessible and plastic portions of the heathen world, — pioneer, and in some sense tentative, missions; and we may well doubt whether, without them, missions would have been soon prosecuted on a large scale among the less accessible people of India and China, whatever may be the popular estimate as to the relative importance of those countries. The providential call to the churches has been most distinctly heard from the Pacific isles, from the wilds of Southern Africa, from the Karens of Burmah, from the Pariahs of India, and recently from the island of Madagascar.

The value of the work of God's grace at the Islands through the gospel of his Son, as set forth in the pages of this volume, is beyond the reach of human calculation. The salvation of a single soul is declared by the Divine Saviour to be worth more than the world; and the gathering of hopeful converts into the churches of those Islands, for the space of fifty years, has averaged more than a thousand a year; and among these converts have been some of the highest and best exhibitions of true piety.

Nor will it be any the less true, that the Hawaiian nation has been evangelized, and that the foreign mission work has therefore been completed, should the nation cease to exist at no distant day. Missions a conserving power for the Islands. The transfer of the arable lands on the Islands into the hands of foreigners, carried much farther, would insure this result. To God's blessing on the Christian mission is it mainly owing, that such a result has not been reached already, and the conserving power of the future will mainly exist in the evangelical churches and the schools. Recent events encourage the hope, that the king and his ministers will see, that the national life depends on the same causes which originally gave it vitality and force. Yet it may ultimately appear, that the national constitution was so fatally impaired by vices before the arrival of the mission, that not even Christianity will prevent the continually recurring fact, that the number of deaths exceeds the number of births.

The nation may, and probably will, fade away. An imperish- able truth. But the facts will remain concerning the success of the gospel. It will be forever true, that the Sandwich Islands were Christianized by evangelical missionaries from the United States; and that, as a consequence of this, the people were recognized, by the leading powers of Christendom, as entitled to the rank and privileges of a Christianized and civilized nation. There is inestimable worth in such a work, with such results. It is not for the present time only, but for all time. Nor will it stand alone. But taking its place beside other missionary efforts in the north and west Pacific, resulting in like wondrous triumphs of the gospel, it will still rank as among the most successful, when all the myriad isles of that ocean shall be won over, as they will be at no distant day, to the kingdom of our blessed Lord.

"Already," says Dr. Mullens, " in more than three hundred islands of eastern and southern Polynesia, the gospel has swept heathenism entirely away. The missionaries of the four great Societies have gathered four hundred thousand people under Christian influences, of whom a quarter of a million are living still, and fifty thousand of these are communicants."

CHAPTER XXXVIII.

THE JUBILEE.

1870.

IT was fitting, at the close of the half century from the landing of the mission on the Sandwich Islands, that there should be a formal recognition of God's signal blessing on the enterprise. A Jubilee celebration was accordingly planned by the Hawaiian Board for some time in the month of June, 1870, the usual time for the annual meeting of the mission; and the Prudential Committee of the American Board, and the English missions in the South Pacific, were invited to be present by their representatives. The difficulty of access for the South Sea missionaries was such as to prevent their coming; and the Prudential Committee did not see their way clear to promise a representative. But in the spring of 1870, the health of Dr. N. G. Clark, Foreign Secretary of the Board, becoming somewhat impaired, a brief visit to the Islands was deemed expedient for him; and he arrived at Honolulu on the 19th of May, in season for the Jubilee. Uniting his efforts with those of brethren on the ground, efficient committees were appointed, composed partly of native gentlemen, to make the needful arrangements. The aim was to secure for the Jubilee a national recognition; and the king kindly consented to make the 15th of June a national holiday, and to be present at the public celebration. He also directed a ,national salute to be fired on that day in honor of the occasion, and made liberal contributions for a grand collation.

On Sabbath morning, June 12th, the two native
Jubilee ser- congregations in Honolulu united, in the
mons. Kawaiahao or great Stone Church, to hear the Rev. Mr. Kuaea, the distinguished native pastor, preach the Jubilee sermon.[1] It was of course in the Hawaiian language. Every seat in the church was occupied, and benches were brought in till all available space was filled. As many as twenty-five hundred persons were seated.

At half past ten, the officiating clergymen, seven in number, entered the pulpit; when there was a voluntary skillfully played, by Mrs. Governor Dominis, on the powerful organ belonging to the church. After a short prayer by the Rev. B. W. Parker, a hymn in the native language, composed for the occasion, was sung by a choir of fifty Hawaiian singers.

Mr. Kuaea's text was Lev. xxv. 11: "A Jubilee shall the fiftieth year be to you." The discourse was not less noticeable for its orderly arrangement, than for its matter, and occupied an hour in the delivery, during which the preacher is said not to have referred to note or memorandum of any kind. In the course of his sermon, he called attention to the wonderful change that had been brought about in the short space of half a century. The Ha-

[1] My account of this celebration is substantially what I find in *The Pacific Commercial Advertiser* of June 18th, *The Friend* of the same date, both published at Honolulu; and a communication from Honolulu to the *Boston Daily Journal.*

waiians, he said, were a law-abiding, Sabbath-keeping people; and so general was education among them, that it was extremely rare to find a man or woman who could not both read and write. On the evening of the same day, the Fort Street Church was filled with a large foreign audience, to hear a Jubilee discourse by the Rev. Dr. Damon, from the same text; in which he reviewed the first fifty years, and recalled many remarkable incidents illustrating God's providential care of the mission.

That church was again filled on Monday and Tuesday evenings, to hear the reminis-cences of Mrs. Thurston and Mrs. Whitney, the surviving members of the first company of missionaries, and of the Rev. Mr. Bishop, of the first reinforcement, then the oldest male missionary on the ground.

Reminiscences of old missionaries.

Wednesday was the Jubilee, and a day long to be remembered on these Islands. The people attended in great numbers, and the day was as pleasant as could have been desired. The Kawaiahao was tastefully decorated by the hands of ladies. A procession was formed at ten o'clock. Two companies of infantry and one of cavalry, all native soldiers, did honor to the occasion. The legislature had adjourned, and the members were in attendance, with the older missionaries, in carriages. The younger ministers, the native preachers and delegates, the faculty of Oahu College, the alumni of Lahainaluna Seminary, and the Mission Children's Society, added numbers and dignity to the display. But the most interesting feature of the procession was the array of children from the Sab-

The procession.

bath-schools of the two native and two foreign churches of the city, eight hundred in number, all in neat holiday attire, and each school with its beautiful banner. The place of martial music was well supplied by hymns, ringing out in a multitude of harmonious youthful voices.

The children occupied the spacious galleries of the church, and the body of the house was filled to repletion by adults. The king then entered the church with Emma, queen dowager, attended by his ministers. He was received by the audience standing, the choir singing a version of "God save the King" in the Hawaiian language. The scene was impressive. On the front of the gallery was the inscription in evergreen, "1820 — JUBILEE — 1870;" and beneath, the national motto, "Ua mau ka ea o ka aina i ka pono," "The Life of the Land is preserved by Righteousness." The king sat at the right of the pulpit, and behind him were the members of his cabinet, and the diplomatic representatives of foreign nations. On the left were the missionaries; and a great mass of natives, numbering perhaps three thousand, crowded the edifice; and there was believed to be a greater number outside.

After prayer in Hawaiian, by Dr. Lowell Smith, and singing by the choir, Dr. Clark, speaking in behalf of the American Board, made the following address; which the Rev. H. H. Parker, pastor of the native church, translated sentence by sentence into the native tongue: —

"It seems to have been left to these Islands to present to the world one of the most remarkable illustrations of the developing

power of Christianity. The procession that has just
moved through your streets — that peaceful army
with banners — and this great assembly, are wit-
nesses to its triumphs. For the hour, local differ-
ences are forgotten; the places of business, the sen-
ate-chamber, and the court-room are deserted; rich
and poor, the high-born and the lowly, meet on the
higher level of a common humanity. We offer our
prayer of thanksgiving; we raise our song of jubilee; royal munificence and private bounty unite to
spread the feast on the nation's holiday.

"This honor we pay to the gospel of Christ, and
to the noble souls who here planted and nurtured
the seeds of a Christian civilization. This is our
recognition of the worth of the sainted dead, and of
the honored living who still wait to put their robes
of glory on.

"The world's method of promoting the social and
moral elevation of men is by commerce and civilization. We like the gospel better, and the culture
that follows in its train. What did all the commerce
and civilization of the world do for Africa before the
introduction of Christianity? Let the midnight glare
of blazing villages and the horrors of the slave-trade
answer. What did they do for China? Witness the
devastations of war and the opium traffic forced upon
an unwilling people. What for the Islands of the
Pacific, but to multiply the causes of disease and
death? What household was made happier, what
home purer, what man or woman raised to a nobler
life?

"But the changes wrought in these Islands during the last fifty years by the introduction of Christianity — who shall measure them? Where else have

changes so great and so beneficent been witnessed in
so short a period? A heathen nation has become
Christian ; the Bible, a Christian literature, schools,
and churches, are open and free to all ; law and order have taken the place of individual caprice; an
independent government shares in the respect and
courtesies of the civilized world ; a poor wretched
barter with a few passing ships, has been changed
for a commerce that is reckoned by millions of dollars: but more than all, and better than all, the
seeds of Christian culture, ripened on this soil, have
been borne by the winds and found lodgment in
lands thousands of miles away — in the Marquesas
and in Micronesia.

" And why these beautiful residences that line the
streets of the capital, and stretch away up the valleys and down the coast? Why these houses of taste
and culture, these gardens teeming with all the richness of a tropical clime, and enriched with the spoils
of many lands? Why has this barren waste of a few
years ago, where was neither tree, shrub, nor flower
to relieve the eye, been changed as into the garden
of the Lord, and made a fitting symbol of the moral
changes that have passed over the Islands? Why
these openings to enterprise and this delightful social life that attracts so many from other lands, but
that Christianity has come with its better thought
and nobler purpose, sending its quickening energies
through every form of human activity, and demonstrating to this age of materialism, to this nineteenth
century, that the highest progress of a nation comes
not from commerce and civilization alone, but when
a new life current has been poured through its heart
and quickened its brain?

" Other men have labored and we are entered into
their labors. We are here to-day, we have come up
to this Jubilee, because of the sacrifices, the patient
toil and the heroic faith of Bingham, one of whose
many monuments is this church edifice in which we
are convened; of Thurston, whose name has gained
new lustre these last few days; of Whitney, whose
ardent zeal is lovingly remembered on Kauai, and because of their successors and compeers; — Andrews,
the lexicographer of the Hawaiian tongue; Coan,
who has been permitted to fill out the largest church
roll allotted to any man in his generation; Alexan
der, the teacher of an able and efficient ministry;
Lyons, the sweet singer of this Israel; and Richards
and Judd and Armstrong, who in troublous times
rendered invaluable aid to the government in the organization and maintenance of civil institutions;
and many other equally devoted followers of Christ,
whose praise is in all the churches.

" We forget not to-day the generous support and
the hearty coöperation in every good work of the
noble men and women, of whom the Hawaiian people
may well be proud; Kalanimoku, whose native courtesy was only equaled by his Christian fidelity; blind
Bartimeus, who saw much and loved much, sitting
at the feet of Jesus; Keopuolani, the daughter, wife,
and mother of kings; Elizabeth Kaahumanu, who
seemed to combine in one character, her imperial
namesake of England and the Saint of Hungary;
Kapiolani, who could alike illustrate the beauty of
the gospel in a well ordered household, and its bold-
ness in braving the wrath of Pele. But time would
fail me to name or number those of high and low
degree whose example, faith, and prayer, sustained

aud cheered the mission circle, and contributed so largely to the success of their labors.

" Nor, as a representative of the American Board, can I forget the fathers and mothers, who gave of their sons and daughters to come to this then far-off land, nor the thousands and tens of thousands, who gave of their wealth and of their poverty, and when they had nothing else to give, gave of their prayers for the welfare of a people, of whom they asked and expected no return.

" What may be the future of this nation, what its place in the future history of the church or the world, we presume not to foretell. He who reads the signs of the times need be at no loss in judging of its importance. For us, the past at least is secure. The story of the gospel on these Islands has gone forth to all lands, and stirred the hearts and quickened the hopes of the Christian world.

"In view of these delightful memories, and the grand result achieved through the blessing of God upon the labors of his servants, shall we not pledge ourselves to maintain and round out into full-orbed completeness the work of the fathers? Shall we not, with larger faith and surer hope, consecrate ourselves to the evangelization of the world?

" Here we fight the battle, and there we wear the crown ; here the faith, the toil, the struggle, there the endless Jubilee."

The choir now sang, in Hawaiian, the hymn commencing

' No mortal eye that land hath seen,
    Beyond, beyond the river."

after which addresses were delivered by Hon. C.
Other ad-   C. Harris, Minister of Foreign Affairs, the
dresses.   Hon. H. A. Pierce, American Minister Res-

ident, the Rev. Artemas Bishop, the oldest of the resident missionaries, the Hon. D. Kalakaua, of the House of Nobles, the Hon. Mr. Aholo, of the Legislative Assembly, and the Rev. Mr. Kauwealoha, who had spent the last seventeen years as a missionary at the Marquesas Islands.

The speeches would occupy more space than can be afforded; but the following extracts from the first two have a historical value, which the reader will at once perceive. Referring to the overthrow of the idolatrous system, Mr. Harris said : —

"At that critical period, a small band of devoted men and women made their appearance here, and by their teaching and example established that Christian church, the foundation of which you this day celebrate with such good reason. You must rejoice in the advent of those, who have truly been to you the Apostles of the Gospel of our Great Master. The teachings of these men and women, and the civilization which they so timely introduced, when the Pacific Ocean was comparatively unknown to the nations, have been the principal cause why you enjoy, to-day, an independent government, and representative institutions. But for them, you might have been, aye, you would have been, in the position of the New Zealand Maories." *Testimony of the Minister for Foreign Affairs.*

To the same purport are the statements of Mr. Pierce, and they will be read with pleasure.

"Forty-five years' knowledge of this Archipelago, enables me to draw a truthful contrast between their former state and present condition. In 1825, Hawaiians were ignorant and debased, though amiable and hospitable, possessing greater intelligence than other Polynesian *Testimony of the American Minister Resident.*

races. In 1870, we see them advanced to a high degree of Christian knowledge, general education, civilization, and material prosperity. The happy result is due, for the most part, under God, to the labors of the American missionaries. On an occasion like this I am permitted to bear personal testimony to their Christian virtues, zeal, devotion, industry, ability, and faithfulness, as illustrated by fifty years of missionary labor, and I am firmly of opinion, that, without their teachings and assistance, this nation would have long since ceased to exist. Hawaiians of this and coming generations may therefore be grateful to God for missionary instruction, and for the great benefits derived therefrom."

Mr. Bishop and the three native gentlemen spoke in the Hawaiian language. Singing was interspersed. On two occasions, the choir and Sunday-school children united in appropriate hymns, and with fine effect. Before the last of the speeches, the choir sang the hymn, " My country 'tis of thee," in Hawaiian, which awakened much enthusiasm in the assembly. At the close, a " Jubilee Hymn for 1870 " was sung, composed by Mr. Lyons in the same language.

After the benediction, the assembly retired to the adjoining well-shaded grounds, where a *The colla-tion.* collation was spread for six or seven thousand people, such as had never before been seen on those Islands. His Majesty the King, and Queen Emma, honored the feast by their presence for a brief space. The king had previously contributed two thousand pounds of poi, with meat and fish, and afterwards he gave a hundred dollars towards expenses. The committee of arrangements had provided bread and fruit, an ample supply of lemonade, and other necessaries; to which the ladies of the city had added various delicacies both for food and decoration.

On Thursday evening there was a reunion at the residence of Mr. Whitney, editor of the "Commercial Advertiser," comprising the American missionaries and their descendants, with the Hawaiian pastors and delegates and their wives from the various islands. The company numbered two hundred and twenty-five. A large tent had been erected on the premises, and tables were spread with ample provision. Natives of Hawaii, America, England, Tahiti, and the Marquesas Islands, mingled in social enjoyment, and the addresses showed a warm and truly Christian spirit uniting them all.

A reunion.

23

CONCLUSION.

THE Jubilee was a fitting testimonial and proof of the triumphs of the gospel in the Hawaiian nation, as a consequence of the divine blessing on the labors of Protestant missionaries from the United States of America. The king, his ministers, the representatives of foreign powers, the Hawaiian legislature in both its branches, the mission, the parent Board, and the Hawaiian people, may all be said to have united in it. The mission itself did not need the celebration, but its history would otherwise have been in a measure incomplete. For eight previous years, a nominally Protestant mission had sought to supplant the work of the American missionaries, had succeeded in alienating the government in some measure from its best friends and benefactors, and had even led many Christian people in England and America to regard the efforts already made as a failure, and to believe that a new mission was needed to evangelize the Islands.

The retiring of the leader of that mission from the Islands, just before the celebration, in circumstances of entire discomfiture, and the occurrence and developments of the Jubilee, were noted providential coincidences. The memorable event of the day, however, was the concurrent testimony, from unquestionable sources, as to the triumphs of the gospel of the grace of God on those Islands. The mission was permitted, in its fiftieth year, to stand forth acknowledged on all hands as a successful Christian enterprise, and as the grand conservator of the nation.

The Sandwich Islands Mission may, therefore, properly connect its close, in its distinctive missionary form, with the NATIONAL JUBILEE of the year 1870, fifty years from the date of its commencement.

" THE LORD REIGNETH, LET THE EARTH REJOICE, LET THE MULTITUDE OF ISLES BE GLAD THEREOF." Ps. xcvii. 1.

THE MISSIONARIES.

THE Rev. JOHN A. VINTON, of Boston, who is distinguished for accuracy, made out, not long since, for the use of the Prudential Committee, an outline statement of the leading facts, so far as attainable, of all the Missionaries, Missionary Physicians, and Assistant Missionaries, who are or have been connected with the missions under the care of the American Board. Their number is about fourteen hundred, and the memoranda would make a volume of respectable size.

What follows, is an abridgment of Mr. Vinton's memoranda of the Missionaries, Missionary Physicians, and Assistant Missionaries, who have been employed in the Hawaiian and Micronesian Islands. Personal friends will see deficiencies; but the wonder is, that materials for so complete a statement were to be found in the archives of the Board.

ORDAINED MISSIONARIES.

HIRAM BINGHAM, born at Bennington, Vt., Oct. 30, 1789; professed religion there, May, 1811; graduated at Middlebury College, 1816, and Andover Theological Seminary, 1819; ordained at Goshen, Ct., Sept. 29, 1819; embarked in the brig *Thaddeus*, Capt. Blanchard, at Boston, Oct. 23, 1819; landed at Honolulu, on Oahu, April 19, 1820; returned to the U. States, Feb. 4, 1841; died at New

Haven, Ct., Nov. 11, 1869, aged 80. See biographical sketch in this volume.

Mrs. BINGHAM (Sybil Moseley), born at Westfield, Mass., Sept. 14, 1792; married at Hartford, Ct., Oct. 11, 1819; emb. with her husband; returned with him Feb. 4, 1841; died at Easthampton, Mass., Feb. 27, 1848, aged 55. — HIRAM BINGHAM, a son, is a missionary in the Gilbert Islands.

ASA THURSTON, born in Fitchburg, Mass., Oct. 12, 1787; prof. rel. 1810; graduated at Yale Coll., 1816; Andover Theol. Sem., 1819; ordained at Goshen, Ct., Sept. 29, 1819; embarked at Boston, in the brig *Thaddeus*, Oct. 23, 1819; landed at Kailua, Hawaii, April 12, 1820; died at Honolulu, March 11, 1868, aged 80. See biographical sketch.

Mrs. THURSTON (Lucy Goodale), born at Marlborough, Mass., Oct. 29, 1795; prof. rel. 1816; married Oct. 12, 1819; embarked Oct. 23, 1819; visited U. States, Feb. 4, 1841; reëmbarked at New York, March 10, 1842; again visited the U. States in 1851; reëmb. at Boston, Nov. 18, 1851; still living at Honolulu. — THOMAS G. THURSTON, a son, is a minister of the gospel in California.

SAMUEL WHITNEY, born at Branford, Ct., April 28, 1793; prof. rel. at Northford, Ct., May, 1814; two years in Yale Coll.; emb. in brig *Thaddeus*, Oct. 23, 1819; at Waimea, on Kauai, July 25, 1820; ordained at Kailua, Nov. 30, 1825; removed to Lahaina, on Maui, in 1827; ret. to Waimea in 1829; died at Lahainaluna, Dec. 15, 1845. See biographical sketch.

Mrs. WHITNEY (Mercy Partridge), born at Pittsfield, Mass., Aug. 14, 1795; prof. rel. 1816; mar. Oct. 4, 1819; emb. Oct. 23, 1819; visited the U. States, 1860; returned to the Islands, and is still living there. — SAMUEL WHITNEY, a son, is a minister of the gospel in the United States.

ARTEMAS BISHOP, born at Pompey, N. Y., Dec. 30, 1795; prof. rel. 1813; Union Coll., 1819; Princeton Theol. Sem., 1822; ord. at New Haven, Ct., Sept. 12, 1822; emb. in ship *Thames*, at New Haven, Nov. 19, 1822; at Kailua, March 11, 1824; removed to Ewa, on Oahu, in 1837; there till 1863, when increasing infirmities led to his removal to Honolulu, where he still resides.

Mrs. BISHOP (Elizabeth Edwards), from Boston, Mass.; born in Marlborough, Mass., June, 1796; mar. Nov., 1822; emb. Nov. 19, 1822; died at Kailua, Feb. 21, 1828. — SERENO E. BISHOP, a son, is Principal of the Lahainaluna Seminary.

Mrs. BISHOP (Delia Stone), from Rochester, N. Y.; born in Bloomfield, N. Y., May 26, 1800; emb. in ship *Parthian*, at Boston, Nov. 3, 1827; labored as a teacher till her marriage at Kailua, Dec. 1, 1828; is still living at . the Islands.

WILLIAM RICHARDS, born in Plainfield, Mass., Aug. 22, 1793; prof. rel. Aug., 1811; Williams Coll., 1819; Andover Theol. Sem., 1822; ord. at New Haven, Ct., Sept. 12, 1822; emb. at New Haven, in ship *Thames*, Nov. 19, 1822; stationed at Lahaina, on Maui, May 31, 1823; visited U. States Dec. 9, 1836; called to labors in connection with the government, and was released July 3, 1838; went to England as Ambassador, 1842, and was thus employed till 1845; Minister of Public Instruction, Sept., 1846; died at Honolulu, Nov. 7, 1847. See biographical sketch.

Mrs. RICHARDS (Clarissa Lyman), born in Northampton, Mass., Jan. 10, 1794; prof. rel. June, 1816; mar. Oct. 30, 1822; emb. Nov. 19, 1822; released July 3, 1838; after her husband's death, returned to this country, and died at New Haven.

CHARLES SAMUEL STEWART, born at Flemington, N. J., Oct. 16, 1798; Princeton Coll., 1815; Theol. Sem., Princeton, 1821 ; emb. at New Haven, Nov. 19, 1822 ; stat. at Lahaina, May 31, 1823. The illness of his wife compelled his return to this country, Oct. 15, 1825 ; rel. Aug. 12, 1830 ; still living.

Mrs. STEWART (Harriet B. Tiffany), from Cooperstown, N. Y.; born at Stamford, Ct., June 24, 1798 ; emb. Nov. 19, 1822 ; ret. to the U. States, Oct. 15, 1825 ; died some time after.

JAMES ELY, born at Lyme, Ct., Oct. 22, 1798 ; studied at Foreign Mission School, Cornwall, Ct.; emb. in ship *Thames,* Nov. 19, 1822 ; stat. at Waimea, on Kauai; afterwards, in 1824, at Kaawalua, on Hawaii; at Honolulu, June 4, 1825 ; ret. to the U. States, Oct. 15, 1828 ; rel. March 24, 1830 ; is still living.

Mrs. ELY (Louisa Everest), born at Cornwall, Ct., Sept. 8, 1792.

JOSEPH GOODRICH, from Wethersfield, Ct.; Yale Coll., 1821 ; emb. in the ship *Thames,* Nov. 19, 1822 ; stat. at Hilo, on Hawaii, Jan. 24, 1824 ; ord. at Kailua, Sept. 29, 1826 ; at Hilo till Jan. 25, 1836 ; ret. to U. States, May 22, 1836 ; rel. Oct. 11, 1836 ; died in 1852.

Mrs. GOODRICH.

LORRIN ANDREWS, born in East Windsor, Ct., April 29, 1795 ; grad. Jefferson Coll., Pa.; Theol. Sem., Princeton, N. J., 1825 ; ord. Washington, Ky., Sept. 21, 1827 ; emb. at Boston, in ship *Parthian,* Nov. 3, 1827 ; at Lahaina, on Maui, till Sept., 1831, when the High School at Lahaina-luna was commenced; was its first Principal, and continued in this school about ten years; released in 1842, and became seamen's chaplain at Lahaina ; in 1845, removed to Honolulu, and was made a judge under the Hawaiian government ; resigned in 1855 ; during many years was Secretary to the Privy Council ; was the author of a Hawaiian grammar and a Hawaiian dictionary; died at Honolulu, Sept. 29, 1868.

Mrs. ANDREWS.

EPHRAIM WESTON CLARK, from Peacham, Vt.; born at Haverhill, N. H., April 25, 1799; prof. rel. 1816; Dart. Coll., 1824; Andover Theol. Sem., 1827; ord. at Brandon, Vt., Oct. 3, 1827; sailed in the *Parthian*, from Boston, Nov. 3, 1827; stat. at Honolulu, devoting part of his time to seamen; was associated with Mr. Andrews in High School at Lahainaluna, in 1835; continued there till May, 1843; at Wailuku, on Maui, from May, 1843, till August, 1848; then took charge of First Church in Honolulu, which assumed his support in 1850; became Sec. of the Hawaiian Missionary Society in 1850, and in 1852 went to Micronesia with the first missionaries, returning to Honolulu in November; visited U. States in 1856, but ret. soon to the Islands. After the death of his wife, again visited the U. States; arriv. May 21, 1859, and ret. before the close of the year. A third time he came in 1864, to superintend the electrotyping of the Hawaiian Scriptures by the American Bible Society; in kindred employment he still continues.

Mrs. CLARK (Mary Kittredge), born at Mount Vernon, N. H., Dec. 9, 1803; mar. Sept. 27, 1827; emb. as above; visited the U. States with her husband, May 22, 1856; died at Honolulu, Aug. 14, 1857.

Mrs. CLARK (Sarah Helen [Richards] Hall), daughter of Levi Richards, of Norwich, Vt., and relict of Rev. Thomas Hall, of Waterford, Vt.; married at St. Johnsbury, Vt., Sept. 13, 1859.

JONATHAN SMITH GREEN, from Pawlet, Vt.; born at Lebanon, Ct., Dec. 20, 1796; prof. rel. 1815; Andover Theol. Sem., 1827; ord. at Brandon, Oct. 3, 1827; sailed from Boston, in the *Parthian*, Nov. 3, 1827; in 1829, in the barque *Volunteer*, Capt. Charles Taylor, explored the northwest coast of America, with a view to a future mission, from Norfolk Sound, in lat. 57° north, to lat. 32°, about the southern limit of the present State of California; from January, 1831, to August, 1832, at Hilo; then went to Wailuku, on Maui, till 1842, when, at his own request, he was rel. from his connection with the Board; still a missionary at the Islands, in connection with the American Missionary Association, at Makawao, in East Maui.

Mrs. GREEN (Theodosia Arnold), born at East Haddam, Ct., April 3, 1792; prof. rel. 1816; mar. Sept. 20, 1827; sailed from Boston, Nov. 3, 1827; deceased. — JOSEPH P. GREEN, a son, is a minister of the gospel at the Islands.

PETER JOHNSON GULICK, born at Freehold, N. J., March 12, 1796; prof. rel. 1818; Princeton Coll., 1825; Theol. Sem., Princeton, 1827; ord. at Freehold, Oct. 3, 1827; emb. at Boston, in the *Parthian*, Nov. 3, 1827; at Waimea, on Kauai, from July, 1828, till some time in 1835; then at Koloa, till 1843; then on Molokai, till 1847; then at Waialua, on Oahu, till 1857; since which time he has resided at Honolulu.

Mrs. GULICK (Fanny Hinckley Thomas), from Westfield, Mass.; born at Lebanon, Ct., April 16, 1798; prof. rel. July, 1826; mar. Sept. 5, 1827; sailed as above, Nov. 3, 1827; still living. — LUTHER H., ORRAMEL H., JOHN T., and THOMAS L. GULICK, sons, are ministers of the gospel; the first a missionary to Micronesia, the second to Japan, the third to China, and the fourth is without charge, in the United States.

DWIGHT BALDWIN, M. D., from Durham, Greene Co., N. Y.; born in Durham, Ct., Sept. 29, 1798; Yale Coll., 1821; prof. rel. Sept., 1826; Theol. Sem., Auburn, 1829; ord. Utica, N. Y., Oct. 6, 1830; emb. in ship *New England*, at New Bedford, Dec. 28, 1830; at Waimea, on Hawaii, from 1831 to 1836; then at Lahaina, where, except a visit to the U. States in 1856 and 1857, he has remained till the present time.

Mrs. BALDWIN (Charlotte Fowler), born at Northford, Ct., 1805 ; prof. rel. 1822 ; mar. Dec. 3, 1820 ; sailed as above ; still at Lahaina.

SHELDON DIBBLE, born at Skeneateles, N. Y., Jan. 26, 1809 ; Hamilton Coll., 1827 ; Theol. Sem., Auburn, 1830 ; ord. Utica, N. Y., Oct. 6, 1830 ; sailed in ship *New England*, from New Bedford, Dec. 28, 1830 ; at Hilo till 1836 ; then connected with seminary at Lahainaluna ; visited the U. States, Nov. 24, 1837 ; reëmb. at New York, Oct. 9, 1839 ; died at Lahainaluna, Jan. 22, 1845.

Mrs. DIBBLE (Maria M. Tomlinson), born April, 1808 ; mar. in 1830 ; died Lahainaluna, Feb. 20, 1837.

Mrs. DIBBLE (Antoinette Tomlinson), from Brooklyn, N. Y. ; sailed from New York with her husband, Oct. 9, 1839 ; ret. to the U. States, April 2, 1848. See biographical sketch.

REUBEN TINKER, born in Chester, Mass., Aug. 6, 1799 ; prof. rel. Aug., 1820 ; Amherst Coll., 1827 ; Theol. Sem., Auburn, 1830 ; ord. at Chester, Nov. 3, 1830 ; emb. in ship *New England*, at New Bedford, Dec. 28, 1830. With Messrs. Whitney and Alexander, sailed from Honolulu, July 18, 1832, for the Society Islands, which they reached Aug. 23 ; then visited Washington Islands, and returned to Honolulu Nov. 17, same year. His station was Wailuku, on Maui, till 1835 ; then Honolulu, till his return to this country, and release, in 1840 ; died 1854.

Mrs. TINKER (Mary Throop Wood), from Madison, Ohio ; born at Chester, Mass., Aug. 24, 1809 ; prof. rel. April, 1830 ; mar. at Chester, Nov. 14, 1830 ; emb. with her husband, Dec. 28, 1830, and returned with him to this country.

WILLIAM PATTERSON ALEXANDER, born near Paris, Bourbon Co., Ky., July 25, 1805 ; prof. rel. Jan., 1825 ; studied at Centre Coll., Danville, Ky., but did not graduate ; Theol. Sem., Princeton, 1831 ; ord. at Cincinnati, O., Oct. 13, 1831 ; emb. in the ship *Averick*, at New Bedford, Nov. 26, 1831 ; accompanied Messrs. Whitney and Tinker to the Washington Islands in 1833 ; again at these islands, with Messrs. Armstrong and Parker, in the same year, but relinquished the project of a mission, and returned to Honolulu in the year following ; stat. at Waioli, on Kauai, Sept., 1834, where he continued till 1843 ; then became a teacher in the seminary at Lahainaluna, where he remained till 1857 ; visited the U. States in 1859 and 1860 ; since 1857, at Wailuku, on Maui.

Mrs. ALEXANDER (Mary Ann McKinney), of Harrisburg, Pa. ; born near Wilmington, Del., Jan. 5, 1810 ; prof. rel. May, 1824 ; mar. Oct. 25, 1831 ; emb. with her husband, Nov. 26, 1831 ; visited her native land, May 2, 1859 ; reëmb. New York, March 20, 1860 ; still with her husband at Wailuku. — WILLIAM DE WITT, a son, is President of the Oahu College, and JAMES McKINNEY ALEXANDER, is a minister of the gospel in California.

RICHARD ARMSTRONG, D. D., born at Turbotville, Pa., April 13, 1805 ; prof. rel. at Carlisle, Pa., Feb., 1827 ; Dickinson Coll., Sept. 27, 1827 ; Theol. Sem., Princeton, 1831 ; ord. at Baltimore, Oct. 27, 1831 ; sailed from New Bedford, Nov. 26, 1831 ; visited the Washington Islands from July 2, 1833, to May 12, 1834 ; at Wailuku, from July, 1835 ; took charge of First Church in Honolulu, in Nov., 1840 ; Minister of Pub. Inst. for Hawaiian Islands, in 1848 ; released from his connection with the Board in 1849 ; visited U. States, Aug. 31, 1857 ; returned to Islands, and died there in 1860.

Mrs. ARMSTRONG (Clarissa Chapman), from Bridgeport, Ct. ; born in Russell, Mass., May 15, 1805 ; prof. rel. at

Monson, Mass., Aug., 1830 ; mar. at Bridgeport, Ct., Sept. 25, 1831 ; emb. Nov. 26, 1831 ; still residing at the Islands.

JOHN S. EMERSON, born in Chester, N. H., Dec. 28, 1800 ; prof. rel. Aug., 1819 ; Dartmouth Coll., 1826 ; Theol. Sem., Andover, 1830 ; agent of the Board one year ; ord. at Meredith Bridge, N. H., May 19, 1831 ; sailed from New Bedford, Nov. 26, 1831 ; at Waialua, on Oahu, from 1832 to 1842 ; Aug., 1842, removed to Lahainaluna, and was there four years ; returned to Waialua in July, 1846, and was there till his death ; visited the U. States, April 26, 1860 ; reëmb. at New York, Dec. 1, 1860 ; died at Waialua, March 28, 1867. See biographical sketch.

Mrs. EMERSON (Ursula Sophia Newell), born at Nelson, N. H., Sept. 27, 1806 ; prof. rel. March, 1829 ; mar. Oct. 25, 1831 ; sailed in the *Averick*, Nov. 26, 1831 ; still at Waialua. — OLIVER EMERSON, a son, is devoted to the gospel ministry, but his field of labor not yet decided.

COCHRAN FORBES, born in Gorham, Chester Co., Pa., July 21, 1805 ; prof. rel. 1824 ; not a college graduate ; Theol. Sem., Princeton, 1831 ; ord. at Baltimore, Oct. 27, 1831 ; emb. at New Bedford, in the *Averick*, Nov. 26, 1831 ; at Kaawaloa, on Hawaii, till 1846 ; then at Lahaina ; ret. to the U. States, April 2, 1848 ; rel. Aug. 10, 1849.

Mrs. FORBES (Rebecca Duncan Smith), of Newark, N. J. ; born at Springfield, Essex Co., N. J., June 21, 1805 ; prof. rel. 1825 ; mar. at Newark, Oct. 9, 1831 ; emb. as above ; ret. to the U. States, April 2, 1848. — ANDERSON O. FORBES, a son, has charge of the Second Church in Honolulu.

HARVEY REXFORD HITCHCOCK, from Manchester, Ct. ; born at Great Barrington, Mass., March 13, 1800 ; prof. rel. 1817 ; Williams Coll., 1828 ; Theol. Sem., Auburn,

1831 ; ord. at Auburn, Sept. 20, 1831 ; emb. at New Bedford, Nov. 26, 1831 ; stat. on Molokai ; visited U. States, April 8, 1853 ; ret. March 31, 1855 ; died on Molokai, Aug. 29, 1855.

Mrs. HITCHCOCK (Rebecca Howard), born at Owasco, Cayuga Co., N. Y., Dec. 2, 1808 ; prof. rel. 1828 ; mar. Aug. 26, 1831 ; emb. with her husband, Nov. 26, 1831 ; visited the U. States, April 8, 1853 ; reëmb. Boston, Nov. 28, 1854 ; still at the Islands.

LORENZO LYONS, born at Coleraine, Franklin Co., Mass., April 18, 1807 ; prof. rel. Montrose, Pa., April, 1823 ; Union Coll., 1827 ; Theol. Sem., Auburn, 1831 ; ord. at Auburn, Sept. 20, 1831 ; emb. at New Bedford, Nov. 26, 1831 ; stat. at Waimea, on Hawaii, where he has labored ever since.

Mrs. LYONS (Betsey Curtis), born in Elbridge, Onondaga Co., N. Y., Jan. 10, 1813 ; prof. rel. Feb., 1827 ; mar. Sept. 4, 1831 ; emb. with her husband as above ; died at Honolulu, May 14, 1837.

Mrs. LYONS (Lucia G. Smith), of Truxton, N. Y. ; born at Burlington, N. Y., 1810 ; was a teacher on the Tuscarora Reservation in 1836 ; went as a teacher to the Sandwich Islands, sailing from Boston in the barque *Mary Frazier*, Dec. 14, 1836 ; married to Mr. Lyons, July 14, 1838 ; still at the Islands.

DAVID BELDEN LYMAN, born at New Hartford, Ct., July 29, 1803 ; prof. rel. 1821 ; Williams Coll., 1828 ; Andover Theol. Sem., 1831 ; ord. at Hanover, N. H., Oct. 12, 1831 ; sailed in ship *Averick*, from New Bedford, Nov. 26, 1831 ; stat. at Hilo, Hawaii, where he has labored ever since, without leaving the Islands ; has been principal of the high-school in Hilo from its establishment in 1836.

Mrs. LYMAN (Sarah Joiner), born at Royalton, Vt., Nov. 29, 1806 ; mar. Nov. 2, 1831 ; emb. as above, and still resides at Hilo.

EPHRAIM SPAULDING, born at Ludlow, Vt., Dec. 10, 1802; prof. rel. June, 1822; Middlebury Coll., 1828; Theol. Sem., Andover, 1831; ord. at New Bedford, Nov. 21, 1831; sailed in the *Averick,* from New Bedford, Nov. 26, 1831; stat. at Lahaina, but ill-health compelled him to leave the Islands, Dec. 26, 1836; reached Boston, June 28, 1837, and died at Westborough, Mass., June 28, 1840.

Mrs. SPAULDING (Julia Brooks), born at Buckland, Mass., April 7, 1810; prof. rel. Aug., 1830; mar. Nov. 11, 1831; emb. as above; ret. to the U. States, June 28, 1837, on account of failure of health; resides at Melrose, near Boston.

· BENJAMIN WYMAN PARKER, born in Reading, Mass., Oct. 13, 1803; prof. rel. at Atkinson, N. H., 1824; Amherst Coll., 1829; Theol. Sem., Andover, 1832; ord. at Reading, Sept. 13, 1832; emb. at New London, Ct., Nov. 21, 1832; accompanied Messrs. Alexander and Armstrong to the Washington Islands; since that time, has not left the Sandwich Islands, except on a visit to the Marquesas Islands in Dec., 1834; stat. at Kaneohe, on Oahu.

Mrs. PARKER (Mary Elizabeth Barker), from Guilford, Ct.; born at Branford, Ct., Dec. 9, 1805; prof. rel. at Branford, 1824; mar. at Guilford, Sept. 24, 1832; emb. as above, and is still with her husband. — HENRY H. PARKER, a son, has charge of the First Church at Honolulu.

LOWELL SMITH, D. D., born in Heath, Mass., Nov. 27, 1802; prof. rel. 1823; Williams Coll., 1829; Theol. Sem., Auburn, 1832; ord. at Heath, Sept. 26, 1832; emb. in ship *Mentor,* at New London, Nov. 21, 1832; stat. on Molokai, with Mr. Hitchcock, June, 1833; at Ewa, on Oahu, Nov., 1834; at Honolulu, July 1, 1836; in charge of Second Church in Honolulu, from its formation in 1838 till 1869; visited the U. States in 1865; reëmb. at New York, April 11, 1866; residing at Honolulu.

24

Mrs. Smith (Abba W. Tenney), from Brandon, Vt.; born at Barre, Mass., Dec. 4, 1809; prof. rel. Jan., 1828; mar. Oct. 2, 1832; emb. as above, and visited U. States as above; with her husband at Honolulu.

Titus Coan, born at Killingworth, Ct., Feb. 1, 1801; prof. rel. at Riga, N. Y., March, 1828; Theol. Sem., Auburn, 1833; ord. in Park Street Church, Boston, Aug. 4, 1833; emb. with Mr. Arms, in the schooner *Mary Jane*, at New York, Aug. 16, 1833, on a voyage of exploration to Patagonia; landed on that coast, near the Strait of Magellan, Nov. 14, 1833; finding that part of the world wholly unpromising for missionary operations, emb. on their homeward voyage, Jan. 25, 1834; reached New London, May 14, 1834. Mr. Coan sailed for the Islands, in ship *Hellespont*, Capt. Henry, from Boston, Dec. 5, 1834; his field of labor, since Aug., 1835, has been in the Hilo and Puna districts, on Hawaii, where he labored till his visit to the U. States in June, 1870.

Mrs. Coan (Fidelia Church), born in Riga, Monroe Co., N. Y., Feb. 17, 1810; prof. rel. Feb., 1829; mar. Nov. 3, 1834; emb. Dec. 5, 1834, and came to the U. States in 1870.

Isaac Bliss, from Virgil, N. Y.; born at Warren, Mass., Aug. 28, 1804; prof. rel. in Amherst College, March, 1827; Amherst Coll., 1828; Theol. Sem., Auburn, 1831; ord. at Victor, N. Y., Oct. 5, 1831; was pastor at Virgil, N. Y., a year or two; emb. in barque *Mary Frazier*, Capt. Sumner, at Boston, Dec. 14, 1836; was four years at Kohala, on Hawaii; sailed with his wife for the U. States, Dec. 2, 1841; arr. April 20, 1842; died in 1851.

Mrs. Bliss (Emily Curtis), born in Elbridge, Onondaga Co., N. Y., July 25, 1811; prof. rel. Feb., 1827; mar. Aug. 14, 1832; emb. Dec. 14, 1836; ret. to the U. States, April 20, 1842.

DANIEL TOLL CONDE, born in Charlton, Saratoga Co., N. Y., Feb. 3, 1807; prof. rel. 1827; Union Coll., 1831; Theol. Sem., Auburn, 1834; ord. at Fredonia, N. Y., Sept. 7, 1836; emb. in the *Mary Frazier*, at Boston, Dec. 14, 1836; at Hana, on Maui, till June, 1848; at Wailuku the eight following years; emb. on his ret. to the U. States after the death of his wife, and arr. March 18, 1857; released Oct. 26, 1858.

Mrs. CONDE (Andelusia Lee), born in Jericho, Vt., June 17, 1810; prof. rel. July, 1824; was a teacher of the Seneca Indians at the Cattaraugus Mission Station, N. Y., in 1835 and 1836; mar. Sept. 13, 1836, and emb. with her husband as above; died at the Islands, March 30, 1855.

MARK IVES, born at Goshen, Ct., Feb. 10, 1809; prof. rel. 1829; Union Coll., 1833; Theol. Sem., East Windsor, 1836; ord. at Sharon, Ct., Sept., 1836; emb. at Boston, Dec. 14, 1836; at Hana, on Maui, till 1840; then at Kealakekua Bay till 1845; then at Kealia, on Hawaii, till 1850; ret. to the U. States, 1851; rel. July 18, 1854.

Mrs. IVES (Mary Anna Brainerd), born at Haddam, Ct., Nov. 18, 1810; prof. rel. Jan., 1831; mar. Nov. 25, 1836; emb. as above; ret. 1851; rel. July 18, 1854.

THOMAS LAFON, M. D., born in Chesterfield Co., Va., Dec. 17, 1801; prof. rel. Sept., 1833; studied medicine at Transylvania University, Lexington, Ky.; ord. at Marion Coll., Sept., 1835; emb. at Boston, Dec. 14, 1836; at Koloa till 1841; rel. June 22, 1841; ret. to this country, and since deceased.

Mrs. LAFON (Sophia Louisa Parker), born at New Bedford, Mass., June 30, 1812; prof. rel. May, 1834; mar. at New Bedford, Nov. 14, 1836; emb. etc., as above.

EDWARD JOHNSON, born in Hollis, N. H., 1813; prof. rel. 1832; emb. in barque *Mary Frazier*, at Boston, Dec.

14, 1836 ; a teacher at Waioli, on Kauai, from 1837 to
1848 ; ord. at Honolulu, May 29, 1848 ; stat. at Waioli ;
visited U. States in 1855 ; ret. to Islands in 1856 ; died on
board the *Morning Star*, while visiting the Micronesian
Mission, Sept. 1, 1867, aged 54.

Mrs. JOHNSON (Lois S. Hoyt), from Warner, N. H. ;
born in Salisbury, N. H., 1809 ; prof. rel., Boston, 1831 ;
mar. Nov., 1836 ; emb. as above ; still at the Islands.

DANIEL DOLE, born in Bloomfield, now Skowhegan,
Me., Sept. 9, 1808 ; prof. rel. July, 1830 ; Bowdoin Coll.,
1836 ; Theol. Sem., Bangor, 1839 ; ord. at Bloomfield in
1840 ; emb. in ship *Gloucester*, from Boston, Nov. 14, 1840 ;
stat. at Punahou, on Oahu, at the head of a school for the
children of missionaries ; since 1855 at Koloa, on Kauai ;
now preaching to men of foreign birth, and has also a
school.

Mrs. DOLE (Emily H. Ballard), from Gardiner, Me. ;
born at Hallowell, Me., June 11, 1808 ; prof. rel. 1829 ;
mar. at Gardiner, Oct. 2, 1840 ; emb. as above, and died
at the Islands, April 27, 1844.

Mrs. DOLE (Charlotte [Close] Knapp, widow of Horton
O. Knapp, an assistant missionary) ; mar. to Mr. Dole,
June, 1846 ; with her husband at Koloa.

ELIAS BOND, born at Hallowell, Me., Aug. 19, 1813 ;
prof. rel. at Lowell, Mass., Jan., 1832 ; Bowdoin Coll., 1837 ;
Theol. Sem., Bangor, 1840 ; ord. at Hallowell, Sept. 30,
1840 ; sailed from Boston, Nov. 14, 1840 ; stat. at Kohala,
and been there till the present time.

Mrs. BOND (Ellen Mariner Howell), born at Portland,
Me., Dec. 29, 1817 ; prof. rel. Feb., 1836 ; mar. at Portland, Sept. 29, 1840 ; sailed as above; is still at Kohala.

JOHN D. PARIS, born in Staunton, Augusta Co., Va.,
Sept. 2, 1809 ; prof. rel. Hebron, near Staunton, 1829 ; at

Hanover College, Ind., two years; Theol. Sem., Bangor, 1839; ord. at Bangor, Aug. 29, 1839; sailed in ship *Gloucester*, from Boston, Nov. 14, 1840; destined to the Oregon mission, but the more urgent necessities of the Islands detained him there; in 1842, at Waiohinu, in the district of Kau, on Hawaii; visited the U. States in 1850; sailed on his return, Nov. 18, 1851; stat. at Kealakekua Bay, in the district of Kona, Hawaii, and there remains.

Mrs. PARIS (Mary Grant), from New York city; born at Albany, N. Y., April 27, 1807; prof. rel. in New York, 1829; mar. at New York, Oct. 25, 1840; emb. at Boston, Nov. 14, 1840; died at Hilo, Feb. 18, 1847.

Mrs. PARIS (Mary Carpenter), from New York city; mar. Sept. 8, 1851; emb. at Boston, Nov. 18, 1851; still at Kealakekua Bay.

JAMES W. SMITH, M. D., emb. at Boston, May 2, 1842; stat. in 1844 at Koloa, on Kauai, where he has resided until now; ord. to the ministry in 1857.

Mrs. SMITH (Melicent K.).

GEORGE BERKLEY ROWELL, born at Cornish, N. H.; Amherst Coll., 1837; Theol. Sem., Andover, 1841; ord. Oct. 22, 1841; emb. at Boston, May 2, 1842; stat. at Waioli, on Kauai, till 1846; then at Waimea, on the same island, till 1865, when his connection with the Board ceased.

Mrs. ROWELL (Malvina J. Chapin).

ASA BOWEN SMITH, born in Williamstown, Vt., July 16, 1809; prof. rel. July, 1831; Midd. Coll., 1834; Andover and New Haven Theol. Sem.; ord. at Williamstown, Vt., Nov. 1, 1837; went from New York overland to the Oregon Indians in 1838; reached Wallawalla, on the Columbia River, after four months; at Kamiah, on the Clearwater River, among the Nez Perces Indians, in May, 1839:

transferred to the Sandwich Islands in 1842 ; at Waialua, on Oahu, till 1846 ; ret. to U. States ; rel. Aug. 11, 1846.

Mrs. SMITH (Sarah Gilbert White), born at West rook-field, Mass., Sept. 14, 1813 ; prof. rel. May, 1835 ; mar. March 15, 1838 ; accompanied her husband as above.

ELIPHALET WHITTLESEY, born in Salisbury, Ct., July 13, 1816 ; prof. rel. July, 1831 ; Williams Coll., 1840 ; Union Theol. Sem., 1843 ; ord. at Salisbury, Sept. 26, 1843 ; emb. in the brig *Globe*, at Boston, Dec. 4, 1843 ; first station at Hana, on Maui ; at Kaupo, on the same island, in 1846 ; again at Hana in 1847 ; ret. to the U. States 1854 ; rel. March 1, 1864.

Mrs. WHITTLESEY (Elizabeth Keene Baldwin), from Newark, N. J. ; born at Frankfort, Sussex Co., N. J., Aug. 29, 1821 ; prof. rel. June, 1840 ; Mount Holyoke Female Sem. ; mar. at Newark, Nov. 16, 1843 ; emb., etc., as above.

TIMOTHY DWIGHT HUNT, from Rochester, N. Y. ; Yale Coll., 1840 ; Auburn Theol. Sem., 1843 ; ord. in 1843 ; emb. in the brig *Globe*, at Boston, Dec. 4, 1843 ; stat. in the district of Kau, on Hawaii, Sept. 11, 1845 ; in Lahai-naluna Seminary from July, 1846 ; preacher to the foreign congregation at Honolulu, 1847 ; went in 1848 to San Francisco, California, to preach to the emigrants there ; rel. 1849.

Mrs. HUNT (Mary Hedge), from Newark, N. J.

JOHN FAWCETT POGUE, born in Wilmington, Del., Dec. 29, 1814 ; prof. rel. Philadelphia, Feb., 1832 ; Marietta Coll., 1840 ; Lane Theol. Sem., 1843 ; emb. (then unmarried) in the brig *Globe*, at Boston, Dec. 4, 1843 : stat. at Koloa, on Kauai, till July, 1847 ; then at Kealakekua Bay ; at Lahainaluna, 1851 ; principal of the seminary in 1852, which position he held till 1866. Afterward sat Waiohinu on Hawaii. Now at Honolulu, Secretary of the Hawaiian Board.

Mrs. Pogue (Maria K. Whitney, daughter of Rev. Samuel Whitney), born at Waimea, on Kauai; educated in U. States; ret. to her parents in the brig *Globe*, Dec. 4, 1843; mar. to Mr. Pogue at Honolulu, May 29, 1848; visited the U. States in 1866; ret. in 1867, by way of the Isthmus and San Francisco; now with her husband at Honolulu.

Claudius Buchanan Andrews, born at Kinsman, Trumbull Co., Ohio, in 1817; Western Reserve Coll., 1840; Lane Sem., 1843; emb. (unmarried) at Boston, Dec. 4, 1843; resided on Molokai till 1847; then a teacher at Lahainaluna; visited the U. States in 1850; reëmb. at Boston, Nov. 18, 1851; on Molokai till 1858; at Lahainaluna till 1861; then at Honolulu; in the seminary at Lahainaluna, 1867, till now.

Mrs. Andrews (Anna Seward Gilson), born in Reading, Vt., Nov. 18, 1823; mar. Aug. 7, 1850; emb. at Boston, Nov. 18, 1851; died at Makawao, East Maui, Jan. 27, 1862.

Mr. Andrews has a second marriage.

Samuel Gelston Dwight, born in Northampton, Mass., Jan. 18, 1815; prof. rel. at Montreal, Canada, 1843; Union Theol. Sem., 1847; ord. at New York, Oct. 17, 1847; emb. in the *Samoset*, at Boston, Oct. 23, 1847; connection with the Board ceased Sept. 26, 1854. Now at the Islands.

Henry Kinney, born at Amenia, Dutchess Co., N. Y., Oct. 1, 1816; prof. rel. Oct., 1832; Yale Coll., 1844; Union Theol. Sem., 1847; ord. at La Grange, N. Y., in 1847; emb. in the *Samoset*, at Boston, Oct. 23, 1847; at Kau, on Hawaii, July, 1848; remained there till health failed; died at Sonora, in California, Sept. 24, 1854, aged 38.

Mrs. Kinney (Maria Louisa Walworth), from West Bloomfield, N. Y.; born at Cleveland, Ohio, May 20, 1822 ·

prof. rel. Oct., 1837 ; mar. Sept. 6, 1847 ; emb. as above; and accompanied her husband to California.

WILLIAM CORNELIUS SHIPMAN, born at Wethersfield, Ct., May 19, 1824; prof. rel. at Barry, Pike Co., Ill., 1846; Mission Institute, Quincy, Ill., 1850 ; Theol. Sem., New Haven, 1853 ; ord. at New Haven, May 14, 1854 ; emb. in ship *Chaica*, at Boston, June 4, 1854 ; at Lahaina, Oct. 19, 1854 ; in the district of Kau, Hawaii, from June, 1855, till his death, Dec. 21, 1861, at the age of 37.

Mrs. SHIPMAN (Jane Stobie), from New Haven, Ct.; born at Aberdour, Fifeshire, Scotland, Dec. 20, 1827; prof. rel. Quincy, Ill., March, 1840 ; mar. at Waverly, Ill., July 31, 1853 ; emb., etc., as above. Still at the Islands.

WILLIAM OTIS BALDWIN, born in Greenfield, N. H., Aug. 25, 1821; prof. rel. Amherst, N. H., 1840; Amherst Coll., 1851 ; Theol. Sem., Bangor, 1854 ; ord. at Amherst, N. H., Oct. 4, 1854 ; sailed from Boston, Nov. 28, 1854; at Hana, till his return to the U. States, April 26, 1860; rel. 1860.

Mrs. BALDWIN (Mary Proctor), born in Lunenburg, Mass., March 14, 1822 ; prof. rel. 1839 ; mar. at Amherst, N. H., Oct. 4, 1854; emb. and ret. as above.

ANDERSON OLIVER FORBES (son of ' Rev. Cochran Forbes, a missionary to the Islands), born at Kealakekua Bay, April 14, 1838 ; came to the U. States in 1848 ; prof. rel., 1849 ; Washington Coll., Pa., 1853 ; Theol. Sem., Princeton, 1858 ; ord. at Philadelphia, May 5, 1858 ; ret. to Islands same year ; stat. on Molokai till 1868 ; at Honolulu, June 14, 1868, in connection with the Second Church.

Mrs. FORBES (Maria Patten, daughter of Levi Chamberlain), born at Honolulu about 1830 ; mar. there, 1859.

CYRUS TAGGART MILLS, born at Paris, Oneida Co.,

N. Y., May, 4, 1819; prof. rel. at Lenox, N. Y., May, 1838; Williams Coll., 1844; Union Theol. Sem., 1847; ord. at New York, Feb. 2, 1848; emb. at Boston for Madras, Oct. 10, 1848; Principal of Batticotta Seminary, in Ceylon, until Sept., 1853; ret. to U. States in 1854; rel. March 11, 1856; from Sept. 1860, for four years, he was President of Oahu Coll.; ill health compelling his return to the U. States, he is now principal of a high-school in California.

Mrs. MILLS (Susan Lincoln Tolman), from Ware Village, Mass.; born in Enosburgh, Vt., Nov. 8, 1825; prof. rel. Ware, 1838; mar. at Ware, Sept. 11, 1848; shared the experience of her husband as above.

LUTHER HALSEY GULICK, M. D. (eldest son of Rev. Peter J. Gulick, a missionary to the Islands), born at Honolulu, June 10, 1828; came to the U. States in early life; prof. rel. at Manchester, Pa., 1844; rec. his degree from the New York University, in March, 1850; ord. in New York, Oct., 1851; emb. for the Sandwich Islands and Micronesia, at Boston, Nov. 18, 1851; arrived at Ponape, or Ascension Island, Sept. 11, 1852; removed to Ebon, Dec., 1859; visited U. States, 1862; after his return to the Sandwich Islands, became Secretary of the Board of the Hawaiian Evangelical Association; resigned in 1870; now agent in U. States.

Mrs. GULICK (Lousia Lewis), born in New York city Nov. 10, 1830; prof. rel. Dec., 1846; mar. Oct. 29, 1850; emb., etc., as above.

ORRAMEL HINCKLEY GULICK (brother of the preceding), born at the Islands; prof. rel. at Honolulu, May 28, 1848; one of fourteen children of missionaries admitted to the church on that day; ord., 1862; stat. at Waiohinu, on Hawaii, in 1862; removed Aug., 1865, to Waialua, on Oahu; with his wife, assisted by Elizabeth Lyons, commenced a female boarding-school in October of that year; came to U. States in 1870, and is now designated to Japan.

Mrs. GULICK (Ann Eliza Clark, daughter of Rev. Ephriam W. Clark), born at Honolulu; has shared the experience of her husband.

WILLIAM DE WITT ALEXANDER (son of Rev. William P. Alexander, missionary at the Islands), prof. rel. at Honolulu, May 28, 1848; Yale Coll., 1855; returned to the Islands in 1858, as Professor of Greek in the Oahu College; became President of the same in 1865.

Mrs. ALEXANDER (Abbie Baldwin, daughter of Dr. Baldwin, a missionary at the Islands); mar. in 1861.

SERENO EDWARDS BISHOP (son of Rev. Artemas Bishop, a missionary at the Islands), born at Kailua, Feb., 1827; educated in the U. States; ord. at the Islands in 1862; at Hana, on Maui, 1862; principal of the seminary at Lahainaluna, 1866.

Mrs. BISHOP.

HENRY H. PARKER (son of Rev. Benjamin W. Parker, missionary to the Islands), ord. pastor of the First Church in Honolulu, June 28, 1863.

MISSIONARY PHYSICIANS.

THOMAS HOLMAN, M. D., from Cooperstown, N. Y.; emb. in brig *Thaddeus*, at Boston, Oct. 23, 1819; stationed at Kailua, April 21; withdrew from the mission, July 30, 1820; dismissed from connection with the Board, May 12, 1822. Since deceased.

Mrs. HOLMAN (Lucia Ruggles), of Brookfield.

ABRAHAM BLATCHLEY, M. D., from East Guilford, Ct.; rec. the degree of M. D. from Yale College in 1816; emb.

in the ship *Thames*, at New Haven, Nov. 19, 1822; at Kailua till his removal to Honolulu, May 10, 1825; ret. to the U. States in 1826; released Oct. 16, 1827; died in 1860.

Mrs. BLATCHLEY (Jemima Marvin), born at Lyme, Ct., March 28, 1791; mar. Nov., 1822; emb., etc., as above.

GERRIT PARMELEE JUDD, M. D., born in Paris, Oneida Co., N. Y., April 23, 1803; prof. rel. New Hartford, N. Y., Aug., 1826; Medical College, Fairfield, N. Y.; emb. in ship *Parthian*, at Boston, Nov. 3, 1827; stationed at Honolulu; rendered eminent services in the government as Minister of Finance, in 1842; released as a missionary of the Board same year; still at the Islands.

Mrs. JUDD (Laura Fish), from Clinton, N. Y.; born in Plainfield, Otsego Co., N. Y., April 3, 1804; prof. rel. 1821; mar. Sept. 20, 1827; emb., etc., as above.

ALONZO CHAPIN, M. D., born at West Springfield, Mass., Feb. 24, 1805; prof. rel. at Amherst College in 1826; grad. at Amh. Coll., 1826; received his medical degree from the University of Pennsylvania in 1831; emb. in ship *Averick*, at New Bedford, Nov. 26, 1831; at Lahaina until the illness of Mrs. Chapin compelled their return; arr. in Boston, May 7, 1836; rel. March 14, 1837; now at Winchester, Mass.

Mrs. CHAPIN (Mary Ann Tenney, of Boston), born in Newburyport, Mass., May 9, 1804; prof. rel. Newburyport, Nov., 1824; mar. at Boston, Oct. 26, 1831; emb., etc., as above.

SETH LATHROP ANDREWS, M. D., born at Putney, Vt., June 24, 1809; Dartmouth College, 1831; grad. at Medical Coll., Fairfield, N. Y.; prof. rel. May, 1834; sailed in the barque *Mary Frazier*, from Boston, Dec. 14, 1836; at Kailua till his return to U. States, May 11, 1849; rel. 1852.

Mrs. Andrews (Parmelly Pierce), born in Woodbury, Ct., Jan. 12, 1807; prof. rel. Jan., 1822; mar. at Pittsford, N. Y., Nov. 11, 1836; emb., etc., as above; died at Kailua, Sept. 29, 1846.

Charles Hinckley Wetmore, M. D., born at Lebanon, Ct., Feb. 8, 1820; prof. rel. May, 1841; studied medicine at the Berkshire Medical Institute, Mass.; emb. at Boston, Oct. 16, 1848; at Hilo, which has been his abode to the present time.

Mrs. Wetmore (Lucy Sheldon Taylor), born at Pittsfield, Mass., Aug. 22, 1819; prof. rel. May, 1836; mar. at Pittsfield, Sept. 25, 1848; emb. as above.

ASSISTANT MISSIONARIES.

Daniel Chamberlain, of Brookfield, Mass.; a farmer; sailed with the first company of missionaries, Oct. 23, 1819; there not being a demand for his labor as a farmer, he left the Islands, March 21, 1823, and was released from connection with the Board Nov. 12, 1823.

Mrs. Chamberlain.

Samuel Ruggles, born in Brookfield, Ct., March 9, 1795; prof. rel. May, 1816; studied at the Foreign Mission School; was one of the first company of missionaries; emb. Oct. 23, 1819; stationed with Mr. Whitney at Waimea, July 25, 1820; with Mr. Goodrich at Hilo, Jan. 24, 1824; at Kaawaloa, on Hawaii, July, 1828; at Waimea, on Hawaii, in 1831. Ill health constrained his leaving the Islands, Jan., 1834; rel. Nov. 29, 1836. Still living.

Mrs. Ruggles (Nancy Wells), born at East Windsor, Ct., April 18, 1791; prof. rel. Jan., 1814; mar. Sept. 22, 1819; emb. and ret. as above.

Elisha Loomis, printer, born in Middlesex, Yates Co., N. Y., Dec., 1799; prof. rel. at Canandaigua, N. Y., 1816;

at the Foreign Mission School, Cornwall, Ct.; emb. in the first company of missionaries; his station at Honolulu; began to print, Jan., 1822; health failing, he returned to the United States in 1827. After his return to America he was employed for a season in printing for the mission; was a missionary to the Indians at Mackinaw, from Nov. 4, 1830, to June, 1832; and died 1837, aged 37.

Mrs. LOOMIS (Maria Theresa Sartwell), from Utica, N. Y.; born in New Hartford, Oneida Co., N. Y., Aug. 25, 1796; prof. rel. Utica, Sept., 1819; mar. Sept. 27, 1819; emb., etc., as above.

LEVI CHAMBERLAIN, from Boston, Mass.; born in Dover, Vt., Aug. 28, 1792; prof. rel. Boston, Sept. 6, 1818; sailed in the ship *Thames*, from New Haven, Nov. 19, 1822. After many years of useful labor in various departments, he died at Honolulu, July 29, 1849, aged 57. See biographical sketch.

Mrs. CHAMBERLAIN (Maria Patten), from Pequea, Pa.; born in Salisbury, Lancaster Co., Pa., March 8, 1803; prof. rel. at Pequea, May, 1821; emb. in the ship *Parthian*, at Boston, Nov. 3, 1827, as an unmarried teacher; was mar. at Lahaina, Sept. 1, 1828; visited the U. States in 1859; rel. Jan. 30, 1855; still at Honolulu. — JAMES P. CHAMBERLAIN, a son, a minister of the gospel in the United States.

STEPHEN SHEPARD, printer, born at Kingsborough, Fulton Co., N. Y., July 26, 1800; prof. rel. Oct., 1822; emb. in ship *Parthian*, Nov. 3, 1827; stat. at Honolulu; died July 6, 1834, aged 34.

Mrs. SHEPARD (Margaret Caroline Stow), from Champion, Jefferson Co., N. Y.; born March 6, 1801; prof. rel. 1821; mar. at Pompey, N. Y., Oct. 24, 1827; emb., etc., as above; arr. in the U. States, June 30, 1835, and soon after released.

ANDREW JOHNSTONE, sailed from New Bedford, Mass., Dec. 28, 1830 ; stat. at Honolulu ; taught a school for the children of foreigners ; rel. from connection with the Board, April 22, 1836 ; died at Honolulu.

Mrs. JOHNSTONE, from New Bedford ; died at Honolulu.

EDMUND H. ROGERS, printer, born at Newton, Mass., 1806 ; sailed, unmarried, in ship *Averick*, from New Bedford, Nov. 26, 1831 ; was associated with Mr. Shepard in the printing-office at Honolulu, where he continued till his own death, Dec. 1, 1853.

Mrs. ROGERS (Mary Ward), from Whitesborough, N. Y.; born at Middlebury, N. Y., in 1799 ; went, unmarried, as a teacher, in the *Parthian*, Nov. 3, 1827 ; was married at Lahaina, 1833 ; died at Honolulu, May 23, 1834.

Mrs. ROGERS (Elizabeth M. Hitchcock), born at Great Barrington, Mass., Oct. 4, 1802 ; went out as a teacher, unmarried, in ship *Hellespont*, Dec. 5, 1834 ; was married on Molokai, July 12, 1836, and died at Honolulu, Aug. 2, 1857.

LEMUEL FULLER, printer, born at Attleborough, Mass., April 2, 1810 ; emb. in ship *Mentor*, Capt. Rice, at New London, Nov. 21, 1832 ; his health failing, returned in 1834, and was released soon after.

HENRY DIMOND, book-binder, born in Fairfield, Ct., in 1808; emb. in the *Hellespont*, Dec. 5, 1834; stat. at Honolulu ; released in 1850 ; still at the Islands.

Mrs. DIMOND (Ann Maria Anner), born in the city of New York, 1808; mar. Nov. 3, 1834; emb. as above.

EDWIN OSCAR HALL, printer and assistant secular agent, born in Walpole, N. H., Oct. 21, 1810 ; prof. rel. at Rochester, N. Y., Jan., 1834 ; sailed in the *Hellespont*,

Dec. 5, 1834 ; stat. at Honolulu ; rel. in 1850 ; still at the Islands.

Mrs. HALL (Sarah Lynn Williams), born at Elizabethtown, N. J., Oct. 27, 1812 ; prof. rel. Nov., 1826 ; mar. in New York city, Nov. 3, 1834 ; emb. as above.

EDWARD BAILEY, teacher, born at Holden, Mass., Feb. 24, 1814 ; prof. rel. Jan., 1830 ; emb. in the *Mary Frazier*, Dec. 14, 1836 ; stat. at Kohala, on Hawaii, on his arrival ; at Lahainaluna in 1840 ; at the Female Seminary at Wailuku, from 1841 to 1849 ; afterwards in a self-supporting school ; visited U. States in 1858 ; still at the Islands.

Mrs. BAILEY (Caroline Hubbard), born in Holden, Mass., Aug. 13, 1814 ; prof. rel. June, 1832 ; mar. Nov. 28, 1836 ; emb., etc., as above ; visited the U. States in 1864 ; at the Islands.

SAMUEL NORTHRUP CASTLE, born at Cazenovia, N. Y., Aug. 12, 1808 ; prof. rel. at Sweden, N. Y., 1831 ; emb. in the *Mary Frazier*, Dec. 14, 1836 ; at Honolulu, as secular agent of the mission many years — at first associated with Mr. Chamberlain, then with Mr. Cooke ; visited the U. States in 1842, and again in 1862 ; still at Honolulu.

Mrs. CASTLE (Angeline Loraine Tenney), born in Sudbury, Vt., Oct. 25, 1810 ; prof. rel. Nov., 1831 ; mar. at Plainfield, N. Y., Nov. 10, 1836 ; emb. as above ; died March 5, 1841.

Mrs. CASTLE (Mary Tenney), from Exeter, N. Y. ; mar. in 1842 ; emb. Nov. 2, 1842 ; still living with her husband.

AMOS STARR COOKE, born in Danbury, Ct., Dec. 1, 1810 ; prof. rel. in New York city, Oct., 1830 ; sailed from Boston, Dec. 14, 1836 ; stat. at Honolulu ; in June, 1839, with Mrs. Cooke, placed in charge of a school for young chiefs, supported by the government, till 1849 ; asso. with Mr. Castle as secular superintendent ; still at Honolulu.

Mrs. COOKE (Juliette Montague), born in Sunderland, Mass., March 10, 1812; prof. rel. June, 1833; mar. at Danbury, Ct., Nov. 24, 1836; emb., etc., as above.

HORTON OWEN KNAPP, born at Greenwich, Ct., March 21, 1813; prof. rel. Aug., 1831; emb. at Boston, in the *Mary Frazier*, Dec. 14, 1836; a teacher at Waimea, on Hawaii, till 1840; afterwards at Honolulu till his death, March 28, 1845. See biographical sketch.

Mrs. KNAPP (Charlotte Close), born at Greenwich, Ct., May 26, 1813; prof. rel. May, 1831; mar. Nov. 24, 1836; emb. as above. After the death of Mr. Knapp, she married Rev. Daniel Dole, June, 1846.

EDWIN LOCKE, born at Fitzwilliam, N. H., June 18, 1813; prof. rel. Nov., 1832; emb. in the *Mary Frazier*, Dec. 14, 1836; at Waialua, as teacher of manual labor school; died at Punahou, Oct. 28, 1843. See biographical sketch.

Mrs. LOCKE (Martha Laurens Rowell), born at Cornish, N. H., Nov. 9, 1812; prof. rel. Nov., 1831; mar. Sept. 2, 1836; emb. as above; died at Waiahea, Oahu, Oct. 8, 1842.

CHARLES McDONALD, born at Easton, Pa., Dec. 24, 1812; prof. rel., Philadelphia, 1831; two years at Marion College, Missouri; emb. in the *Mary Frazier*, Dec. 14, 1836; died at Lahaina, Sept. 7, 1839.

Mrs. McDONALD (Harriet Treadwell Halsted), born in the city of New York, Dec. 6, 1810; prof. rel. March, 1832; mar. in New York, Aug. 25, 1836; emb. as above.

BETHUEL MUNN, born in Orange, N. J., Aug. 28, 1803; prof. rel. Newark, N. J., 1825; emb. in the *Mary Frazier*, Dec. 14, 1836; a teacher four years on Molokai; returned to U. States, April, 1842.

Mrs. MUNN (Louisa Clark), born at Skeneateles, N. Y.,

March 3, 1810 ; prof. rel. 1832 ; mar. Nov. 21, 1836 ; emb. as above ; died Aug. 25, 1841.

WILLIAM SANFORD VAN DUZEE, born in Hartford, N. Y., Jan. 12, 1811 ; prof. rel. Oct., 1831 ; one year at University of Vermont; emb. in the *Mary Frazier*, Dec. 14, 1836 ; a teacher at Kaawaloa, on Hawaii, July 10, 1837 ; ret. to U. States in 1840.

Mrs. VAN DUZEE (Oral Hobart), born at Homer, N. Y., Feb. 3, 1814; prof. rel. Oct., 1830 ; mar. at Gouverneur, N. Y., Aug. 9, 1836 ; emb., etc., as above. — Their daughter CYRENE is now a missionary teacher at Erzrûm, in Eastern Turkey.

ABNER WILCOX, born in Harwinton, Ct., April 19, 1808 ; prof. rel. Sept., 1831 ; emb. in the *Mary Frazier*, Boston, Dec. 14, 1836 ; teacher at Hilo till 1845 ; then transferred to Waialua, on Oahu ; removed to Waioli, on Kauai, in July, 1847, where he taught a select school more than twenty years ; visited the U. States in 1851 ; his next visit was in 1869 ; and he died at Colebrook, Ct., Aug. 20, of that year.

Mrs. WILCOX (Lucy Eliza Hart), from Norfolk, Ct.; born at Cairo, N. Y., Nov. 17, 1814; prof. rel. Nov., 1831 ; mar. Nov. 23, 1836 ; emb. as above. She came to the U. States with her husband in 1869, and died at Colebrook, Ct., Aug. 13, one week before his decease.

MARIA C. OGDEN, born in Philadelphia, Pa., Feb. 17, 1792 ; prof. rel. at Woodbury, Oct., 1816 ; emb. in the ship *Parthian*, Nov. 3, 1827 ; stat. at Waimea, on Kauai, from July 15, 1828 ; at Lahaina, 1829 ; transferred to the Female Seminary at Wailuku, June, 1838, and taught there twenty years or more ; afterwards in charge of a school at Honolulu, till rendered unable by the pressure of age.

25

LYDIA BROWN, born at Wilton, N. H., in 1780; prof. rel. 1808; emb. in ship *Hellespont*, Dec. 5, 1834; a teacher at Wailuku till 1840; on Molokai from 1840 to 1857; afterwards resided at Lahaina; died at Honolulu, 1869.

MARCIA MARIA SMITH, born at Burlington, N. Y., Sept. 20, 1806; prof. rel. at Gouverneur, N. Y., April, 1824; went out in the *Mary Frazier*, in 1836; a teacher at Kaneohe, from Sept. 1, 1837; in the school at Punahou, from 1842 till 1853; ret. to United States, 1853; rel. June 6, 1854.

WILLIAM HARRISON RICE, born at Oswego, N. Y., Oct. 12, 1813; prof. rel. at Granby, N. Y., March, 1832; emb. in ship *Gloucester*, from Boston, Nov. 14, 1840; was first a teacher at Hana, on Maui, till 1845; then till 1854, in the high-school at Punahou; in secular employment on Kauai till his decease in 1863.

Mrs. RICE (Mary Sophia Hyde), from Wales, N. Y.; born at Seneca Village, Erie Co., N. Y., Oct. 11, 1816; prof. rel. 1830; mar. Sept. 28, 1840; emb. as above; now in the United States.

WILLIAM AVERY SPOONER, born at West Brookfield, Mass., June 2, 1828; prof. rel. at W. Brookfield, March, 1848; emb. at Boston, April 16, 1855; steward at Oahu College until 1860; rel. Feb. 14, 1860; still at the Islands.

Mrs. SPOONER (Eliza Ann Boynton), born in Shirley, Mass., July 9, 1828; prof. rel. July, 1846; mar. at Shirley, Dec. 8, 1851; emb. as above.

MISSION TO MICRONESIA.

MISSIONARIES.

BENJAMIN GALEN SNOW, born in Brewer, Me., Oct. 4, 1817; prof. rel. June, 1834; Bowdoin Coll., 1846; Theol. Sem., Bangor, 1849; ord. at Brewer, Sept. 25, 1851; emb. at Boston, Nov. 18, 1851; reached Kusaie, on Strong's Island, Aug. 22, 1852; removed to Ebon, one of the Marshall Islands, in Sept., 1862; visited the Sandwich Islands, Jan. 16, 1865; ret. to Ebon, Aug. 29, 1865; visited the United States in May, 1870.

Mrs. SNOW (Lydia Vose Buck), born in Robbinston, Me., Oct. 26, 1820; prof. rel. March, 1839; mar. Sept. 1, 1851; emb., etc., as above; visited the United States, May 26, 1868.

LUTHER HALSEY GULICK, M. D., heretofore mentioned as a missionary on the Sandwich Islands, was previously a missionary at Ponape, one of the Caroline Islands, from 1852 to 1859, and afterwards at Ebon for a year or two.

Mrs. GULICK (already given).

ALBERT A. STURGES, born in Granville, Ohio, Nov. 5, 1819; prof. rel. 1832; Wabash Coll., Indiana, 1848; Theol. Sem., New Haven, 1851; ord. Nov. 11, 1851; emb. at Boston, Jan. 17, 1852; arr. at Ponape, Sept. 11, 1852; on a visit to the United States in 1870.

Mrs. STURGES (Susan Mary Thompson), born in Granville, Ohio, June 1, 1820; prof. rel. 1832; mar. Dec. 26, 1851; emb., etc., as above; visited the Sandwich Islands in 1861; ret. June 19, 1862; now on a visit to the United States.

EDWARD TOPPIN DOANE, born at Tompkinsville, on Staten Island, N. Y., May 30, 1820; prof. rel. at Niles,

Mich., 1839; Illinois College, 1848; Union Theol. Sem., 1852; ord. in New York city, Feb. 26, 1854; emb. at Boston, June 4, 1854; reached Ponape, Feb. 6, 1855; rem. to Ebon, one of the Marshall Islands, Dec. 5, 1857; visited the United States, 1863; returning, wrecked on Roneador Reef, near Providence Island, in the Caribbean Sea, May 30, 1865; reached Ebon, Aug. 27, and Ponape, Sept. 19, 1865.

Mrs. DOANE (Sarah Wells Wilbur), born at Franklinville, Long Island, N. Y., May 20, 1835; prof. rel. 1853; mar. at Brooklyn, N. Y., May 13, 1854; emb. as above; came sick to the Sandwich Islands, June, 1861, and died at Honolulu, Feb. 16, 1862.

Mrs. DOANE (Clara Hale Strong), born in Monroe Co., N. Y., Oct. 4, 1841; prof. rel. Rockford, Ill., May, 1861; educated in Rockford Female Seminary; mar. April 13, 1865; emb. at New York in steamer *Golden Rule*, May 20, 1865; wrecked, etc., as above.

GEORGE PIERSON, M. D., born at Cedarville, N. J., May 10, 1826; prof. rel. Jacksonville, Ill., May, 1848; Illinois College, 1848; Theol. Sem., Andover, 1851; ord. at Jacksonville, Nov. 9, 1851; a missionary to the Choctaw Indians in 1852, but, health failing, he returned home; sailed from Boston, Nov. 28, 1854, for Micronesia; reached Strong's Island, Oct. 6, 1855; joined Mr. Doane at Ebon, Dec. 5, 1857; failure of Mrs. Pierson's health constrained their removal to California in 1860; released Aug. 27, 1861.

Mrs. PIERSON (Nancy Annette Shaw), born at Delhi, N. Y., June 10, 1828; prof. rel. at Meredith, N. Y., 1849; mar. at Unadilla, Sept. 10, 1854; emb., etc., as above.

HIRAM BINGHAM, Jr., son of Rev. Hiram Bingham, born at Honolulu, Oahu, Aug. 16, 1831; came to the United States in early life; prof. rel. in New Haven, Ct., in 1850;

Yale Coll., 1853; Theol. Sem., Andover; ord. Nov. 9, 1856; sailed for the Pacific in *Morning Star*, from Boston, Dec. 2, 1856; arr. at Honolulu, April 24, 1857; reached Ponape, in the same vessel, Sept. 23, 1857; commenced a missionary station at Apaiang, Nov. 19, 1857; health failing, visited the United States, Sept. 8, 1865; sailed again from Boston for the Pacific, Nov. 12, 1866, in the new packet *Morning Star*, of which he went as commander; and arrived at Honolulu, March 13, 1867; still in the mission.

Mrs. BINGHAM (Minerva Clarissa Brewster), born at Northampton, Mass., Oct. 19, 1834; prof. rel. Feb., 1850; mar. Nov. 18, 1856; emb., etc., as above.

EPHRAIM PETER ROBERTS, born in Danby, Vt., Oct. 28, 1825; prof. rel. at Dorset, 1845; Williams Coll., 1854; Theol. Sem., Bangor, 1857; ord. at Bangor, Me., July 28, 1857; emb. at Boston, Oct. 30, 1857; arr. at Ponape, Sept., 1858; connection with the Board discontinued July 30, 1861.

Mrs. ROBERTS (Myra Holman Farrington), born at Holden, Me., Sept. 22, 1835; prof. rel. June, 1854; was mar. Sept. 6, 1857; emb., etc., as above; rel. July 30, 1861.

CATALOGUE OF PUBLICATIONS

IN THE

HAWAIIAN, MARQUESAN, GILBERT ISLANDS, MARSHALL ISLANDS, KUSAIE, AND PONAPE LANGUAGES.

(See p. 327.)

THE following Catalogue was compiled for this work by Rev. Luther H. Gulick, M. D., and brought down to June, 1870. The sources of information are, —

1. Minutes of the General Meeting of the Sandwich Islands Mission, to 1863.

2. Annual Reports of the Board of the Hawaiian Evangelical Association ; 1864 to 1870.

8. "Bibliography of the Hawaiian Islands, printed for James F. Hunnewell ; " 1869.

IN THE HAWAIIAN LANGUAGE.

The Four Gospels, 1828, 12mo.

The New Testament : —

First edition, 1837, pp. 520, 12mo. Numerous portions of this edition were put in circulation before the completion of the volume. Out of print.

Second edition, 1843, pp. 320, 12mo. Out of print.

Third edition, 1868, pp. 823, 8vo. Part of the " Family Bible."

Fourth edition, 1868, pp. 339, 18mo. "School edition."

Hawaiian-English Testament, with references, 1857, pp. 727, 12mo.

The Bible : —

First edition, completed May 10, 1839, pp. 2431, 12mo. Numerous portions of this edition were circulated before its completion. Out of print.

Second edition, 1843, pp. 1451, 8vo, and 4to.

Third edition, 1868, " Family Bible," marginal references, pp. 1456, royal 8vo, and 4to.

A B C Primer (Piapa), 1822, pp. 4, 8, and 12, 12mo. Very many editions.

First Teacher (Kumu Mua), by Mr. Bingham, pp. 16, 16mo. Many times revised and reprinted.

First Lessons (Ikemua), 1835, pp. 48, 12mo.

First Book for Children (Palapala Mua), by Mr. Bingham, pp. 36, 18mo. Several editions.

Second Teacher (Kumu Lua), 1844, pp. 32, 16mo.

Reading Book (Palapala Heluhelu), by Mr. Dibble, pp. 48, 12mo. Four editions.

Reading Book (Palapala Heluhelu), by L. Andrews and J. S. Green, 1842, pp. 340, 12mo.

First Steps in Reading (Alakai Mua), 1854, pp. 16, 12mo.

The American Tract Society Primer (Kumumua Hou), by Mr. Bond, 1860, pp. 80, 16mo.

The New Primer (Kumumua Ano Hou), by Mr. Fuller, 1862, 12mo.

Lessons in Punctuation (Ao Kiko), 1844, pp. 24, 12mo. Several editions.

Catechism (Ui), 1824. Many editions, pp. 4 and 8, 16mo.

Historical Catechism (Ninauhoike), by Mr. Bingham, 1831. Third edition, 1864, pp. 189, 24mo.

Catechism (Ui no ka Moolelo Kahiko a ke Akua), 1832, pp. 56, 18mo.

Catechism on Genesis (Ninauhoike no Kinohi), 1833, pp. 56, 16mo.

Daily Food (Ai-o-ka-la). An annual, 1833 to 1860.

Daily Food, by Dr. L. Smith, 1861, stereotyped, two editions, pp. 154, 18mo.

Union Questions, by Mr. Dibble, 1835. Two editions, pp. 156, 16mo.

Abbott's & Fisk's Bible Class Book, Nos. 1 and 2, by Mr. Andrews, pp. 100, 16mo.

Scripture Helps (Huliano), 1835. Two editions, pp. 112, and 152, 18mo.

Child's Catechism on Genesis (Haawina Kamalii), by Mr. L. Lyons, 1838, pp. 152, 12mo.

Proof Texts (Kuhikuhi no ka Pal. Hem.), 1839, pp. 35, 12mo.

Bible Lessons (Haawina Pal. Hem.), 1840, pp. 83, 12mo.

Heavenly Manna, 1841, pp. 69, 18mo.

Doctrinal Catechism (Ui Ekalesia), 1841, pp. 32, 32mo. Several editions.

Doctrinal Catechism (Ui no ke Akua, etc.), by Dr. Armstrong, 1848. Several large editions, pp. 48, 12mo.

Catechism on Genesis (Haawina Baibala), by Mr. L. Lyons, 1852, pp. 132, 12mo.

Sabbath-school Question Book, No. 1 (Ui Kamalii), 1866, by Mr. Bond, pp. 140, 12mo.

Sabbath-school Book, No. 2 (Haawina Kamalii), 1867, pp. 174, 12mo.

Sabbath-school Book, No. 3, by Mr. Bond, 1869, pp. 132, 12mo.

Sabbath-school Book No. 4, by Mr. W. P. Alexander, 1869, pp. 12, 12mo.

Sabbath-school Books, No. 5, by Mr. O. H. Gulick, 1870, pp. 103, 12mo.

A Word from God, 1825, 8vo.

Thoughts of the Chiefs, 1825, pp. 8, 18mo.

History of Joseph, 1826, pp. 32, 18mo.

Scripture History, 1830. Several editions, pp. 86 to 144, 12mo.

On Marriage, by Mr. Clark, 1833, pp. 12, 12mo.

Exposition of Ten Commandments, 1834, pp. 15, 12mo.

On the Sabbath, by Mr. J. S. Green, 1835, pp. 12, 12mo.

Church Covenant. Many editions, pp. 16, 12mo.

Church Covenant for Molokai, by Mr. Hitchcock, 1837, pp. 16, 32mo.

On Intemperance, by Dr. Baldwin, 1837, pp. 18, 12mo.

On Lying, by Mr. Lyman, 1838, pp. 8, 12mo.

On Experimental Religion, 1839, pp. 12, 12mo.

Letter to the Churches, 1840, pp. 24, 12mo.

Attributes of God, 1841, pp. 12, 12mo.

Eighty-four Questions, 1841, pp. 12, 12mo.

Keith on the Prophecies, 1841, pp. 12, 12mo.

Church Government, for Kauai, 1841, pp. 20, 12mo.

For Parents, 1842, pp. 12, 12mo.

Three tracts on Popery, 1842, pp. 12, 8vo.

Address to Women of Hawaii, by Mrs. Anderson, 1863, pp. 12, 18mo.

Series of Tracts, No. 1 to 16.

Counsels for Children (Olelo Ao Liilii), 1865, pp. 32, 18mo.

On Popery, by Dr. Armstrong, 1841. Several editions, pp: 23, 12mo.

Thoughts on Popery, by Mr. Pogue, 1867, pp. 56, 12mo.

The True Church, by Mr. Pogue, 1867, pp. 26, 12mo.

Bunyan's Pilgrim's Progress, by Mr. A. Bishop, 1842, pp. 410, 16mo.

Clark's Scripture Promises, 1858, pp. 309, 12mo.

Evidences of Christianity (Na Hoike o ka Pal. Hem.), by Mr. W. P. Alexander, 1849. Two editions, pp. 116, 12mo.

System of Theology (No ko ke Akua Ano, etc.), by Mr. W. P. Alexander, 1848. Two editions, pp. 219, 12mo.

Volume of Sermons, 1835, pp. 64, 12mo. Second edition, 1841, pp. 296, 12mo.

Dying Testimonies, by Mr. Dibble, 1832, pp. 40, 12mo.

Memoir of Bartimeus, by Mr. J. S. Green, 1844. Two editions, pp. 64, 18mo.

Memoir of Obookiah (Opukahaia), 1867, pp. 103, 12mo.

Pastor's Hand-Book, 1869, pp. 104, 16mo.

Church History, by Mr. J. S. Green, 1835, pp. 205, 12mo. Several editions.

Annual Reports of Board of Hawaiian Evangelical Association, 1864 to 1870.

Hymn Book (Himeni Hoolea). First edition, by Messrs. Bingham & Ellis, 1823, pp. 60, 12mo. Very many editions. Last edition by Mr. L. Lyons, 1867, 400 hymns.

Hymn and Tune Book, with Elementary Lessons (Himeni Hawaii), by Mr. Bingham, 1834, pp. 360, 12mo.

Child's Hymn Book (Himeni Kamalii), 1837, pp. 72, 24mo.

Child's Hymn Book, with Tunes, 1842, pp. 101, 16mo.

Child's Hymn and Tune Book (Lira Kamalii), 1862, pp. 192, 16mo.

Book of Tunes, with Elements of Music (Lira Hawaii), 1846. Three editions, 1855, pp. 104.

Arithmetic, 1827, pp. 8, 16mo.

Fowle's Child's Arithmetic (Helu Kamalii), by Mr. A. Bishop, 1844, pp. 48, 24mo. Many editions.

Colburn's Mental Arithmetic (Helu Naau), by Mr. A. Bishop, 1835. Many editions, pp. 68 to 132, 18mo.

Colburn's Sequel (Hailoaa), by Mr. A. Bishop, 1835, pp. 116, 12mo. Two editions.

Leonard's Arithmetic, by Mr. A. Bishop, 1852, pp. 244, 12mo.

Thompson's Higher Arithmetic, by Mr. C. J. Lyons, 1869.

Algebra, by Mr. A. Bishop, 1838, pp. 44, 12mo.

Mathematics, 1838, by Mr. E. W. Clark, pp. 168, 8vo.

Bailey's Algebra, by Mr. A. Bishop, 1843–1858, pp. 160, 8vo.

First Lessons in Geometry, by Mr. L. Andrews, 1833, pp. 64, 16mo. Two editions.

Geometry, Surveying, and Navigation, by Mr. L. Andrews, 1834, pp. 122, 8vo.

Astronomy, by Mr. E. W. Clark, pp. 12, 12mo.

Geography, by Messrs. Whitney & Richards, 1832, pp. 44, 12mo.

Geography and Maps, by Mr. L. Andrews, 1835, pp. 216, 12mo.

Woodbridge's Geography, by Mr. S. Whitney, 1836, pp. 203, 12mo. Two editions.

Questions on Geography, by Mr. L. Andrews, 1833. Many editions, pp. 24 to 48, 12mo.

Skeleton Maps, by Mr. L. Andrews, 1834, pp. 13, 4to.

Atlas of Colored Maps, by Mr. L. Andrews, 1836, pp. 9, 4to. Several editions.

Keith's Study of the Globes, by Mr. L. Andrews, 1841, pp. 80, 16mo.

Worcester's Geography of the Bible, by Mr. Dibble, 1834, pp. 99, 16mo. Two editions.

Maps of Sacred Geography, by Mr. L. Andrews, 1837, pp. 6, 4to. Several editions.

Scripture Geography, by Mr. Dibble, 1839, pp. 52, 8vo.

Scripture Chronology and History, by Mr. Dibble, 1837, pp. 216, 12mo.

Animals of the World, by Mr. L. Andrews, 1833, pp. 12, 12mo. With Chart.

Comstock's History of Quadrupeds, by Mr. Dibble, 1834, pp. 192, 12mo.

Stories about Animals, by Mr. Dibble, 1835, pp. 84, 12mo. Three editions.

Lessons in Drawing, with Copper-plate Illustrations, by Mr. L. Andrews, 1837, pp. 36, 12mo.

Anatomy, Illustrated, by Dr. Judd, 1838, pp. 60, 12mo.

Abbott's Little Philosopher, by Mr. E. W. Clark, 1837, pp. 40, 12mo.

Gallaudet's Natural Theology (Hoike Akua), by Mr. Dibble, 1840, pp. 178, 12mo. Two editions.

Gallaudet's Child's Book on the Soul (Hoike Uhane), by Mr. S. Whitney, 1840, pp. 68, 18mo.

Wayland's Moral Philosophy, by Messrs. Armstrong & Dibble, pp. 288, 12mo. Two editions.

Political Economy, 1839, pp. 128, 8vo.

Compendium of History, by Mr. J. S. Green, 1842, pp. 76, 12mo.

Hawaiian History by Hawaiians, 1838, pp. 86, 8vo. Two editions.

History of Hawaiian Islands, by S. M. Kamakau. Published in the newspaper Kuokoa, 1866-68.

Antiquities of Hawaiian Islands, by Hawaiians. In the newspaper Kuokoa, 1865-66.

Lady of the Twilight (Laiekawai): a Romance, by a Hawaiian.

Almanac, 1834 to 1862, 12mo.

The Constitution, 1840, pp. 24, 12mo.

The Constitution and Laws, 1841, pp. 196, 12mo.

Volumes of Statute Laws, 1845 to 1870.

Penal Code, 1851, pp. 136, 8vo.

Civil Code, 1859, 2 vols., 8vo.

Decisions of the Supreme Court, 1857 to 1865, 2 vols., 8vo.

Legal Form Book, by J. W. H. Kauwahi, 1857, 12mo.

Records of Constitutional Convention, 1864, pp. 72, folio.

Reports of Govermental Departments, 1845 to 1870.

The Hawaiian Teacher, 1834.   A monthly.

The Juvenile Teacher, 1837.   A monthly.

The Hawaiian Luminary, 1834.   A monthly.

The Ant, 1841 to 1845.   A monthly.

The Hawaiian Messenger, 1845-55.

The News, 1854.   A weekly.

The Hawaiian Banner, 1856-61.   A weekly.

The Morning Star, 1854-62, and 1864.   A monthly.

The Hawaiian Missionary, occasional, 5 or 6 numbers.

The Star of the Pacific, 1861. A weekly.
The Independent Press, 1861–70. A weekly.
The New Era, 1865–70. A weekly.
The Day Spring, 1866–70. A monthly.

Lessons on the English Language (Haawina no ka Olelo Beretania), 1837, pp. 36, 12mo. Three editions.

Hawaiian English Grammar, 1837, pp. 40, 8vo.

Foreign Primer (Kumu Kahiki), by Mr. L. Andrews, 1837, pp. 36, 12mo.

Latin Lessons for Hawaiian Children, 1839, pp. 132, 18mo.

English and Hawaiian Lessons, 1841, pp. 40, 16mo.

Exercise Book for Learning English (Oke kokua, etc.), 1843, pp. 104, 18mo.

Spelling Book (Ao Spella), by Mr. Emerson, 1846, pp. 48, 12mo.

Hawaiian-English Phrase Book, by Mr. A. Bishop, 1854, pp. 112, 16mo.

Hawaiian-English Vocabulary, by Mr. L. Andrews, 1835, pp. 132, 8vo.

English-Hawaiian Vocabulary, by Mr. Emerson, 1845, pp. 184, 8vo.

English-Hawaiian Grammar, by Mr. L. Andrews, 1854, pp. 32, 8vo.

Hawaiian-English Dictionary (with Eng.-Haw. Vocabulary), by Mr. L. Andrews, 1865, pp. 560, 8vo.

Notes on Hawaiian Grammar, Parts 1 and 2, by Pres. W. D. Alexander, 1865.

IN THE MARQUESAN DIALECT.

Elementary Primer, 1833, by Mr. W. P. Alexander, pp. 12mo.

Elementary Primer, 1834, pp. 8, 12mo.

Elementary Primer, 1853, pp. 12, 12mo.

Elementary Primer (Piapa), by Mr. J. Bicknell, pp. 48, 12mo.

Gospel of Matthew.
Second edition of *Piapa*, 1868, pp. 48, 12mo.
Elementary Arithmetic, 1869, pp. 46, 16mo.
Elementary Geography, 1869, pp. 24, 16mo.
Hymn Book, 1870, pp. 30, 16mo.

IN THE GILBERT ISLANDS DIALECT, BY MR. AND MRS. BINGHAM.

Primer, 1860, pp. 20, 12mo.
Hymn Book, 1860, pp. 12, 16mo.
Eleven Chapters in Matthew, 1860, pp. 43, 12mo.
Hymn Book, 1863, pp. 27, 16mo.
Gospel of Matthew, 1864, pp. 124, 16mo.
Gospel of John, 1864, pp. 108, 16mo.
Ephesians, 1864, pp. 20, 16mo.
Bible Stories, 1864, pp. 72, 16mo.
Primer, 1865, pp. 48, 12mo.
Gospel of Matthew, 1866, pp. 49, 16mo.
Gospel of John, 1866, pp. 39, 16mo.
Ephesians, 1866, pp. 7, 16mo.
Bible Stories, 1866, pp. 155, 16mo.
Catechism, by Rev. Mr. Mahoe, 1866, pp. 75, 16mo.
Extracts from Luke, 1869, pp. 24, 12mo.
Gospel of Mark, 1869, pp. 69, 12mo.
Acts of the Apostles, 1869, pp. 41, 12mo.
Arithmetic, 1870, pp. 3, 16mo.
Geography, 1870, pp. 36, 12mo.
Catechism, 1870, pp. 24, 12mo.
Primer, 1870, pp. 24, 12mo.
Reading Book, 1870, pp. 72, 12mo.
Luke, 1870, pp. 92, 12mo.
Romans, 1870, pp. 40, 12mo.

IN THE MARSHALL ISLANDS LANGUAGE.

Primer, by Dr. Pierson, 1858, pp. 8, 16mo.
Primer and Hymns, by Mr. Doane, 1860, pp. 44, 12mo.

First Lessons, by Mr. Doane, 1861.
Ten Chapters of Matthew, by Mr. Doane, 1861 and '62.
Arithmetic, by Messrs. Aea & Doane, 1863, pp. 24, 16mo.
Hymns, by Mr. Doane, 1863, pp. 24, 16mo.
Mark, by Mr. Doane, 1863, pp. 47, 12mo.
Primer, by Mr. Doane, 1863, pp. 10, 12mo.
Geography, by Mr. Doane, 1863, pp. 24, 16mo.
Matthew, by Mr. Doane, 1865, pp. 79, 12mo.
Primer, by Mr. Snow, 1866, pp. 34, 12mo.
Hymns, by Mr. Snow, 1866, 16mo.
Acts, by Mr. Snow, 1867, pp. 75, 16mo.
Hymns, by Mr. Snow, 1869, pp. 42, 16mo.
John, by Mr. Suow, 1869, pp. 52, 12mo.
Mark, by Mr. Snow, 1869, pp. 41, 12mo.
Primer, by Mr. Snow, 1869, pp. 48, 12mo.

IN THE KUSAIE DIALECT, BY MR. B. G. SNOW.

Primer, 1860, pp. 32, 12mo.
John, 1863, pp. 38, 12mo.
Primer, 1864, pp. 24, 12mo.
Matthew, 1865, pp. 50, 12mo.
Hymn Book, 1865, pp. 32, 16mo.
Articles of Faith and Covenant and Names of Church Members, 1866, pp. 13, 12mo.
Primer, 1867, pp. 48, 12mo.
Mark, 1868, pp. 50, 12mo.
John, 1868, pp. 64, 12mo.
Acts, 1869, pp. 60, 12mo.
Epistles of John, 1869, pp. 20, 12mo.

IN THE PONAPE LANGUAGE.

Primer, by Dr. L. H. Gulick, 1857–58, pp. 26 and 12, 16mo.
Hymn Book, by Dr. L. H. Gulick, 1858, pp. 19, 16mo.
Old Testament Stories, by Dr. L. H. Gulick, 1858, pp. 59, 16mo.

New Testament Stories, by Dr. L. H. Gulick, 1859, pp. 40, 12mo.

Both Stories, reprinted, by Dr. L. H. Gulick, 1865, pp. 61, 12mo.

Eight Chapters in Matthew, by Dr. L. H. Gulick, 1859, pp. 20, 12mo.

Primer, by Mrs. Gulick, 1858–59, pp. 36 and 20, 12mo.

Gospel of John, by Mr. A. A. Sturges, 1862, pp. 39, 8vo.

Nine Chapters Mark, by Mr. Sturges, 1864, pp. 24, 8vo.

Hymns, by Mr. Sturges, 1864–65, pp. 8 and 27, 16mo.

Luke, by Mr. Sturges, 1866, pp. 51, 8vo.

Acts, by Mr. Sturges, 1866, pp. 48, 8vo.

Arithmetic, by Mr. Sturges, 1869, pp. 36, 16mo.

Geography, by Mr. Sturges, 1869, pp. 24, 16mo.

Matthew, by Mr. Sturges, 1870, pp. 48, 12mo.

Mark, by Mr. Sturges, 1870, pp. 27, 12mo.

Primer, by Mrs. Sturges, 1867, pp. 60, 12mo.

INDEX.

26